Wildlife of

Galápagos

Second Edition

Julian Fitter, Daniel Fitter & David Hosking

Princeton University Press
Princeton and Oxford

Dedication
To Mary and the people of the Galápagos

Published in the United States, Canada, and the Philippines
by Princeton University Press
41 William Street
Princeton, NJ 08540

Published in the United Kingdom by William Collins
An imprint of HarperCollins*Publishers*
1 London Bridge Street
London SE1 9GF

First published in the United Kingdom by Collins in 2000
First published in the United States by Princeton University Press in 2002
This fully revised and updated edition published in 2016

Line illustrations by Martin B. Withers
Maps and diagrams by Shane O'Dwyer

ISBN 978-0-691-17042-8

Library of Congress Control Number: 2015946911

British Library Cataloging-in-Publication Data is available

Printed on acid-free paper.

Edited and designed by D & N Publishing, Baydon, Wiltshire
Color reproduction by FMG
Printed and bound in Bosnia and Herzegovina by GPS Group

10

CONTENTS

FOREWORD

Visitors to the Galápagos Islands can enjoy amazing wildlife. The experience of living alongside nature while in the Galápagos can also be an acute experience. Nature's forces – from volcanoes to evolution – are at work here and can be experienced. My great-great grandfather, Charles Darwin, was so inspired by Galápagos wildlife that his theory of evolution subsequently changed the way we see the world. Thus, getting so close to animals and plants makes for unforgettable experiences, and might even change your life.

Over the past 20 years, I have been fortunate enough to spend time in the Galápagos Islands with Daniel and Tina Fitter. While undertaking fieldwork, as part of research work on Galápagos Tomatoes at the Natural History Museum, London, I was lucky enough to visit some of the more remote parts of the archipelago. I have benefitted greatly from Daniel's knowledge and experience. Daniel, Julian Fitter and David Hosking have written this wonderful book, offering their enormous wealth of knowledge and experiences of nature in Galápagos to everybody.

The Galápagos is now the richest and healthiest province of Ecuador. Many of the local people (who have settled in the Galápagos in the last 70 years) embrace their newfound wildlife. The Charles Darwin Research Station initiated Gardening for Galápagos as one of their outreach programs. This has encouraged locals to grow native plants in municipal areas and gardens; not only does this support other wildlife but is also symbolic, encouraging visitors and locals alike to recognise the native wildlife.

I hope this excellent book will help the countless visitors to the Galápagos Islands to enjoy this wild nature experience, and will encourage them to pause and think about how they could adapt their own lives to be more ecologically friendly. This way the Galápagos Islands could become a beacon for sustainable living, showing us how to live with nature.

I always take this book with me in the field; it is compact, accurate and contains the wisdom and understanding of many years of Galápagos living and exploration by the three authors. Whether the purpose of your visit to the Galápagos Islands is as a tourist or scientist this book, *Wildlife of the Galápagos*, is a 'must'.

Sarah Darwin

THE AUTHORS

Julian Fitter

Julian arrived in Galápagos in May 1964 on the Charles Darwin Foundation's first support vessel, *Beagle*. It had not been his intention to stay there, but falling in love changed all that, and after a brief spell in Quito, teaching at the Central University, he returned to Galápagos with his wife, Mary Angermeyer. Julian spent the next fourteen years travelling the islands and building the first yacht charter business in Galápagos. He returned to England in 1979, and became involved in attempting to develop tourism in the Falkland Islands. Being ahead of his time, he turned to a more mundane means of earning a living, as a financial adviser. Julian maintained his links with Galápagos and in 1995 was instrumental in establishing the Galápagos Conservation Trust in the UK. He served as its first Chairman and is now an Ambassador. He also helped establish Falklands Conservation, served as its first secretary, and is now a Vice President of that organisation. Retiring from financial services in 2004 he moved to New Zealand in 2005 and established Friends of Galápagos New Zealand, He has written three books on New Zealand wildlife, one on walks around Auckland and contributed to a major volume on Albatrosses. More recently he has helped to establish and develop the Maketu Ongatoro Wetland Society which works on a variety of ecological restoration projects in the Bay of Plenty, New Zealand. He has a strong and committed interest in the conservation of the natural environment, particularly the Galápagos Islands, and of the need to include the local population in a sustainable use of resources to that end.

Daniel Fitter

Daniel was born in Galápagos. From a very young age he was able to explore islands while accompanying his father (Julian) on his charter yachts. This helped him to develop a keen interest in their flora and fauna. A keen birdwatcher and photographer, Daniel has one of the largest photographic libraries on Galápagos subjects. He is also author of *Creative Force Galápagos* and has contributed to various other books with his work. He is currently living in Ecuador with his wife Tina and working as a tour leader and photographer.

David Hosking

David first visited the Galápagos in 1970 with his late father, Eric Hosking OBE, Hon FRPS, and as direct result of this visit decided to follow in his father's footsteps and pursue a career in wildlife photography. He has visited Galápagos many times since as a naturalist and photographic guide. David is a Fellow of the Royal Photographic Society and the British Naturalists' Association. His reputation as a master photographer has been enhanced by the publication of his work in a wide range of books, including two other Collins Traveller's Guides on the wildlife of East and Southern Africa. With his wife Jean he is deeply involved in the administration of the Frank Lane Picture Agency, one of the oldest libraries specialising in natural history photographs. David is also chairman of the Eric Hosking Charitable Trust: www.erichoskingtrust.com

ACKNOWLEDGEMENTS

A book such as this needs a lot of help to compile; general information is readily available but the details are often hard to locate. Additionally the names of species change as our knowledge of the biology of the islands increases. Since the first edition of this work, the Waved Albatross, Masked Booby, Dark-rumped Petrel and Audubon's Shearwater have all had changes to their English and/or scientific names. The generic name of the lava lizards changed recently and all the snakes were reclassified in 1997 – there is still disagreement about the nomenclature of the tortoises!

A big thank you must go the various scientists, all associated with the Charles Darwin Research Station, who willingly responded to our queries, helped with identification of species and corrected sections of text relating to their field. In particular we would like to thank Dr Alan Tye, Dr Rodrigo Bustamante, Dr Lazaro Roque-Albelo, Dr Marco Altamirano B, Dr Hernan Vargas, Dr Charlotte Causton and Dr Ivan Aldace. Dr Howard Snell and Dr Heidi Snell also deserve a special mention. In Canada Dr Stewart Peck and Dr Bernard Landry and in Belgium Dr Leon Baert helped with invertebrates. Dr Patty Parker was a mine of information on the Galápagos Hawk. Christian Caceres from the Galápagos National Park service gave invaluable help and we would particularly like to thank Dr Eliecer Cruz, formerly the Director of the Galápagos National Park Service, and Dr Robert Bensted-Smith, formerly Director of the Charles Darwin Research Station, for their help and co-operation.

Thanks also to Godfrey Merlen and David Day, two scientists who have lived many years in Galápagos and have come to know and love them with an intimacy that is hard to appreciate. Their help with the cetaceans in particular is much appreciated. The late Gayle Davies, the CDRS Librarian, was the patient recipient of many emails, to all of which she replied quickly and helpfully.

My thanks also to Conley McCullen and Michael Jackson, whose books on the plants and the biology of the islands have been invaluable. In the production of the text, we owe a considerable debt to my late father, Richard Fitter and to Jane Riddell who went through most of it with helpful suggestions, corrections, queries and above all patience. Tina Fitter was a vital contributor in Galápagos. Our thanks also to the production team, without whom the mass of information would never have become a book.

For the second edition I was also helped by many of the above, especially Alan Tye but also Dr Josh Donlan, Dr Donna Harris and Dr Karl Campbell, rodents, Dr Christine Parent, land snails, Cruz Marquez, reptiles, and Julia Koppitz at HarperCollins.

This third edition has introduced a new fish section and has greatly expanded the Visitor Sites section in line with developments in Galápagos. My thanks to Robert Dowler for his help on the thorny question of the classification of the rice rats, an issue as tricky as with the snakes and tortoises. As always my thanks to Myles Archibald at HarperCollins whose patience and forbearance is legendary – or becoming so.

And a special thanks to my fellow authors, who while mainly involved in the photographic side of the book provide an invaluable support service on the text side.

Julian Fitter, Maketu, New Zealand, September 2015

CONSERVATION PLEA

Biol. Eliecer Cruz
PAST DIRECTOR
Galápagos National Park Service

Dr Robert Bensted-Smith
PAST DIRECTOR
Charles Darwin Research Station,
Galápagos

The visitor to Galápagos does not need a field guide to identify such unmistakable creatures as the Marine Iguana or the Flightless Cormorant! But the islands are home to many more unique but less prominent species of reptiles, birds, plants and insects. Furthermore, it is the subtle differences between species that reveal the secrets of evolution, the most famous case being the finch species that inspired Charles Darwin. This guide is an excellent companion for the visitor who wants to go a step beyond the superficial look and observe more closely the nature of the archipelago. And Galápagos is the perfect place for such observation, for here the wildlife nonchalantly permits our scrutiny; we can enjoy closeness to wildlife here, as nowhere else.

These characteristics, and the fact that the Galápagos Islands, unlike the rest of the world's archipelagos, still has 95 per cent of its original pre-human quota of species, make this a truly special place, which has been recognised as a National Park, Marine Reserve, Whale Sanctuary, Man and Biosphere Reserve and World Heritage Site. But the isolation that engendered the unique flora and fauna of Galápagos has long since ended and the islands now face the threat of invasive alien species, from the notorious goats and pigs to insidious enemies such as insects, weedy plants and diseases. The worldwide problem of over exploitation of the marine ecosystem has also reached Galápagos. These threats must be kept at bay. The preservation of Galápagos is the shared mission of the Galápagos National Park Service and the Charles Darwin Foundation for the Galápagos Islands. The Park Service is the government agency charged with managing the Park and the Marine Reserve. Its partner, the Charles Darwin Foundation, is an independent international organisation, providing scientific research, training, education and advisory services.

Our two organisations are dedicated to the conservation of Galápagos, but we need the commitment and co-operation of others. We need the active participation of the local island community to help tackle the root causes of the threats to biodiversity, and we need the co-operation of all who are lucky enough to visit the Galápagos Islands. We hope that, if you care enough about Galápagos to identify and observe its plant and animal life, you will also care enough to help the conservation effort by becoming a *Friend of Galápagos*. To find out more about conservation of the islands and about the worldwide Friends of Galápagos movement, please visit our websites on *www.galapagos.org* or send an e-mail to *cdrs@fcdarwin.org.ec*.

Welcome to the wonders of Galápagos!

INTRODUCTION

Putting together a book like this takes an amazing amount of time and a lot of help from other people. I spent fifteen years with Galápagos as my home; I thought I knew them pretty well, but in writing and researching this book I have found out how little I really knew and how much we still have to learn about the biology of the Galápagos ecosystem.

I arrived in Galápagos 129 years after Charles Darwin. I came by sea, on a small sailing vessel with the same name, *Beagle*, and our landfall, San Cristóbal, was the same. Thereafter our experiences were very different, but what is amazing about Galápagos, what impressed Charles Darwin, is still there to amaze and impress the visitor of the 21st century. While much has changed, much was the same for me in 1964 as it was for Darwin in 1835 and is the same for the visitor today. But it is only the same because of a lot of hard work and effort by the people of Galápagos, the Ecuadorian authorities, the Galápagos National Park Service and the Charles Darwin Foundation and many more.

As we seek to preserve the unique Galápagos ecosystem, we are faced with two main problems: alien species and ourselves. Obvious alien species are the feral goats that devastated Santiago and Northern Isabela. Less obvious are the fire ants *Wasmannia auropunctata* and Quinine tree *Cinchona succirubra,* and an untold number of other invasive invertebrate and plant species that threaten to destroy this fragile ecosystem while our backs are turned.

The Galápagos National Park and the Charles Darwin Foundation have had considerable success in ridding the islands of introduced mammals: goats, donkeys, pigs, cattle, dogs and to a lesser extent, cats; these are the 'easy' species to eradicate. In 2000 the number of introduced plants was around 550, similar to the number of native species; they now number more than 720. No one really knows how many introduced invertebrates there are: we know of at least 460 introduced insect species, six of which are invasive and a threat to the ecosystem. The task is huge, we need funding for a serious programme of control and eradication of invasive species and education and effective controls to stop the importation of new alien species.

The other problem is 'us': we are the most invasive and destructive creature of all. The population of Galápagos, while officially just over 25,000, is probably approaching 40,000 and still growing. The Galápagos National Park has had to release small amounts of land to allow for this rapid population growth. It is not just the size of the population that is cause for concern, but their economic activities. Often the problem is caused by businesses based in Ecuador or elsewhere who are just looking to make

money out of Galápagos, with little thought for the wildlife or the people who live there.

Fishing has been a serious problem in the past, but is less so now because the fishermen have used up so much of the resource that it is a less attractive economic activity than it was previously. The new problem is tourism, not the economically sustainable variety that uses smaller boats owned and crewed by local people, but the ever increasing number of larger boats owned and crewed by people from outside Galápagos and which bring relatively little benefit to the islands, but take a lot out of them. While the threat of very large, 500 passenger or more, cruise ships has been removed, the threat of Galápagos being opened to mass tourism is ever present. The key for the islands must be 'sustainability' and the tourism industry itself must fight to ensure that it remains sustainable.

The key to the future of the Galápagos, both as a natural laboratory for the study of evolution and as the world's most amazing zoo, is how we deal with these two 'problems'. Clearly the only answer to invasive species is their control or preferably eradication. Population growth and economic activity is far more difficult. If we put our heads in the sand and ignore it, then it will surely make the conservation of the ecosystem academic. If however we stop seeing the people as the problem, and look on them as the solution, then we have a chance of succeeding. If we can help the people of Galápagos to appreciate fully the importance of conservation and their environment, of not importing alien species, of developing economically sustainable businesses that directly benefit the local people, then we will have a chance to save this remarkable, inspiring and thought-provoking group of islands.

What, you may ask, is such an 'appeal' doing in the introduction to a guide to the animals and plants of the Galápagos? Quite simply this; it is only by understanding the issues that you can fully appreciate the importance and value of Galápagos. I hope that by using this guide to help to identify the plants and animals of Galápagos you will come to appreciate ever more deeply the amazing nature of the biology of the islands, their significance and the importance of preserving them.

One of the attractions of the Galápagos for the novice is that there are relatively few species; this makes identification a great deal easier. Iguanas are very straightforward; the black ones are Marine, the yellow ones are Land, and if it's pink, then you must be on Volcán Wolf! Lava lizards and tortoises vary according to the island they are on, as do Scalesia and cacti. Darwin's finches are probably the trickiest, especially as they vary so much and even cross-breed at times. This book is not just about identification, it is about the animals and plants themselves, why they are interesting or important. Take a closer look at your surroundings, understand it a little better, look after it a lot better and your children and grandchildren will be able to visit these wonderful islands and see and appreciate what you have seen, what I first saw in 1964 and what Charles Darwin saw back in 1835.

Julian Fitter, Maketu, New Zealand, September 2015

GALÁPAGOS ISLANDS
(Ecuador)

roads
✈ airports
▲ 113   height in metres
(3700) height in feet
Floreana location name

0   34 Km

P A C I F I C   O C E A N

Equator

I. Darwin
I. Wolf

I. Pinta
▲ 777 (2550)

I. Marchena
▲ 343 (1125)

I. Genovesa
Bahía Darwin

Roca Redonda

C. Berkeley
Pta. Albemarle
▲ Volcán Wolf 1707 (5600)
Volcán Ecuador ▲
Pta. Vicente Roca
Caleta Webb
I. Fernandina
Bahía
▲ Volcán La Cumbre 1494 (4900)
Urvina
C. Douglas
Pta. Espinosa
C. Hammond
Pta. Mangle

James Bay
▲ 907 (2974)
I. Santiago
I. Bartolomé
Sullivan Bay
Rocas Bainbridge
I. Daphne Mayor
I. Seymour
I. Baltra
I. Sombrero Chino
✈

Bahía Cartago
▲ Volcán Darwin 1326 (4350)
I. Rabida
I. Pinzón

Caleta Tagus
▲ Volcán Alcedo 1125 (3700)
Isla Isabela
Bahía Elizabeth
Pta. Moreno

▲ Cerro Azul 1689 (5540)
Volcán Sierra Negra
Volcán Chico 1491 (4890)
Santo Tomás
Puerto Villamil
I. Los Hermanos
I. Tortuga
C. Rosa
Pta. Cristóbal
Pta. Essex

Isla Eden
Cerro Dragón
▲ 863 (2830)
Santa Rosa
Bellavista
Camote
Puerto Ayora
Bahía Tortuga
I. Santa Cruz
Islas Plazas
I. Santa Fé

Post Office Bay
Pta. Cormorán
I. Enderby
I. Champion
Puerto Velasco Ibarra
▲ Cerro Pajas 640 (2080)
I. Floreana
I. Gardner

Bahía Hobbs
Pta. Pitt
La Galapaguera
I. San Cristóbal
León Dormido
Puerto Baquerizo Moreno
El Progreso ▲ 717 (2350)
✈

Arecife McGowan
I. Española
B. Gardner
Pta. Cevallos
Pta. Suárez

Island Names and Origins

Most of the islands in Galápagos have more than one name – Santa Cruz has had up to thirteen different names over the years. In 1892, on the quatercentenary of Columbus' voyage, the Ecuadorian government renamed the islands El Archipelago de Colon and gave all the islands official names. With two exceptions these are the names in common usage today. The exceptions are Santiago, whose official name is San Salvador, and Floreana, which has the official name of Santa Maria.

COMMON NAME	ENGLISH NAME	DERIVATION
Pinta	Abingdon	One of Columbus' ships; The Earl of Abingdon
Isabela	Albemarle	Isabela of Castille; The Duke of Albemarle
Baltra	South Seymour	
Santa Fé	Barrington	Holy Faith; Admiral Samuel Barrington, RN
Beagle	Beagle	HMS *Beagle*
Marchena	Bindloe	Fray Antonio Marchena; Captain John Bindloe
Tortuga	Brattle	Spanish for turtle; Nicholas Brattle
Bartolomé	Bartholomew	Lt David Bartholomew, RN
Caldwell	Caldwell	Admiral Caldwell, RN
Champion	Champion	Andrew Champion, whaler
Floreana	Charles	King Charles II
San Cristóbal	Chatham	Christopher Columbus; William Pitt, First Earl of Chatham
Cowley	Cowley	Ambrose Cowley, buccaneer
Crossman	Crossman	Richard Crossman
Darwin	Culpepper	Charles Darwin; Lord Culpepper
Daphne	Daphne	HMS *Daphne*
Pinzon	Duncan	The brothers Pinzon; Admiral Viscount Duncan, RN
Eden	Eden	
Enderby	Enderby	Samuel Enderby, whaler
Gardner	Gardner	Lord Gardner
Guy Fawkes	Guy Fawkes	Guy Fawkes, the English conspirator
Española	Hood	España – Spain; Admiral Viscount Samuel Hood, RN
Santa Cruz	Indefatigable	Holy Cross; HMS *Indefatigable*
Santiago	James	Spanish for James; King James II
Rábida	Jervis	Convent of La Rábida; Admiral John Jervis
Sin Nombre	Nameless	
Fernandina	Narborough	Admiral Sir John Narborough
Onslow	Onslow	Richard Onslow, 3rd Baron Onslow
Plaza	Plaza	Leonidas Plaza, President of Ecuador
Seymour	North Seymour	
Genovesa	Tower	Genova, birthplace of Columbus
Watson	Watson	
Wolf	Wenman	Theodor Wolf/Lord Wenman

Sources: Slevin, J. R. *The Galápagos Islands. A History of their Exploration* (1959).

NATIONAL PARK RULES

The Galápagos Islands are one of the few places in the world that remain relatively untouched by human exploitation. The preservation of the environment is everybody's responsibility. You can help, by following some simple rules which will help to maintain the archipelago's fragile ecosystem intact. The future depends on you.

This is a summary of the Galápagos National Park rules – you can obtain a full copy online or from your tour operator, or on arrival in Galápagos. Please respect them – the islands are only in such pristine condition because the several million visitors who arrived before you respected and stayed within the rules. Thank you.

- Any visit within the protected area of the Galápagos National Park (GNP) must be accompanied by a naturalist guide, authorised by the Galápagos National Park Directorate (DPNG).
- Use only tourism operators who are authorised by the DPNG.
- Keep to marked trails and areas, and respect the signage at all times.
- To avoid disturbing animals, stay at least 2 m away from them, and respect their space and freedom. The animals are used to humans walking on the trails and so feel comfortable with this, but as soon as you go off the trail you are doing something not normal and this can agitate them. This rule applies to the distance between the subject and any recording equipment, such as your camera lens or microphone.
- Take photos and videos without flash or additional lighting to avoid disturbing the animals. Any commercial or professional photography or video requires a licence from the DPNG.
- There are designated areas for camping; to use these you should request authorisation from the DPNG (San Cristóbal, Santa Cruz, Isabela) at least 48 hours in advance.
- It is your responsibility to avoid introducing food, animals or plants to the archipelago. Please cooperate with the inspection and quarantine officials at airports and docks in the islands.
- Do not buy any products or souvenirs made from banned substances such as coral, shell, lava rock, animal parts or endemic materials. This is an illegal activity.
- Removing native animals and/or plants in any form without national park authorisation is illegal. There is an inspection of all luggage at the airports.
- Please do not leave any trace of your presence on the island: take only photos and memories; leave only footprints.
- Please take your trash with you. The centres of all towns and villages have effective waste-management systems. It is best if you return to your country with your old batteries and other contaminating items.
- Smoking and lighting campfires in the protected areas of the GNP is strictly prohibited, as there is a serious risk of causing major fire damage.
- Fishing is not allowed except on recreational fishing boats authorised by the DPNG.
- Motorised aquatic sports, mini-subs, drones and aerial tourism are not permitted in the GNP.

The Galápagos National Park thanks you for respecting these rules. Think about others who come after you; they'll be grateful to you for your conservationist attitude.

PHOTOGRAPHY NOTES

Pre-planning

You will have given a lot of thought to your Galápagos holiday, so it is well worth spending a little time considering how to record what you see. Consider whether you want still images, underwater images and/or video. Also how you will transfer and edit this data.

Before you set off, make sure you have insurance cover for all your equipment, checking that your policy fully covers loss or damage and travel in South America. Keep a checklist of all the equipment you are taking – remember that most cameras and lenses have serial numbers and that these will be required should you have to make a claim. If any of your equipment is stolen, report the theft to the local police and obtain a statement confirming the incident, as some insurance companies need this information.

Equipment

Cameras

The choice of cameras today is vast, but you can begin to narrow down the search by deciding how much you want to spend and whether your interest is in stills or video. For still images, decide between a single-lens reflex (SLR) camera, which has interchangeable lenses, or a compact camera, which does not.

Most top brands have two or three levels of SLR, usually reflected in the price and function. Pay particular attention to the sensor that is used to record the image, its size and the number of pixels, and whether the camera automatically cleans the sensor. This last aspect is very important, as each time you change a lens, dust can enter, and this will then show up on every image until the sensor is cleaned. Top-of-the-range SLR cameras use a full-frame sensor similar in size to 35 mm film; other sensor sizes are the smaller 1.6, 1.3 and Micro Four Thirds (MFT). The advantage of smaller sensors is that the subject size is bigger in the recording area, but the disadvantage is that a lot of pixels are crammed into a smaller area. Entry- and mid-level SLR cameras are likely to have 12–20 million pixel sensors, while the top-level full-frame sensor may have 35 million pixels or more. If you are interested in underwater photography, check that an underwater housing is available for the SLR model you choose.

Entry-level SLR cameras can still offer an impressive array of options and are competitively priced – they are often less expensive than many top-end compact cameras. Entry-levels SLRs usually have a plastic body, which is fine provided you do not throw them around, and they are usually smaller than the mid-level models. The sensor size is generally 1.6.

Mid-level SLRs are the most popular models, with a mix of basic and advanced options in a more robust body construction. Top-level SLRs are expensive but offer outstanding performance and quality. They are usually water- and dust-resistant, with a full-frame or 1.3 sensor, and have the very best auto-focus and metering technology. The downside is their size and weight, which can be double that of the entry-level models.

When it comes to compact cameras, the choice is vast. These cameras mostly come with some form of zoom lens: this is ideal for composition as you can make your subject bigger or smaller. This change in subject size is normally achieved optically by an increase or decrease in lens size, which produces the best results. Some compact cameras achieve the zoom digitally by cropping the sensor, but the results are not as good. Increasingly popular are bridge cameras, which handle like an SLR but have a 24× or even 50× fixed super-zoom lens. Finally, if you are likely to take your compact with you when you go swimming, look for one that is waterproof.

Mobile-phone and tablet cameras

Most mobile phones now come with a built-in camera. Some are very basic in quality but can be fine for sending images to another mobile device, while many smartphones record good-quality images that can be downloaded at home and printed. Similarly, most tablets have built-in cameras. While these are great fun to use, their screens can be difficult to manipulate in the bright Galápagos sunlight. To minimise camera shake, it could be worth investing in a mobile- or tablet-specific stand or even a selfie stick. Don't forget to use a protective case for your device.

Do ensure that your device has enough internal memory. If you don't have a laptop with you, the opportunity to transfer images to your cloud account will be limited as Internet and Wi-Fi service in Galápagos is confined to the three main towns. Some mobile phone signal is available in many locations, apart from the far west and some distant islands. However, aside from the cost, 3G signal is erratic and has low capacity, so it is best to plan that you won't have any access. When you are out of signal, it's worth putting your phone onto flight mode to save battery usage.

Camcorders

All the new camcorders available on the market shoot in high definition (HD), and some video is saved in advanced video coding high definition (AVCHD), which is used by many professional film-makers but may not be compatible with some home computer software programs. The other commonly used video compression format is H.264 (often known as MPEG-4), which saves footage more efficiently, thereby using less memory. Check what memory cards are available for your camcorder, along with the battery life and the cost of spare batteries. Also look at what optics are available – 5× or 10× zooms are normal, but some zooms go up to 35×, which is great for capturing distant action.

Today, there is a lot of cross-over between SLRs, compacts and camcorders. It is quite common for the latest SLRs to take HD video, which is great if you mainly want stills but also want to record video action, and the same is true of compacts, tablets and mobile phones. Many camcorders also have the option to record still images, and some of the very latest cameras allow photo-quality freeze-framing, with pre-10-second record memory.

Lenses

If you have an SLR camera, think about what interchangeable lenses to take with you. To some extent this will be dictated by the manufacturer, although there are some very good independent manufacturers who make lenses to fit most models.

Your lens options can be broken down into three main types: short, medium and long (see below). Within these types there are zoom or fixed-focal-length lenses. Zoom lenses have many advantages; particularly, that one lens can cover a multitude of different situations. For the very best optical results, a fixed-focal-length lens is considered ideal, but this

A medium zoom is going to be the most useful, 70–200mm.

does involve carrying several lenses. Lenses with image stabilisation (IS) or (OS), while costing extra, are worth considering. The most suitable for Galápagos would be a short and a medium lens.

Short lenses With zoom lenses ranging from between 8–16 mm and 18–300 mm there is lots of choice. Something between 18 mm and 70 mm will be the most useful. It is worth remembering that some of these lenses are not compatible with full-frame-sensor cameras.

Medium lenses These lenses tend to be in the 70–300 mm to 100–400 mm range. Some medium lenses have wide apertures, such as f2.8, and are compatible with converters, which increase the effective focal length by a factor of either 1.4× or 2×.

Long lenses Most of the wildlife in Galápagos is very tame, so very long fixed-focal-length lenses are not necessary. That said, there are some very good own-brand 200–400 mm lenses, often combined with 1.4× or 2× converters. If your budget does not stretch to these expensive lenses, look at the long zoom lenses made by some of the independent manufacturers, such as the 150–600 mm.

If you are interested in photographing the world in close up, look at the shorter 70 mm macro lens for plants and the longer 180 mm lens for subjects that move.

Professional photographers need to buy a permit from the Galápagos National Park. If you are using professional-looking equipment, be prepared to explain yourself to officials. For more details, visit www.galapagospark.org.

Memory cards

Camera memory cards come in a number of different types, the most common being CompactFlash (CF) and Secure Digital (SD). The card capacity is measured in gigabytes (GB) – the more gigabytes it has, the more images can be stored. Memory cards also come in different speeds, indicating the time it takes to transfer the picture information onto the card ('read' it) and from the card to your computer ('write' it); these speeds are measured in kilobytes or megabytes per second (KB/sec or MB/sec). The

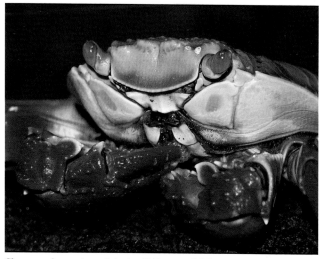

Close-up and macro lenses help view Galápagos wildlife in a different way: this is a Sally Lightfoot Crab.

main advantage of the faster MB cards is the speed at which the picture information is moved around. If you are taking lots of pictures in quick succession, you don't want to be held up by a slow transfer rate. Don't forget your card reader or transfer lead if you plan to download or back up to a laptop. Some modern cameras are Wi-Fi- or Bluetooth-enabled.

Treat the memory card with care – do not squash or drop it, and keep the connecting terminals free from dust. Its a good idea to store your cards in purpose-made cases, which will protect them from damp and dust. Take plenty of memory cards, you will take many more pictures than you expect.

Batteries

As most digital cameras use rechargeable batteries, don't forget to pack chargers. Most boats and hotels in Galápagos use the US system of a two-pin flat plug and 110V. Another alternative is to take a solar charger. Remember to have enough spare rechargeable batteries to allow for those days when mains electricity may not be available. If you are using disposable batteries, take them home with you.

Camera bags

There are a large number of camera bags available and purchasing one is a matter of personal choice. However, consider buying one that doubles as a rucksack, as this is a more comfortable way of carrying equipment over rough ground. Some camera bags of this type also have a built-in waterproof cover, which provides useful extra protection for wet landings. In selecting a suitable bag, resist the temptation to purchase one that is too big – you will only feel obliged to fill it! Check it comes within the recommended size of the airline you are using.

A photographic waistcoat is a handy garment for keeping photographic accessories readily to hand. Waist-mounted camera and lens pouches can

A rucksack-style camera bag is the most comfortable way of carrying equipment.

help to spread the load. Waterproof stuff bags, available in varying sizes, offer an additional form of protection. Alternatively, a supply of large plastic bags can be a useful way of protecting equipment or even your entire camera bag. Just check they do not have safety holes in them.

Camera supports

The commonest cause of picture failure is lack of definition as a result of camera shake. The most effective way of overcoming this is by using a good tripod – there are many light yet sturdy models on the market. The delicate volcanic rock of the Galápagos is easily damaged by tripod legs that have metal spikes, so choose one with rubber feet. Monopods are also a good means of steadying a camera. Rifle stocks and pistol grips are another form of support and allow freedom of movement when photographing moving subjects.

Flashes

The Galápagos National Park has a 'no flash' rule. With the ambient light generally being very good and modern cameras offering adjustable ISO settings (see below), it is easy to manage without a flash. If your camera has a built-in flash, make sure this is switched off.

Other camera accessories

A cable release is an excellent way of reducing camera shake – your camera should accept either an electronic or mechanical type. To help distribute the weight of your camera and lens while you are carrying it around, choose

While autofocus is a great help for photographing birds in flight, don't forget to use a faster shutter speed.

a wide camera strap with some elasticity. A small hot-shoe spirit level for checking straight horizons can be a great aid to landscape photographers.

Technique

For the most part, the secret to successful photography lies in the ability to master and control several major factors – those of exposure, lighting, depth of field, definition and composition.

ISO and noise

The ISO system sets how sensitive the image sensor is to the amount of light present. This affects the shutter speed/aperture combinations you can use to obtain correct exposure. However, the price you pay for using a high ISO is 'noise'. This is apparent by the presence of colour speckles where there should be none. It's worth doing some tests to see how high you can push the ISO before noise becomes noticeable. On most cameras, this will be 400 ISO, but on some it may be much higher.

Exposure

Your camera will have a mode dial, which gives options to automate your exposure. Remember that obtaining the correct exposure is a combination of aperture and shutter-speed settings. Aperture controls the depth of field by making the aperture of the lens iris larger or smaller, and the shutter controls the length of time the light is allowed to pass through the aperture. If you set the mode dial to 'Av', you set the aperture and the camera works out how long to allow light through. 'Tv' works in the opposite way, while 'P' allows the camera to work both settings out for you. 'M' is totally manual, so you have to determine both the shutter speed and the aperture. Some mode dials also include small symbols: if you select a flower or mountain symbol, the camera will set a small aperture, which will give great depth of field; if you select the running person symbol, the camera will use a faster shutter speed to freeze the movement.

There are situations in Galápagos where even the most complex metering system is going to struggle. A good example would be a white bird like a

Nazca Booby on very dark volcanic rock: the meter will try to adjust the exposure correctly for the rock, but this will then overexpose the bird. This is where a good understanding of your camera comes into play. Most SLR cameras will have a +/− (overexposure/underexposure) override and, in the situation outlined above, you will need to underexpose by about one to two stops to ensure the correct exposure. The same effect can be obtained by doubling the sensor speed (for example, from 100 ISO to 200 ISO), but remember to change these settings back before moving on.

Regularly check your results on the camera's LCD monitor, as this will give you an instant indication of what your pictures look like. Badly exposed results can then be deleted and retaken.

Lighting

The Galápagos Islands are on the Equator, where the sun rises quickly to the point where it is directly overhead. This overhead lighting is not ideal for photographing wildlife or landscapes; low side lighting is better for showing detail in wildlife subjects and creates interesting shadows in landscapes. So for the best photographic conditions it's important to get ashore at sunrise and again in the late afternoon. While most wildlife photographs are taken with the sunlight behind the photographer, so that the subject is fully lit, remember that some spectacular images can be taken using side or back lighting, particularly using the warm glow created at sunrise and sunset.

Depth of field

The range of apertures, or 'f' stops, available on each individual lens determines depth of field. In most landscape pictures, taken with wide-angle or standard lenses, maximum depth of field is generally selected to render as much of the foreground, middle ground and far distance as sharp as possible. To achieve this result, it is necessary to select a small aperture of f16 or f22. This will consequently result in a slow shutter speed, so ensure you use some means of support.

For individual images of birds or mammals taken using longer lenses, it is often better to select a large aperture of f5.6 or f4. This will result in the background being thrown well out of focus, which in turn will help to isolate your subject.

Composition

Unlike many elements of a photograph, which are automatically selected by the camera itself, composition demands an active input from the photographer. It is therefore in your own interest to be fully conversant with the factors relating to good composition.

Many newcomers to photography tend to produce all their images in a horizontal (landscape) format. Don't forget that cameras work equally well in a vertical (portrait) format.

Also remember to consider changing your viewpoint. Explore the possibilities of photographing a subject by kneeling or even lying on the ground. When it comes to precise framing, zoom lenses are very useful, allowing control over subject size and perspective. In some cases, the size of the main subject can be quite small within the picture space, provided that the inclusion of more of the surroundings adds information or pictorial interest. Any animal portrait will be greatly improved if you can make your exposure when a 'highlight' is visible in the eye.

Try to avoid placing your subject in the centre of the picture space. Instead, mentally divide the space into thirds, both vertically and horizontally, and place your main point of interest where the lines cross. Do pay attention to the horizon, particularly in landscapes, and keep it along the thirds. Ensure the horizon is always level. Computer programs make it easy to stitch together two or three images to make interesting panoramic landscapes.

Raw or JPEG formats

The most common formats for recording your images are JPEG or Raw. You will have the option in your camera set-up to select the format you prefer. The JPEG format is popular because it is a very space-efficient way of recording your images, but it does this by using varying degrees of compression to reduce the file sizes, at the expense of fine image detail. Raw files contain all the data collected by the sensor and give more flexibility for later correction of exposure, colour and sharpness of image.

Camera care and maintenance

All your equipment will be subjected to the potentially damaging effects of the environment. Remember that a single piece of dust or grain of sand on the image sensor will show as a dark speck on every image. A rubber blower brush or mini-vac sucking device is ideal for keeping the inside of your camera clean, while lens elements and filters are best cleaned with specially purchased cleaning fluid and tissues, alcohol or even fresh water as a last resort.

Keeping notes

The identification of Galápagos species often depends on where the subject was photographed. If you have set the date and time correctly on your camera, this information should be embedded in the background information stored on each image. By keeping detailed notes of what you saw and which island you were on each day, you will then be able to sort out and identify species much more easily.

KEY TO SPECIES' STATUS

(e)   Endemic – found only in Galápagos.

(es)   Endemic subspecies – found only in Galápagos, but other closely related members of the species found elsewhere.

(n)   Native – found in Galápagos and elsewhere, but arrived in Galápagos by natural means (plants and invertebrates).

(r)   Resident – equivalent to Native; breeds in the islands (birds).

(pr)   Possible resident – seen throughout the year, but has not yet been recorded as breeding.

(v)   Vagrant.

(i)   Introduced – brought to Galápagos by people, either deliberately or inadvertently.

(ip)   Introduced pest – introduced species that is a serious threat to the Galápagos ecosystem.

(m)   Migrant – regular visitor, normally in the northern winter.

(ro)   Regularly observed (cetaceans and turtles).

20   (oo)   Occasionally observed (cetaceans and turtles).

BIRDS

One of the most attractive features of birdwatching in the Galápagos is that you can identify most species without being an expert. There are only about 60 resident species and 13 of these are the finches! The finches themselves constitute 50% of all the resident land species and several of them can be identified by location: which island and which vegetation zone. Some species like the penguin and Flightless Cormorant identify themselves; others like the mockingbirds and finches can be identified by location. So while you will be able to identify most species quite easily, for others, including some of the finches, you need a good view and a good guide to help in their identification.

Yellow Warbler sitting on a nest.

The relative paucity of species is in reality one of the beauties of Galápagos birds. The finches and mockingbirds are excellent examples of adaptive radiation where one species has developed differently on different islands as a result of their isolation. This development, which is not surprising with reptiles and mammals that cannot fly, is quite surprising with birds that can move from island to island relatively easily. You should though, not look on adaptive radiation, or the evolution of new species, as a thing of the past – it is almost certainly continuing even now, but so slowly that it may be hundreds or thousands of years before any visible differences are evident.

Interestingly the number of resident species of bird is growing. Two species have been introduced: pigeons, which have now been eradicated, and the Smooth-billed Ani; one species, the Cattle Egret, has arrived unaided. It is too early to be sure of the longer term impact of these new arrivals on the Galápagos ecosystem, but Anis eat lizards, eggs and small birds as well as spreading seeds of introduced pest plants such as Mora or Blackberry.

In addition to the resident species, there are a number of regular visitors, mainly migratory waders from North America and as such they will generally be seen in winter plumage making identification tricky. Some can be found in the islands year round and these may eventually become resident and breed in the islands.

To date no endemic bird species has become extinct, however there are several species that are vulnerable due to their restricted breeding range and habitat. Both the Mangrove Finch (<100 individuals), found in only a few patches of mangrove on Isabela, and the Floreana Mockingbird (300 individuals), found only on two small islands off Floreana, are very vulnerable. The Waved Albatross is threatened due to fishing activity. Other species, such as the Flightless Cormorant and the Galápagos Rail or Crake, are vulnerable due to climate and habitat change or the introduction of new predators. Complacency is a real danger and many more species must be viewed as vulnerable. Apart from the finches and the boobies, relatively little work has been done on Galápagos bird species. It is only when armed with accurate information and a full understanding of the species can we feel at all confident of their future.

SEA BIRDS

(e) Galápagos Penguin *Sphensicus mendiculus*

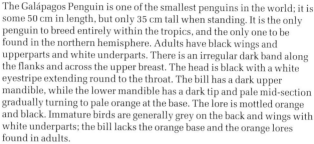

The Galápagos Penguin is one of the smallest penguins in the world; it is some 50 cm in length, but only 35 cm tall when standing. It is the only penguin to breed entirely within the tropics, and the only one to be found in the northern hemisphere. Adults have black wings and upperparts and white underparts. There is an irregular dark band along the flanks and across the upper breast. The head is black with a white eyestripe extending round to the throat. The bill has a dark upper mandible, while the lower mandible has a dark tip and pale mid-section gradually turning to pale orange at the base. The lore is mottled orange and black. Immature birds are generally grey on the back and wings with white underparts; the bill lacks the orange base and the orange lores found in adults.

The call is a soft donkey-like bray, similar to its cousin the Jackass or Magellanic Penguin (*Sphensicus magellanicus*).

Galápagos Penguins are opportunistic breeders and may breed at any time of the year when the food supply is abundant, most commonly starting in April or May when the water temperature is below 23°C. They nest in small colonies in holes or crevices in the rocks close to the shore. The normal clutch is two eggs of which only one chick generally survives. Incubation takes around 40 days and is performed by both parents who look after the chick(s) for a further 60 days before it is able to fend for itself. After becoming independent the chick may stay in a small group with its parents for appreciably longer.

Penguins are found mainly on Fernandina and the north and west of Isabela, although they do breed in small numbers on Bartolomé, Floreana and possibly on Santiago and are seen occasionally elsewhere in the islands. They feed mainly on small fish, including herring (*Sandinops sagax*), piquitingas (*Lile stolifera*) and mullet (*Mugil* spp.), caught within 2 km of the shore and at depths of up to 50 m.

The current population is thought to be in the region of 2,000 individuals but was seriously affected by the 1982/3 and 1997/8 El Niño events, which affected its food supply and reduced the population by 75% and 65%, respectively. Numbers have since recovered but it is a slow breeder and breeding success is influenced by the strength or otherwise of the annual El Niño. One problem identified by researchers is a lack of suitable nesting sites and, to this end, they are experimenting by building 'nesting caves' out of lava rock. Preliminary results are encouraging. The above factors, combined with a slow reproductive rate and a breeding area restricted by the presence of introduced predators such as cats, rats and dogs on the main islands, mean that the Galápagos Penguin is clearly endangered.

Best viewed: Fernandina – Punta Espinosa; Isabela – Bahia Elizabeth, Tagus Cove, Punta Albemarle; Santiago – Bahia Sullivan; Bartolomé – Sombrero Chino; Floreana – Punta Cormorán.

(e) Waved Albatross *Phoebastria irrorata*

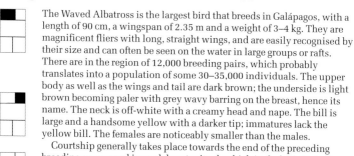

The Waved Albatross is the largest bird that breeds in Galápagos, with a length of 90 cm, a wingspan of 2.35 m and a weight of 3–4 kg. They are magnificent fliers with long, straight wings, and are easily recognised by their size and can often be seen on the water in large groups or rafts. There are in the region of 12,000 breeding pairs, which probably translates into a population of some 30–35,000 individuals. The upper body as well as the wings and tail are dark brown; the underside is light brown becoming paler with grey wavy barring on the breast, hence its name. The neck is off-white with a creamy head and nape. The bill is large and a handsome yellow with a darker tip; immatures lack the yellow bill. The females are noticeably smaller than the males.

Courtship generally takes place towards the end of the preceding breeding season and is an elaborate ritual, which includes bill circling and clacking, a formalised dance (waddle) and a cow-like 'moo' with the bill raised vertically. The breeding season is dictated both by the presence of the south-east trade wind and the cool nutrient-rich waters of the South Equatorial current. Males return to breed in mid-March followed by the females; a single egg is laid on the bare ground between mid-April and late June. Incubation, which is shared, takes some 60 days. When incubating, the egg is held between the tarsi and may be moved considerable distances whilst in this position. The young are fed almost daily when first hatched; feedings become further apart as the chick grows rapidly to become a large ungainly fluffy brown ball. They are fed with pre-digested oil manufactured by the parents from fish and squid, the principal constituents of their diet. Fledging takes place some 170 days after hatching and adults and young leave the island in December. Young birds do not start breeding until their sixth year. Recent studies have shown that 15–20% of young are raised by male birds that are not their natural parent. This is due to 'extra pair copulation' (EPC), which is surprisingly common given that they are generally monogamous.

The Waved Albatross is found only on Española, with a very small population of just a few pairs on Isla La Plata off the coast of Ecuador, and has the smallest range of any albatross: during the chick brooding period (2–3 weeks) the adults forage in a narrow quadrant NNW, and within 100 km, of Española; once the chick is old enough to be left alone and during the non-breeding season, they forage in the nutrient-rich waters off Peru. They feed mainly on small fish and squid, often scavenging close to fishing boats, which can cause mortality.

The waved Albatross is a long-lived bird with a low reproductive rate, breeding in one location; this makes it a vulnerable species. In addition it suffers significant loss in its main foraging area off the coast of Peru where it is targeted as a food species by fishermen as well as suffering as a by-catch in larger fishing operations.

Best viewed: Española – Punta Suarez; also at sea in the southern half of the archipelago.

ⓔ Galápagos Petrel *Pterodroma galapagensis*

Previously the Dark-rumped or Hawaiian Petrel. A large (length 43 cm, wingspan 90 cm) graceful petrel, with black upperparts, white underneath and a distinctive white forehead. Breeds in the Miconia Zone on Santa Cruz, Santiago, San Cristóbal, Floreana and Isabela during the Garua season (May–November); its distinctive 'kee-kee-kee' call can be heard only at night when it comes to the nesting area. Single egg hatches after 50 days; fledging takes five months; sexual maturity is reached after five or six years. Mates for life, and uses the same burrow each year. Population is less than 2,000 pairs. Feeds mainly on small fish and squid. The species is vulnerable, due to small population, predation and loss of habitat.
Best viewed: At sea around the islands.

ⓔ Galápagos Shearwater *Puffinus subalaris*

Small shearwater (length 30 cm, wingspan 70 cm) often seen feeding in large flocks with Common Noddies and pelicans. Black upperparts, white underneath; underside of wings has black edging. Breeds in colonies. One large egg laid in a hole or crevice in a cliff. Incubation takes 50 days, fledging 75 days. Feeds on fish, crustaceans and squid caught underwater.
Best viewed: Santa Cruz – Puerto Ayora; Genovesa. Widespread.

Storm Petrels

Small, swallow-like birds. Three species breed in Galápagos. All are 15–20 cm long with a wingspan of about 40 cm. The plumage is black with a white rump. They have pronounced tubular nostrils, characteristic of all petrels. Feed on plankton, crustaceans, fish and squid larvae.

ⓔⓢ White-vented Storm Petrel *Oceanites gracilis galapagoensis*

Smallest of the resident species, best identified by its square-ended tail and, in flight, by feet projecting beyond tail; white or grey line on undersides from breast to vent. Likes to feed around boats at anchor. Hovers close to surface with legs hanging down. Breeds in islands, most likely in small scattered colonies, sites unknown.
Best viewed: Widespread at sea and in sheltered anchorages.

ⓔⓢ Galápagos Storm Petrel *Oceanodroma tethys tethys*

Has large triangular white rump extending almost to the end of the slightly notched tail. Easily identifiable at its nesting sites as it is the only diurnal storm petrel. Breeds between April and October. A single white egg is laid in a small burrow or cavity in the rocks. The colony on Genovesa numbers up to 200,000 pairs.
Best viewed: Genovesa – Darwin Bay; San Cristóbal – Isla Pitt.

ⓡ Madeiran Storm Petrel *Oceanodroma castro*

The largest of the resident species, the white rump is almost square and the tail is noticeably forked; underwing dark. Less likely to be seen inshore than the other two resident species. Shares the same nesting site on Genovesa as the Galápagos Storm Petrel, but comes to the area only at night.
Best viewed: Widespread throughout the islands.

ⓡ Red-billed Tropicbird *Phaethon aethereus*

One of the most beautiful and spectacular birds, found throughout the islands. The Latin name derives from the legend of Phaeton, son of Helios, the sun god of Greek mythology, the first *enfant terrible*, who nearly set the earth on fire by driving his chariot too close to the sun. A largely white bird (length 48 cm) with a large bright-red bill and two extremely long tail feathers (length 50 cm). It has black barring on the back and black primary feathers on the wings (wingspan 50 cm). The immature lacks the long tail feathers and has a yellowish bill. The legs are very short, hence the need to breed on cliffs. Tropicbirds are plunge divers, feeding on small fish such as herring and mackerel.

Nests in cracks and holes in cliffs throughout the islands. On South Plaza it has an annual cycle, eggs being laid between August and February, elsewhere in the islands breeding is year round, dependent on food supply. A single egg is incubated by both parents and takes some 40–45 days to hatch; chicks fledge at 12–15 weeks. Courtship is a spectacular aerial display with the birds gliding with wings held upwards in a deep 'V', whilst emitting a high-pitched 'kree-kree-kree'. Not threatened. The upper middle right photograph shows a Red-billed Tropicbird being attacked by a frigatebird to force it to disgorge its catch.
Best viewed: Genovesa; South Plaza; Española; North Seymour.

ⓔⓢ Brown Pelican *Pelecanus occidentalis urinator*

An unmistakeable, large brown bird (length 110 cm, wingspan 230 cm), which flies with its neck held in an 'S' shape. It has a long neck and an even longer bill, the lower mandible of which is partly made up of a large pouch, which enables it to catch fish up to 35 cm in length. Adults are largely dark brown with a paler head and neck, which changes in the breeding season to a striking chestnut neck and a white or creamy coloured head, the wings taking on a silvery tint. The immature is a rather drab brown, paler on the underside. The Brown Pelican has very large webbed feet. The adults make virtually no vocal noise, though the young may mew for food, or hiss and clap their bills when disturbed. Widespread throughout the islands, particularly where there are mangrove lagoons, and also in most of coastal tropical America.

They fish by what looks to be an entirely graceless, though actually very effective, plunge dive, filling their pouch with a large amount of seawater and then filtering out small fish and crustaceans. They commonly attend ships and fishing boats as well as the fish dock in the main ports, knowing these to be a ready source of food.

The Brown Pelican breeds in small colonies or individually in mangroves or small bushes, occasionally on rocks. The nest is an untidy affair of twigs and small branches into which two or three eggs are laid and incubated by both parents. Incubation takes about 30 days and the remarkably unattractive and noisy young, on which you can often see biting flies, fledge at about 10 weeks. Breeding is year round with most pairs in a colony breeding simultaneously.
Best viewed: Most anchorages and visitor sites.

The Boobies

The Galápagos are the home of three species of booby, large diving seabirds with dagger-like bills in the same family as the Gannet found in both the Northern and Southern Hemispheres. Visitors are likely to see all three species. It is interesting to note that the three species, while breeding close to each other, do not generally fish close to each other. Blue-foots generally fish inshore, often in spectacular numbers and in conjunction with skipjack tuna, pelicans and noddies. The Nazca Booby fishes further out within the islands while the Red-footed is rarely seen fishing within the islands, preferring to fish far out at sea. A fourth species, the Brown Booby *Sula leucogaster*, is also seen occasionally in the islands. The name 'booby' derives from the Spanish word *bobo*, meaning a fool or clown.

(es) Blue-footed Booby *Sula nebouxii excisa*

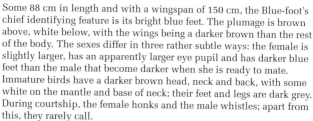

Some 88 cm in length and with a wingspan of 150 cm, the Blue-foot's chief identifying feature is its bright blue feet. The plumage is brown above, white below, with the wings being a darker brown than the rest of the body. The sexes differ in three rather subtle ways: the female is slightly larger, has an apparently larger eye pupil and has darker blue feet than the male that become darker when she is ready to mate. Immature birds have a darker brown head, neck and back, with some white on the mantle and base of neck; their feet and legs are dark grey. During courtship, the female honks and the male whistles; apart from this, they rarely call.

Blue-foots nest in dispersed colonies close to the sea. Their courtship display is a truly clown-like performance, with their blue feet much in evidence. These are lifted one at a time in a solemn dance, just like a clown wearing an enormous pair of shoes. The pair then 'skypoint'. This involves pointing their tails and beaks vertically upwards, half-opening their wings and honking or whistling according to their sex. Breeding is opportunistic and takes place at any time of the year when the food supply is abundant. Up to three eggs are laid and are incubated by both parents for 42 days. The young are quite capable of eating their siblings if food runs short. They take 102 days to fledge and start breeding after three to four years.

The Blue-foot population in Galápagos is in serious decline, from an estimated 10,000-plus pairs in the 1960s to around 3,000 pairs in 2011–12. The decline seems to be the result of a massive decline in breeding success, apparently triggered by a dramatic decline in their main food source of sardines. This appears to date from the large El Niño event in 1997–8. While the continental population *S. n. nebouxii* is stable, the Galápagos subspecies is clearly endangered. Distribution: Found throughout the islands. They breed on the islands south of the Equator, though they have been known to breed on Genovesa.
Best viewed: Coastal waters throughout the islands. Española – Punta Suarez; San Cristóbal – Punta Pitt; Daphne; North Seymour; Baltra.

(v) Brown Booby *Sula Leucogaster*

Similar in size to the Red-footed Booby, with a dark brown back, head, neck, throat and upper breast, white underparts, and a distinctive hard line separating the upper and lower breast. The underwing is dark brown around the edges and white inside. The bill and legs are pale yellow to horn-coloured. Adult males may have a whitish head.

ⓔ Nazca Booby *Sula granti*

The largest of the three species of booby found in the islands (length 92 cm, wingspan 155 cm), the Nazca Booby is arguably the handsomest. The adult is almost entirely white with a black tail and black ends to the primary feathers on the wing. The bill is yellow, rather paler in the female than in the male. The skin at the base of the bill is black, thus giving it a masked appearance. It was previously thought to be a subspecies of the Masked Booby (*Sula dactylatra*). The immature is largely brown on top and pale underneath (photo top right). They give an indignant squawk if you approach too closely. Conservation status: not threatened.

As with the other boobies, the Nazca Booby feeds almost entirely on fish, which it catches by plunge diving. Unlike the Blue-footed Booby, which fishes close inshore, the Nazca Booby fishes further offshore and so is less frequently observed fishing.

Breeding takes place on an annual cycle but not quite the same cycle on all islands. The courtship is along the same lines as the Blue-footed Booby but far less elaborate. Two eggs are laid but only one chick is reared. Laying takes place on Genovesa between August and November, while on Española, most eggs are laid between November and February.
Best viewed: At sea throughout the islands and at the breeding colonies. Española – Punta Suarez; San Cristóbal – Punta Pitt; Genovesa.

ⓔⓢ Red-footed Booby *Sula sula websteri*

The Red-footed Booby is the smallest of the three Galápagos boobies (length 74 cm, wingspan 97 cm), and is easily identifiable on land by its bright red feet. It is semi-nocturnal and nests and perches in trees, and is rather more graceful than the other two species of booby found on the islands. The Red-footed Booby has two distinct plumage phases: the brown phase, which is by far the commonest in Galápagos, is almost entirely mid-brown in colour with red feet and legs and a blue-grey bill with pink facial skin. The white phase is almost entirely white apart from the tips of the primary feathers and the tail, which are black. An intermediate plumage stage can also occur. The Red-footed Booby (white phase) can be differentiated from the Nazca Booby in flight by its smaller size; also it has a blue-grey rather than yellow bill and a whiter appearance. Its call is a strange 'quacking' sound, which is higher pitched and more nasal in the male.

Red-footed Boobies feed out in the open ocean, well away from land, often on the 'bajos' or submarine volcanoes that are found to the north and east of the archipelago. They feed exclusively on fish, sometimes catching flying fish leaping out of the water.

The breeding cycle of the Red-foot is long and can often last for 12 months or more. Courtship involves head shaking and skypointing, but is not as dramatic as in the Blue-foot, and is performed in the trees. A single egg is laid on a platform of twigs and is incubated by both parents for 45 days. The chick fledges after 130 days but is still dependent upon the adults for a further 90 days. This is clearly linked to the far ranging, semi-nocturnal, deep-sea fishing habits of the species. The population is thought to number in excess of 140,000 pairs, and it breeds on Tower, San Cristóbal, North Seymour, Wolf and Darwin.
Best viewed: At sea. Genovesa; San Cristóbal – Punta Pitt; North Seymour; Wolf; Darwin.

ⓔ Flightless Cormorant *Nannopterum harrisi*

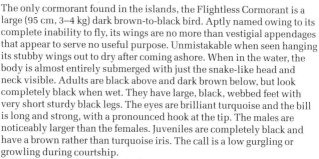

The only cormorant found in the islands, the Flightless Cormorant is a large (95 cm, 3–4 kg) dark brown-to-black bird. Aptly named owing to its complete inability to fly, its wings are no more than vestigial appendages that appear to serve no useful purpose. Unmistakable when seen hanging its stubby wings out to dry after coming ashore. When in the water, the body is almost entirely submerged with just the snake-like head and neck visible. Adults are black above and dark brown below, but look completely black when wet. They have large, black, webbed feet with very short sturdy black legs. The eyes are brilliant turquoise and the bill is long and strong, with a pronounced hook at the tip. The males are noticeably larger than the females. Juveniles are completely black and have a brown rather than turquoise iris. The call is a low gurgling or growling during courtship.

The Flightless Cormorant feeds on small fish, eels and octopus, which it catches close inshore. It dives from the surface with a jack-knife movement and uses only its large and powerful webbed feet to pursue its prey.

The Flightless Cormorant nests in small colonies close to the shore, and has an elaborate courtship ritual, which normally starts in the water with an aquatic dance. The necks are held in a snake-like pose known as 'snake necking' and the birds swim back and forth past each other. The dance is continued on land and a large bulky nest is made of seaweed, which is largely brought by the male and presented to the female as part of the courtship ritual. This is added to by the male, who brings more seaweed when he takes over the incubation. Breeding takes place year round, though most eggs are laid between May and October. Incubation takes about 35 days and initially both parents feed the young. If, however, the food supply is good, the female may leave and mate with another male, while the first male continues to look after and feed the young, for up to nine months.

Its status is vulnerable: it is found only on Fernandina and northern and western Isabela (population of around 900 individuals), and is susceptible to high mortality during major El Niño events. It also faces the threat posed by introduced species, cats and dogs, on Isabela.
Best viewed: Fernandina – Punta Espinosa; Isabela – Urvina Bay, Punta Moreno to Punta Garcia.

(es) Magnificent Frigatebird *Fregata magnificens*

The larger of the two frigatebirds found in Galápagos, up to 114 cm long and with a wingspan of up to 245 cm. Frigatebirds have the largest wingspan-to-weight ratio of any species of bird and are extremely able and skilled fliers. It is also known as the 'man of war' bird due to its piratical habits. The male (upper left photo) is entirely black with a purplish sheen on its back and a red gular (throat) pouch, which is only visible during the breeding season. The female (upper right photo) is slightly larger than the male and has a white breast and shoulders, but is otherwise completely black. Immatures (middle right photo) have a white head and neck and breast. Males have a shrill ululating call during courtship; young birds squeal when requesting food. The species is pantropical, widespread throughout the islands, with a possible population of several thousand pairs.

Frigatebirds eat a wide range of food including fish, small crustaceans and newly hatched Green Turtles (*Chelonia mydas*), which they pick up off the beach almost as soon as they emerge from the nest. They may fish directly from the surface of the sea, or will frequently chase other species, such as Blue-footed Boobies (*Sula nebouxii*) or Red-billed Tropicbirds (*Phaeton aethereus*), and force them to disgorge their recent catch, often by actually holding the tail feathers, shaking them until the bird disgorges its catch, and then catching it before it hits the water.

Breeding can occur at any time of the year. Courtship is spectacular with several males sitting close together, inflating their scarlet gular pouches, lifting their heads and emitting their shrill ululating trill, this progressing to an acrobatic aerial display by the pair who then build an insubstantial nest of twigs in low trees or shrubs close to the shore, often using twigs stolen from other frigatebirds. A single egg is laid, which is incubated by both parents for some 42 days. The young fledge after some 90 days but are often looked after for up to six months by the parents. *Best viewed:* Throughout the islands, and at their breeding sites. North Seymour; Floreana – Gardner; San Cristóbal – Wreck Bay, Kicker Rock, Punta Pitt; Genovesa.

(r) Great Frigatebird *Fregata minor ridgwayi*

Very similar but slightly smaller than *F. magnificens*, up to 114 cm in length and with a wingspan of up to 230 cm. The adult (pair, middle photo; male bottom left photo) is indistinguishable from the Magnificent Frigatebird except when seen close up. The Great Frigatebird has a greenish sheen on its back, while the Magnificent has a purplish one. It also has brownish primary coverts. Female all black apart from white breast and throat. The juvenile (bottom right photo) has rust-coloured patches on the head and breast. The population, range and call is similar to that of *F. magnificens*.

Similar feeding habits to *F. magnificens*, but less likely to be seen in coastal waters as it feeds at sea on fish, especially flying fish, and squid. It too is involved in kleptoparasitism, stealing from anyone and everyone. Both species also feed on Sea Lion placenta.

Courtship is similar to the Magnificent Frigatebird but the egg takes 55 days to incubate. The young are dependent on the parents for up to 18 months after fledging as the feeding technique is much more difficult to master than that of the inshore-fishing Magnificent Frigatebird. The Spanish name, *Pajaro Pirata*, translates as 'Pirate Bird', an apt description. *Best viewed:* At sea throughout the islands. Española – Punta Suarez; North Seymour; Genovesa; San Cristóbal – Punta Pitt; Fernandina – Punta Espinosa.

ⓔ Swallow-tailed Gull *Larus furcatus*

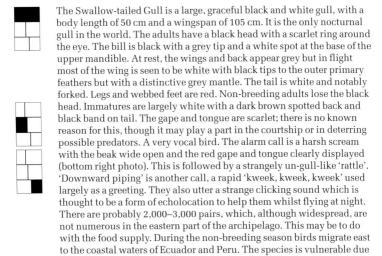

The Swallow-tailed Gull is a large, graceful black and white gull, with a body length of 50 cm and a wingspan of 105 cm. It is the only nocturnal gull in the world. The adults have a black head with a scarlet ring around the eye. The bill is black with a grey tip and a white spot at the base of the upper mandible. At rest, the wings and back appear grey but in flight most of the wing is seen to be white with black tips to the outer primary feathers but with a distinctive grey mantle. The tail is white and notably forked. Legs and webbed feet are red. Non-breeding adults lose the black head. Immatures are largely white with a dark brown spotted back and black band on tail. The gape and tongue are scarlet; there is no known reason for this, though it may play a part in the courtship or in deterring possible predators. A very vocal bird. The alarm call is a harsh scream with the beak wide open and the red gape and tongue clearly displayed (bottom right photo). This is followed by a strangely un-gull-like 'rattle'. 'Downward piping' is another call, a rapid 'kweek, kweek, kweek' used largely as a greeting. They also utter a strange clicking sound which is thought to be a form of echolocation to help them whilst flying at night. There are probably 2,000–3,000 pairs, which, although widespread, are not numerous in the eastern part of the archipelago. This may be to do with the food supply. During the non-breeding season birds migrate east to the coastal waters of Ecuador and Peru. The species is vulnerable due to its small numbers and restricted range.

The Swallow-tailed Gull is the only night-feeding gull in the world. It leaves the nest site at dusk and fishes well out to sea, generally some 15–30 km from land. Little is known about its feeding habits, but it may have special visual and sonar facilities. Its diet consists largely of small fish and squid. The gulls possibly make use of the bioluminescence of these light-emitting animals in the water. In this context, the red ring around the eye may help them locate their prey more precisely, red being commonly associated with improved night vision. When the bird returns to the nest site, the white spot at the base of the upper mandible may help the young to locate the food source. Additionally, the fact that the young are white (the only gull to have white young) may help the adult locate them.

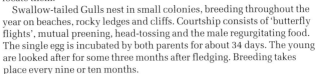

Swallow-tailed Gulls nest in small colonies, breeding throughout the year on beaches, rocky ledges and cliffs. Courtship consists of 'butterfly flights', mutual preening, head-tossing and the male regurgitating food. The single egg is incubated by both parents for about 34 days. The young are looked after for some three months after fledging. Breeding takes place every nine or ten months.

Best viewed: Genovesa; South Plaza; Española – Punta Suarez.

ⓔ Lava Gull *Larus fuliginosus*

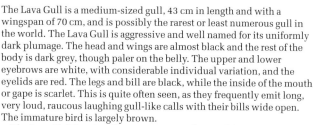

The Lava Gull is a medium-sized gull, 43 cm in length and with a wingspan of 70 cm, and is possibly the rarest or least numerous gull in the world. The Lava Gull is aggressive and well named for its uniformly dark plumage. The head and wings are almost black and the rest of the body is dark grey, though paler on the belly. The upper and lower eyebrows are white, with considerable individual variation, and the eyelids are red. The legs and bill are black, while the inside of the mouth or gape is scarlet. This is quite often seen, as they frequently emit long, very loud, raucous laughing gull-like calls with their bills wide open. The immature bird is largely brown.

The Lava Gull is primarily a scavenger and nest robber. It will also eat lizards and newly hatched iguanas and turtles, and will on occasion catch fish and small crustaceans in shallow lagoons and beaches.

A solitary nester on sheltered beaches and lagoons, its two olive, heavily blotched eggs blend in with their surroundings and are difficult to pick out. Incubation takes around 30 days and the young fledge at about 60 days. They are then looked after by the adults for a short period. Being scavengers, immature Lava Gulls are more naturally self-sufficient than some species with more specialised feeding habits. The total population is thought to be only around 400 pairs spread around the islands, with concentrations near the ports where their scavenging habits pay off. However, they are considered to be vulnerable, in view of the small population and ground nesting.

Best viewed: Widespread. South Plaza; Santa Cruz – Puerto Ayora, Bahia Tortuga; Isabela – Villamil; Genovesa.

ⓜ Franklin's Gull *Larus pipixcan*

A small gull (37 cm) that is found in Galápagos mainly during the northern winter and therefore in non-breeding plumage. The wings and back are grey with a grey patch behind the eye. The rest of the plumage is white, with dark bill and legs with just a hint of red. In breeding plumage, the head is black with white eyelids, the legs and bill dark red. Wings in flight show white tips to the primary feathers, followed by a broader band of black, and then a white band. The rest of the wing is mid- to dark grey.

Franklin's Gull is not known to breed in Galápagos.

Best viewed: Widespread from October to March.

ⓜ Laughing Gull *Larus atricilla*

This is not a common gull. In winter plumage, the Laughing Gull is similar to Franklin's Gull but larger (42 cm). In flight, it is distinguishable from Franklin's Gull by the completely dark wing tips. First-year birds are rather browner on the head, neck and breast than Franklin's Gull. The bill is clearly larger with a more downcurved upper mandible than the bill of Franklin's Gull; this is the best way of distinguishing the two species in non-breeding plumage when not in flight. Breeding plumage is similar to Franklin's Gull, apart from the wings. Call is a series of laughter-like 'screams', hence its name.

The Laughing Gull is not known to breed in Galápagos.

Best viewed: Widespread from October to March.

(es) Brown Noddy *Anous stolidus galapagensis*

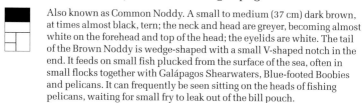

Also known as Common Noddy. A small to medium (37 cm) dark brown, at times almost black, tern; the neck and head are greyer, becoming almost white on the forehead and top of the head; the eyelids are white. The tail of the Brown Noddy is wedge-shaped with a small V-shaped notch in the end. It feeds on small fish plucked from the surface of the sea, often in small flocks together with Galápagos Shearwaters, Blue-footed Boobies and pelicans. It can frequently be seen sitting on the heads of fishing pelicans, waiting for small fry to leak out of the bill pouch.

The Brown Noddy breeds throughout the year on rock ledges and in small caves in cliffs, generally in small colonies, often quite close to the water. Courtship includes a lot of nodding and bowing, hence the common name. A single off-white blotched egg is laid on the bare rock. They breed less than once a year.

Best viewed: Widespread throughout the islands. South Plaza; Santa Cruz – Puerto Ayora; Rábida; Isabela – Tagus Cove; Bartolomé.

(r) Sooty Tern *Sterna fuscata*

A strikingly plumaged tern with black upperparts, white underparts and forehead, and a deeply forked tail. The bill and legs are black. Immature Sooty Terns have wing and mantle feathers tipped with white. They feed on small fish by plunge diving. Sooty Terns have a characteristic flight pattern with slow continuous wing beats, giving the impression of the body moving up and down with each beat.

The Sooty Tern is found only on the northern islands of Darwin and Wolf, where it breeds in large numbers.

Best viewed: Darwin; Wolf. Rarely seen elsewhere in the islands.

(m) Royal Tern *Sterna maxima*

Large (51 cm) tern seen in Galápagos only during the northern winter, in non-breeding plumage. Royal Terns have large orange bills, white forehead, black further back on the head, turning into a distinct crest. Generally white underparts and grey wings and mantle, but black primary feathers. Tail is deeply forked, but less so than the Sooty Tern. Legs and feet are black.

The Royal Tern is not known to breed in Galápagos.

Best viewed: Isabela – Quinta Playa. From January to March.

(m) Common Tern *Sterna hirundo*

Small (30cm) slim tern with grey mantle and wings and black primary feathers. The head has an incomplete black cap and the bill is black in winter, sometimes with a red base. In breeding plumage, the black cap is complete and the bill scarlet with a black tip. The feet and legs of the Common Tern are scarlet. Underparts are white, with a deeply forked tail.

The Common Tern is not known to breed in Galápagos. It is seen only in small numbers from December to March.

Best viewed: Southern islands.

COASTAL BIRDS

(r) Great Blue Heron *Ardea herodias*

The largest heron in the islands, the Great Blue stands nearly 1-m high with a wingspan of nearly 2 m. It is largely blue-grey on the wings and back, the underparts being paler. The head is black and white, the breast streaked with rufous, and black on the folds of the wings. The thighs are rufous. It has distinctive head plumes during the breeding season. The legs are long and dark grey. The bill is orange-yellow but darker on top. In flight, the neck is pulled back in an S-shape. The Great Blue Heron feeds on small fish, crabs, lizards, young iguanas and young birds

Breeding occurs all year round on a large untidy platform of twigs in mangroves or sometimes on cliffs. It nests solitarily, laying two or three eggs that hatch after 28 days. Incubation and feeding is shared by both parents.
Best viewed: On beaches and lagoons on all the main islands.

(r) Great White Egret *Ardea alba*

Also known as the Common Egret. A large elegant all-white heron, at 85 cm it is slightly smaller than the Great Blue Heron. The plumage is all white with long elegant plumes on the back during the breeding season, the bill is large and yellow, the feet and legs black.

Feeding habits are similar to the Great Blue Heron, but will also eat locusts, grasshoppers and other insects.

The Great White Egret breeds in small colonies near the shore, on all of the main islands, generally in mangroves. The clutch is normally two eggs, incubation takes 25–26 days with fledging in 6–9 weeks.
Best viewed: Lagoons and intertidal zones on Santa Cruz, San Cristóbal, Isabela, Santiago and Floreana. Also found in the highlands in farming areas.

(m) Snowy Egret *Egretta thula*

Small (60 cm) all-white heron (though larger than Cattle Egret) with slender black bill and yellow lores (the area of skin just behind bill). The legs are black with yellow feet. The Snowy Egret is not known to breed in Galápagos.
Best viewed: Irregular visitor, rocky shorelines and lagoons.

(r) Cattle Egret *Bubulcus ibis*

Probably the most recent natural arrival in Galápagos, as part of a worldwide expansion of this species. The species was first recorded in 1964 and the first breeding recorded in 1986. It is now known to breed in several locations and the population is rapidly expanding. It is too early to say if this species will have a significant impact on any other species in Galápagos. The smallest (50 cm) all-white heron found in the islands. The bill is yellow. Legs and feet are dull yellow to red (when breeding) in adults but darker in immature birds. Breeding birds have a buff tinge to the head and back. Rather stubbier appearance than other egrets.

The Cattle Egret feeds on locusts, grasshoppers and other insects; also lizards and probably the young of iguanas and Green Turtles.

It is a colonial nester, normally in trees or bushes, laying two or three eggs. Incubation takes 22–26 days and fledging occurs around 4–5 weeks.
Best viewed: Agricultural areas on San Cristóbal, Santa Cruz, Floreana and Isabela. By mangroves and lagoons, and on South Plaza.

ⓔ Lava Heron *Butorides sundevalli*

Small (44 cm) blue-grey heron found throughout the islands on rocky shores and mangrove lagoons. Previously thought to be the same species as *B. striatus*. Dark blue-grey on wings and back, paler underneath, particularly on the breast. It has a bright yellow eye, and the soles of the feet are noticeably bright orange in flight. In breeding plumage, the legs are orange. The bill of the male is black, that of the female silver-grey. In non-breeding plumage, the legs are grey and the bill silver-grey. The immature bird is brownish and striated all over with greenish-brown upperparts and lighter underparts. It can easily be confused with the Striated Heron, but it lacks the yellow-orange lores between the bill and the eyes. It is more widespread than the Striated Heron. Its call is a loud 'squawk' or 'skeow', hence its local name of 'squacco'.

The Lava Heron feeds mainly on small fish, crabs, lizards and insects. When fishing from mangrove roots or rocks, it may jump or dive into the water to ensure the capture of its prey. It is often seen stalking Sally Lightfoot crabs on coastal rocks.

The Lava Heron is a solitary nester in mangroves or around lagoons, and is quite territorial. Nesting can be year round but generally starts between September and March. The clutch size is one to three eggs; incubation takes 20–25 days with fledging in five weeks. Pairs may breed more than once a year.

Best viewed: On coast and in mangrove lagoons throughout the islands.

ⓡ Striated Heron *Butorides striatus*

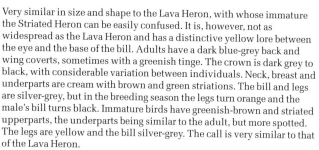

Very similar in size and shape to the Lava Heron, with whose immature the Striated Heron can be easily confused. It is, however, not as widespread as the Lava Heron and has a distinctive yellow lore between the eye and the base of the bill. Adults have a dark blue-grey back and wing coverts, sometimes with a greenish tinge. The crown is dark grey to black, with considerable variation between individuals. Neck, breast and underparts are cream with brown and green striations. The bill and legs are silver-grey, but in the breeding season the legs turn orange and the male's bill turns black. Immature birds have greenish-brown and striated upperparts, the underparts being similar to the adult, but more spotted. The legs are yellow and the bill silver-grey. The call is very similar to that of the Lava Heron.

The Striated Heron feeds on small fish, crabs, lizards and insects.

Breeding habits are similar to the Lava Heron, but it is recorded as nesting only on Isabela, Santa Cruz, Fernandina, Pinta and Pinzón, but possibly elsewhere. It is not thought to be threatened.

Best viewed: Mangrove lagoons and on rocky shorelines.

(es) Yellow-crowned Night Heron *Nyctanassa violacea*

Larger (60 cm) than the Lava or Striated herons and with a similar habitat, but largely nocturnal. The body is mainly grey, with brown and black feathers, especially on the scapulars. Very distinctive head markings: mainly black but with a broad white stripe running back from the underside of the eye and a cream-coloured crown with long cream-coloured plumes. The bill is dark, the legs orange-yellow, and the eye bright red-orange. The immature bird is generally grey-brown and striated all over, with a dark bill and dull orange-brown legs. The immature may occasionally be confused with the Striated Heron, however, its larger size and lack of the yellow/orange lores and yellow legs are diagnostic. Both adult and immature birds adopt a characteristic hunched position, often on one leg. The call is a sharp 'quock' or 'guaque', as in the Spanish name.

It feeds on crabs, scorpions, locusts and other insects, caught mainly at night. It favours mangrove lagoons and towns or villages with streetlights, which attract the painted locust, *Schistocerca melanocera*, and other insects.

The Yellow-crowned Night Heron is a solitary nester. The nest of twigs is built in low mangroves or in a crevice under a rock. A clutch of two to four blue-green eggs is incubated for 22–25 days by both parents; fledging occurs in four weeks.

Best viewed: Widespread on coast and occasionally inland. Not found on Darwin and Wolf.

(r) American Flamingo *Phoenicopterus ruber*

An unmistakable bird (130–145 cm in height), with immensely long legs, a long neck and striking pink to vermilion plumage. The plumage coloration varies with the amount of carotinoid pigment consumed in their diet of crustaceans and micro-organisms, filtered out of the saline waters of the coastal lagoons where they are found. The black wing primaries are only visible in flight. The legs and feet are pink or grey or flesh coloured; the feet are webbed, enabling the birds to swim. The bill is pink with a black tip and is strongly down-curved; when feeding, it is inverted and used as a filter. The young are much paler and gradually assume the pink coloration as they mature. In flight the neck is held out straight, unlike herons. The call is a soft goose-like honk, mainly in flight.

The diet is quite varied, with crustaceans, molluscs, annelid worms, insects and plant material, algae, diatoms, seeds, etc.

Nests are built in small colonies in a number of saline coastal lagoons. The nest of mud is conical and some 20–25 cm high. A single egg is incubated by both adults for 30 days. The chick leaves the nest soon after hatching and its initially straight bill starts to curve after three weeks or so; fledging takes 65–90 days. Breeding is often disrupted by El Niño, when the water level rises in the lagoons and floods the nests. The population appears to be declining with the latest count (February 2014) showing just over 300 individuals. However, the species is vulnerable, due to very small numbers.

Best viewed: Isabela – Villamil, Punta Moreno; Santa Cruz – Bahia Tortuga, Las Bachas; Floreana – Punta Cormorán; Rábida; Santiago – Puerto Egas; Rocas Bainbridge.

ⓟ Pied-billed Grebe *Podilymbus podiceps*

The only grebe found in Galápagos, the Pied-billed is a short (35 cm), dumpy, brownish bird. It is secretive and reluctant to fly, preferring to dive or hide in vegetation. The plumage is generally light greyish-brown, with a dark neck and short tail, and a distinctive black band around the heavy bill when in breeding plumage. The non-breeding adult has white under the chin. The immature plumage is as a non-breeding adult but with irregular stripes on side of head.

The Pied-billed Grebe feeds on a wide variety of prey, including aquatic insects, crustaceans, fish and leeches.

There are no records of breeding in Galápagos but, as sightings occur year round including immature individuals, it probably has. Elsewhere breeds year round.

Best viewed: Brackish and mangrove lagoons: Santa Cruz – Puerto Ayora, Bahia Tortuga; Floreana – Punta Cormorán; Isabela – Villamil; San Cristóbal – highlands.

ⓔⓢ White-cheeked Pintail *Anas bahamensis galapagensis*

Also known as the Galápagos Pintail. A small (41–51 cm), largely brown duck, one of only two found regularly in Galápagos. The plumage is all brown with a speckled breast, white cheeks and throat and a brown top to the head giving it a capped appearance. There is a conspicuous bright green patch or speculum on the wings. The bill is dark, with a pink or reddish base. The female is duller than the male; the immature is like the female, but the speculum is less iridescent.

The White-cheeked Pintail feeds on vegetable matter and invertebrates on the surface of water and by dabbling, but may also dive in deeper freshwater lakes and ponds to escape predators. The species is vulnerable, due to its restricted range and small population.

It is an opportunistic breeder, nesting when conditions are suitable. Up to ten pale brown eggs are laid in a well-hidden nest at the edge of the pond, lagoon or lake. The female incubates for 25 days and once hatched the chicks are able to feed for themselves. The White-cheeked Pintail is found on saltwater, brackish and freshwater lagoons, ponds and lakes, both permanent and temporary, throughout the islands.

Best viewed: Santa Cruz – Puerto Ayora, Turtle Bay, Las Bachas; Isabela – Villamil, Quinta Playa; Santiago – Puerto Egas; San Cristóbal – El Junco.

ⓜ Blue-winged Teal *Anas discors*

The Blue-winged Teal is slightly smaller (37–41 cm) than the White-cheeked Pintail. The male has a speckled chestnut body, darker on back and wings, a distinctive white crescent on the side of the head and a smaller white patch near the tail; the female is mid-brown with a paler head and neck and darker cap. Both sexes have a distinctive blue patch on the wing as well as a green speculum. The bill is dark, almost black.

It feeds on vegetable matter, and small invertebrates on the surface and by dabbling. Although a regular visitor to Galápagos, the Blue-winged Teal is not known to have bred, but the presence of groups of both sexes suggests it may have, or will do so shortly.

Best viewed: It is found in similar areas to the White-cheeked Pintail, but is less common; mainly on inland freshwater ponds, less common on coastal lagoons.

(es) American Oystercatcher *Haematopus palliatus galapagensis*

Heavily built shorebird. Underparts white, but otherwise largely black. A white wing patch and rump are visible in flight. Long, powerful red bill, laterally flattened to help open bivalves. Eyes yellow with red eyering. Feet and legs flesh coloured. The call is a shrill 'kle-e-ep'. Nesting takes place between October and March. Chicks leave nest on hatching.
Best viewed: Widespread throughout the islands.

(r) Black-necked Stilt *Himantopus mexicanus*

Also known as the Common Stilt. Elegant very long-legged wader. Distinctive plumage. Underparts white, upperparts mainly black with white forehead and patch behind the eyes. Legs and feet red. Bill long, straight, slender, pointed and black. Feeds on small invertebrates and fish. Breeds between December and June and courtship is preceded by an elaborate and acrobatic air dance. Four green-brown eggs are laid.
Best viewed: Coastal lagoons throughout the islands.

(m) Semi-palmated Plover *Charadrius semipalmatus*

Small, stocky shorebird, largely grey-brown with white underparts, white neck ring, forehead and a line over the eyes. Legs and feet dull orange-yellow. Bill dark with an orange base. Immature birds have all-dark bill. Breeding plumage similar with black on the upper breast, cheeks and forehead. A pale wingbar is visible in flight. Characteristic behaviour is to run a few metres and then stop. The call is a sharp 'chi-we'.
Best viewed: Throughout the islands from August to April.

(m) Black-bellied Plover *Pluvialis squatarola*

Also known as the Grey Plover. Breeding plumage jet-black underparts and breast, contrasting with silver-grey back and wings. Winter plumage much less striking, with grey-and-white upperparts and pale-grey underparts. The bill, legs and feet are black. In flight, a differentiating feature is the black patch under the wings where they join the body.
Best viewed: Coastal Lagoons throughout islands.

(m) Ruddy Turnstone *Arenaria interpres*

Small (24 cm) stocky wader with short legs. Breeding plumage, tortoise-shell back and wings, black-and-white patterned head, white underparts. Winter plumage grey or brown back and head, white underparts and dark breast. Bill dark with orange base in adults, all-dark in immatures. It appears to be up-turned. Legs orange-yellow, paler in winter. Feeds on small molluscs and crustaceans. Not known to breed in Galápagos.
Best viewed: Widespread throughout the islands.

(m) Wandering Tattler *Heteroscelus incanus*

Medium-sized (28 cm) strong-legged wader. Back and wings slate-grey. Breast and underparts heavily barred in the breeding plumage, breast grey and underparts white in winter plumage. Bill is dark, of medium length and heavy. Legs and feet yellow. Not known to breed in Galápagos.
Best viewed: Widespread on coasts throughout the islands.

ⓜ Western Sandpiper *Calidris mauri*

A small pale sandpiper. The winter plumage is almost indistinguishable from the Semi-palmated Sandpiper but the Western has an appreciably longer bill with a hint of a down-curve at the tip. Breeding plumage a much more rufous colour on back and head. Bill, legs and feet are black. This bird is not known to breed in Galápagos.
Best viewed: Beaches and coastal lagoons, December to March.

ⓜ Least Sandpiper *Calidris minutilla*

The commonest of the 'peep' sandpipers in Galápagos. Upperparts and head are much darker and browner than the Western or Semi-palmated Sandpipers. Winter plumage has red-brown cap. Bill black, very short and sharp. Legs are yellow, which distinguishes Least from the other two, which have black legs. The Least Sandpiper is not known to breed in Galápagos.
Best viewed: Beaches and coastal lagoons, December to March.

ⓜ Solitary Sandpiper *Tringa solitaria*

A medium-sized (22 cm) wader with dark upperparts and white under-parts, breast grey in winter plumage but barred in breeding. Fine white band above and around the eyes. Bill is dark, the legs greenish-yellow. Not to be confused with the Lesser Yellowlegs. Bobs a little like yellow legs. In flight, distinctive black-and-white barring to sides of tail. This bird is not known to breed in Galápagos.
Best viewed: Highlands, December to March.

ⓜ Spotted Sandpiper *Actitis macularia*

A small (19 cm) neat wader. In winter plumage, it has olive-brown upperparts and white underparts. Bill is short, sharp and dark. Legs are dull orange-yellow. White eyestripe above eyes. Breeding plumage has dark brown spots on the breast and flanks. In flight, narrow white wingbar and white sides to the tail are visible. Characteristic short glide after several short wing beats. Watch for bobbing or teetering movements. It is not known to breed in Galápagos.
Best viewed: Beaches and coastal lagoons, December to March.

ⓜ Sanderling *Calidris alba*

A small tide-line wader, frequently seen following waves up and down the beach rather like a clockwork toy. Winter plumage is largely white with a grey back and head; dark primary feathers. Breeding plumage much darker on the back with brown and black. Marked white wingbar in flight, the underside of the wing is very white! Bill, legs and feet are black. Not known to breed in the islands but is present all-year round.
Best viewed: Widespread on beaches.

ⓜ Short-billed Dowitcher *Limnodromus griseus*

Snipe-like wader. Winter plumage generally grey, upperparts darker. Distinctive pale eyestripe and barring on tail, particularly visible in flight. Long, thin, dark, pointed bill. Breeding plumage reddish brown. Legs are olive-yellow. This bird is not known to breed in Galápagos.
Best viewed: Coastal lagoons and beaches.

ⓜ Willet *Catoptrophorus semipalmatus*

Large (38 cm) non-descript wader, especially in winter plumage. Grey-brown back and head, paler undersides and neck. Long, heavy black bill. Legs dark in winter, bluish in breeding plumage, which is more barred on the back and flanks. In flight, black-and-white wing pattern shows on both upper- and undersides of wings. Not known to breed in Galápagos.
Best viewed: Beaches and coastal lagoons, December to March.

ⓜ Whimbrel *Numenius phaeopus hudsonicus*

Also called Hudsonian Curlew or Seven Whistler after its evocative call. Large (42 cm), brown wader with long, markedly down-curving bill. Underparts are pale brown; upperparts darker. Crown is striped dark and pale brown. Not known to breed but present all year.
Best viewed: Beaches, coastal lagoons and highlands, best on Isabela.

ⓜ Greater Yellowlegs *Tringa melanoleuca*

Large (36 cm) brown wader. Long, yellow legs and long, thin, pointed bill. Dark on top pale underneath with brown flecked breast. White eyeline in front of and above eyes. In flight, shows white rump and pale tail, but no wingbar. Not known to breed in Galápagos.
Best viewed: Beaches and coastal lagoons.

ⓜ Lesser Yellowlegs *Tringa flavipes*

Smaller (27 cm) than Greater, and commoner. Similar plumage to Greater, with distinctive yellow legs, long, fine, pointed bill, white rump, pale tail and no wingbar. Not known to breed in Galápagos.
Best viewed: Beaches, coastal lagoons and highlands, December to March.

ⓜ Surfbird *Aphriza virgata*

Plump plover-like wader. In winter, slate-grey back and breast, underparts white. Breeding plumage, brown above with golden scapulars, breast white with dark markings. Bill dark with orange base. Legs stout and yellow. In flight, note white wingbar, white rump and black tail tip.
Best viewed: Rocky coasts, December to March.

ⓜ Red-necked Phalarope *Phalaropus lobatus*

Small (20 cm) swimming wader. Winter plumage dark grey and white, black crown and distinctive black eye patch. Legs dark, bill short and dark. Phalaropes hold their head in a distinctively upright way, with bill parallel to water. Swims in circles to assist catching small fish and crustaceans. Distinctive white wingbars in flight. Not known to breed in Galápagos.
Best viewed: At sea and coastal lagoons, December to March.

ⓜ Wilson's Phalarope *Phalaropus tricolor*

Less common and slightly larger (24 cm) than Red-necked, with longer bill and generally paler. The dark eye patch less noticeable, white eye-stripe narrower and more distinctive. No wingbar but white rump and dark end to the tail. Legs yellowish. Not known to breed in Galápagos.
Best viewed: Mangrove lagoons especially on Santa Cruz.

LAND BIRDS

(e) Galápagos Hawk *Buteo galapagoensis*

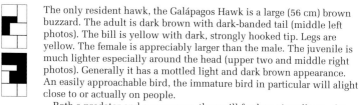

The only resident hawk, the Galápagos Hawk is a large (56 cm) brown buzzard. The adult is dark brown with dark-banded tail (middle left photos). The bill is yellow with dark, strongly hooked tip. Legs are yellow. The female is appreciably larger than the male. The juvenile is much lighter especially around the head (upper two and middle right photos). Generally it has a mottled light and dark brown appearance. An easily approachable bird, the immature bird in particular will alight close to or actually on people.

Both a predator and a scavenger, they will feed on virtually anything, especially young iguana, lizards, birds, especially doves and finches, rats (endemic and introduced), centipedes, locusts and on carrion such as dead goats, donkeys or sea lions and frequently on sea lion placenta.

The Galápagos Hawk nests on all the major islands apart from Genovesa, which it has probably never reached, and San Cristóbal and Floreana, as a result of eradication by humans. The nest is a large untidy pile of twigs and branches in a tree or on a rocky outcrop. A territory will have several nests, only one of which will be used at a time. Each female will mate with up to four males, all of whom help with incubation and rearing the young. This is known as 'co-operative polyandry', and clearly increases the chances of reproductive success. Two or three eggs are laid and hatch after some 50–60 days. The young birds are expelled from the territory after three to five months and spend two years or more in non-territorial areas before breeding. It is these immature birds that are most likely to approach humans. While breeding only takes place in the arid zone, individuals are frequently observed in all areas. There are thought to be only some 120–150 'pairs' but around 800 individual birds. This makes it a very vulnerable species.

Best viewed: South Plaza; Española – Punta Suarez and Gardner Bay; Fernandina – Punta Espinosa; Santa Fé.

(m) Osprey *Pandion haliaetus*

Also known as the Fish Eagle. Though not a common bird, the Osprey may be seen near mangrove lagoons. A large (60 cm) hawk, the Osprey is dark brown above, with white underparts, a head largely white with a black mark through the eyes and cheek. The tail is barred, black-brown above, black-white on underside. It has very long (150–180 cm) broad wings, often held with a marked crook in them. The Osprey fishes by plunge diving feet first.

The Osprey is not known to breed in Galápagos, though an occasional bird will stay over the summer.

Best viewed: Santa Cruz; San Cristóbal; Isabela.

ⓜ Peregrine Falcon *Falco peregrinus*

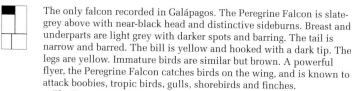

The only falcon recorded in Galápagos. The Peregrine Falcon is slate-grey above with near-black head and distinctive sideburns. Breast and underparts are light grey with darker spots and barring. The tail is narrow and barred. The bill is yellow and hooked with a dark tip. The legs are yellow. Immature birds are similar but brown. A powerful flyer, the Peregrine Falcon catches birds on the wing, and is known to attack boobies, tropic birds, gulls, shorebirds and finches.

The Peregrine Falcon is not known to breed in Galápagos.
Best viewed: Widespread but uncommon near cliffs and bird colonies.

ⓔⓢ Barn Owl *Tyto alba punctatissima*

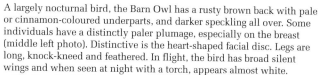

A largely nocturnal bird, the Barn Owl has a rusty brown back with pale or cinnamon-coloured underparts, and darker speckling all over. Some individuals have a distinctly paler plumage, especially on the breast (middle left photo). Distinctive is the heart-shaped facial disc. Legs are long, knock-kneed and feathered. In flight, the bird has broad silent wings and when seen at night with a torch, appears almost white.

The Barn Owl feeds entirely at night on rats, mice, small birds and larger insects.

Barn Owls are known to nest in all months of the year. Preference is for the arid and transitional zones but it will also nest in the highlands. It nests in holes, especially lava tubes and other volcanic features. The clutch of three eggs is incubated for about 30 days and the young fledge after 10–12 weeks.
Best viewed: At night on Santa Cruz, San Cristóbal and Isabela. (Visitors are not allowed ashore on the other islands at night!)

ⓔⓢ Short-eared Owl *Asio flammeus galapagoensis*

A dark brown owl, much more likely to be seen than the nocturnal Barn Owl. It has some lighter streaking above, paler underneath with dark markings. The dark facial disc emphasises the yellow eyes. The bill is dark, and the legs feathered. The short ear tufts are difficult to see. It is most likely to be seen in flight, hunting.

The Short-eared Owl feeds mainly on small birds, and particularly preys on storm petrel colonies, rats and mice (introduced) as well as some larger insects.

Nests on all the major islands apart from Fernandina. It prefers highlands. The nests are in open ground. The bird lays three or four eggs, though normally only two chicks survive to fledging.
Best viewed: Genovesa; highlands of Santa Cruz; San Cristóbal; Floreana; Isabela.

ⓔ Galápagos Dove *Zenaida galapagoensis*

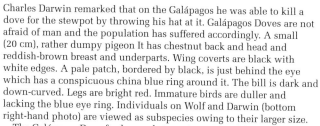

Charles Darwin remarked that on the Galápagos he was able to kill a dove for the stewpot by throwing his hat at it. Galápagos Doves are not afraid of man and the population has suffered accordingly. A small (20 cm), rather dumpy pigeon It has chestnut back and head and reddish-brown breast and underparts. Wing coverts are black with white edges. A pale patch, bordered by black, is just behind the eye which has a conspicuous china blue ring around it. The bill is dark and down-curved. Legs are bright red. Immature birds are duller and lacking the blue eye ring. Individuals on Wolf and Darwin (bottom right-hand photo) are viewed as subspecies owing to their larger size.

The Galápagos Dove feeds on whatever is most readily available, including insect larvae, seeds, pollen, and cactus fruit. It is a reluctant flier, which explains Darwin's ability to knock it down with his hat! The call is a repetitive soft 'cooing' by the males.

The Galápagos Dove nests all-year round depending on food supply, but mainly in the rainy season, February to June, when food is most abundant. Typical pigeon courtship including an aerial display and much bowing and cooing. It nests on the ground under an overhanging rock ledge or in Opuntia cactus, sometimes using old mockingbird nests. The normal clutch is two eggs, with a two-week incubation period and a further two weeks to fledging.

Best viewed: Drier parts of all the main islands.

ⓔ Galápagos Rail *Laterallus spilonotus*

Also known as the Galápagos Crake. A very small (15 cm) and secretive bird which is at the same time remarkably unafraid. Chocolate brown on its back, dark slate grey elsewhere, with white speckling on wings and flanks. Eyes are bright red-brown, the bill is black, and the legs are dark flesh-coloured. Immature birds are paler and not speckled. While not completely flightless, the Galápagos Rail is very reluctant to fly and very vulnerable to introduced predators such as rats and cats. While originally found in most vegetation zones, it is now found only in the highlands of the major islands though it is possibly extinct on Floreana. Conservation status: threatened.

The Galápagos Rail feeds on small invertebrates and seeds.

Ground nesting occurs on the major islands, and has been recorded in all months of the year though predominantly in the period June to February. Up to five eggs are laid in a covered nest. Incubation takes up to 25 days and the young birds reach maturity after a further 12 weeks or so.

Best viewed: Highland areas of Santa Cruz, San Cristóbal and Isabela.

(r) Paint-billed Crake *Neocrex erythrops*

Slightly larger (20 cm) than Galápagos Rail, plumage dark grey, bill yellow with red base, legs red; feeds on insects and other invertebrates.

Nests are found in thick vegetation, the bird laying six or seven eggs, which hatch within three weeks. The young leave the nest immediately. The main breeding period is December to May.

Best viewed: Farming zones: Santa Cruz; San Cristóbal; Floreana; Isabela.

Common Gallinule *Gallinula chloropus*

(r) Also known as the Moorhen. A medium-sized (34 cm) aquatic bird with long, olive-yellow legs and semi-webbed feet. Plumage is brown-black above, black on head, slate-grey underneath and on the breast and neck. The undertail is white and visible when swimming. There is also a white stripe along the flank. The bill, which is chicken-like, is bright red with a yellow tip. There is a red frontal shield extending onto the forehead. The immature bird is browner and paler underneath, and the bill is olive-yellow.

The Common Gallinule feeds on invertebrates, mainly in soil and leaf litter. It flies reluctantly.

The bird nests between May and October, close to the shore of a pond or lagoon, or in mangroves. Seven or more eggs are laid in a clutch. The young leave the nest as soon as all the eggs have hatched.

Best viewed: Coastal lagoons, highland ponds and mangroves on Santa Cruz, Isabela, San Cristóbal and Floreana. San Cristóbal – El Junco, La Toma.

Belted Kingfisher *Ceryle alcyon*

(m) A large (33 cm), strikingly plumaged bird and the only kingfisher found in Galápagos. Plumage is grey-blue above, white underparts. A blue-grey band extends across the breast. Neck white, head blue-grey with prominent crest and white spot just in front of eyes. The female has an additional cinnamon band across the abdomen. The outer tail feathers are barred dark grey and white. The primary feathers are black. The bill is long, stout and sharp.

The Belted Kingfisher feeds by plunge-diving either after hovering or directly from a branch. It is not known to breed in Galápagos.

Best viewed: Mangrove lagoons on Isabela and Santa Cruz.

Dark-billed Cuckoo *Coccyzus melacoryphus*

(r) A slender, elegant, long-tailed, skulking bird. Chestnut-brown above, grey-black cap to head, white below the eye. Underparts are pale beige with more rufous coloration on breast and neck. The bill is black and slightly downcurved. The tail is long, brown and with white tips to outer tail feathers.

Found largely in the arid zone where it feeds on insects. Population fluctuates with increases after wet periods. Nesting is linked to the onset of the rainy season, it lays up to six bluish-chalky-white eggs, the last egg may be laid after the first has hatched. Incubation lasts 10–12 days and chicks leave the nest when barely able to fly after a further 10–12 days.

Best viewed: On all major islands. Santa Cruz – Puerto Ayora. The Charles Darwin Research Station is one of the best places to see it.

Mockingbirds

There are four species of endemic mockingbird found in Galápagos, all with very similar plumage. They will eat almost anything including seeds, invertebrates, baby turtles, Sea Lion placenta, eggs and even ticks off the Land Iguana. They are excellent mimics and have even learnt to imitate the introduced Smooth-billed Ani.

(e) Galápagos Mockingbird *Mimus parvulus*

A slim, thrush-like bird with grey-brown plumage, the upperparts rather darker brown than the underparts. There is a distinct dark-brown patch in front of, and behind, the eye. The legs, bill and feet are dark, the bill being slightly downcurved. The eyes are yellowish-green. It nests in trees or cacti, generally after the start of the annual rains (December–April). Three or four eggs are laid and incubated for about two weeks. The young fledge in 17 days but remain dependent upon parents for five to six weeks, by which time the parents may be incubating a second clutch if the rains continue. The species has an unusual social structure whereby older offspring help to feed younger ones. The group stays together as a family after the end of the breeding season. There are six subspecies restricted to specific islands: *barringtoni* (Santa Fé), *bauri* (Genovesa), *hulli* (Darwin), *parvulus* (Santa Cruz, Seymour, Daphne, Isabela, Fernandina), *personatus* (Pinta, Marchena, Santiago, Rabida), *wenmani* (Wolf).
Best viewed: Santa Cruz; South Plaza, Santiago; Santa Fé; Isabela; Fernandina; Pinta; Marchena; Genovesa; Darwin; Wolf.

(e) Floreana Mockingbird *Mimus trifasciatus*

Virtually identical to *M. parvulus* but with red-brown eyes, the Floreana Mockingbird has rather browner plumage with conspicuous dark patches on the side of the breast. It is found exclusively on the small islands of Champion and Gardner, off Floreana. It was previously found on Floreana (English name Charles) itself, but it has become extinct there, presumably through the depredations of cats and rats. The total population is probably in the region of 150 individuals.
Best viewed: Champion; Gardner by Floreana.

(e) Española Mockingbird *Mimus macdonaldi*

Slightly larger than the other mockingbirds, the Española Mockingbird also is at times rather scrawny looking. The tail feathers have less white on them than other species. The longer legs are distinctive, and the bill more down-curved. The eyes are hazel. Outside the breeding season it may gather in large groups of up to 40 individuals. It is well known to follow tourists and is quite reluctant to fly. Found only on Española (English name Hood) and neighbouring Gardner island. When boats anchor at Gardner, they nearly always receive a delegation of mockingbirds.
Best viewed: Española; Gardner by Española.

(e) San Cristóbal Mockingbird *Mimus melanotis*

Very similar to other species, the San Cristóbal Mockingbird's plumage is mid-way between that of *M. parvulus* and *M. macdonaldi*. The eyes are greenish-yellow. It is found exclusively on San Cristóbal.
Best viewed: San Cristóbal.

(r) Vermilion Flycatcher *Pyrocephalus rubinus*

The adult male Vermilion Flycatcher is unmistakable, with brilliant undersides, breast, neck and cap. The back is black and there is a black eyeband running back to, and joining, the black on the nape of the neck. The bill, legs and feet are also black. The female is much less colourful, having yellow underparts, an off-white breast and neck and a brown head and back. The bill, neck and feet of both sexes are black. The immature bird resembles the female.

The Vermilion Flycatcher feeds on insects mainly caught on the wing, but it is also known to feed on the ground.

The bird breeds mainly during the warm season, December to May, on the coast, but may nest year all round in the highlands. It is known to breed frequently during heavy El Niño years. The population appears to be in decline, precise cause is unknown, but the parasitic fly *Philornis downsi*, which is affecting finch breeding success, may be at least part of the problem.

Best viewed: Widespread on main islands in dry areas and in highlands.

(e) Galápagos Flycatcher *Myriarchus magnirostris*

Also known as the Large-billed Flycatcher. Slightly larger than the Vermilion Flycatcher, and with a superficial resemblance to the female or immature bird of that species, the Galápagos Flycatcher has a mid-brown back and head, grey breast and pale-yellow underparts. The bill, legs and feet are dark, the bill being appreciably larger than that of the Vermilion Flycatcher. A double wingbar is visible on the closed wing.

The Galápagos Flycatcher feeds on flying insects and also larvae. It will often approach very close to humans and even accept insects from the hand.

Nests are constructed during the warm season, December to May, generally in a hole in a tree cactus or lava rock.

Best viewed: Widespread on all main islands, except Genovesa. Commoner in dry zones.

(es) Yellow Warbler *Dendroica petechia aureola*

A small (12 cm) bright-yellow bird commonly seen in all areas of the major and many of the smaller islands, particularly where it is dry. The adult Yellow Warbler has bright yellow underparts and head, is more olive-yellow above, and the wings have dark primary feathers and primary coverts. The male has red streaking on the crown and on the flanks. The bill and legs are dark. The bill is finely pointed, typical of most warblers.

Immatures are greyer, with very pale underparts; some yellow is always visible. It feeds on insects and is often seen feeding on flies in the intertidal zone. Frequently, it is seen entering houses to feed.

Nesting takes place during the warm season, December to April, and is largely dictated to by the annual rains (El Niño). In a major El Niño, breeding will take place several times. The nest is cup-shaped and generally located well off the ground in the canopy of a tree or bush. Two or three buff-spotted eggs are incubated by the female. The young are fed by both parents.

Best viewed: Widespread on all major islands and many small ones.

ⓘ Smooth-billed Ani *Crotophaga ani*

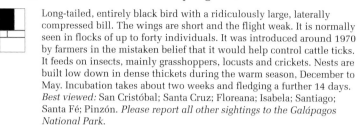

Long-tailed, entirely black bird with a ridiculously large, laterally compressed bill. The wings are short and the flight weak. It is normally seen in flocks of up to forty individuals. It was introduced around 1970 by farmers in the mistaken belief that it would help control cattle ticks. It feeds on insects, mainly grasshoppers, locusts and crickets. Nests are built low down in dense thickets during the warm season, December to May. Incubation takes about two weeks and fledging a further 14 days.
Best viewed: San Cristóbal; Santa Cruz; Floreana; Isabela; Santiago; Santa Fé; Pinzón. *Please report all other sightings to the Galápagos National Park.*

ⓟⓡ Bobolink *Dolichonyx oryzivorus*

A large sparrow-like bird, at first sight it may look like a large Darwin's finch. The breeding male is mainly black with a yellow nape and white on the rump and the back. The female is heavily streaked, rich buff-brown on the upperparts. Underparts are paler with some streaking. Immature birds and non-breeding males resemble a slightly pale female. The bill is rather more pointed than a finch or sparrow, black in the breeding male, mid-brown otherwise. No records of breeding, but year-round presence on San Cristóbal makes the Bobolink a good candidate.
Best viewed: San Cristóbal; highlands.

ⓔ Galápagos Martin *Progne modesta modesta*

The only resident member of the swallow family. Males are almost entirely blue-black, with slightly paler underwings. The wings are pointed and the tail narrow, with a shallow fork. Females are similar but dark brown below. Flight is typical of other martins: a series of quick wing-beats followed by a glide. The Galápagos Martin feeds on insects, always caught while on the wing. Widespread, but not common, most frequently seen in highland areas. Not found in the northern islands.
Best viewed: Isabela – Sierra Negra, Punta Moreno, Tagus Cove.

ⓜ Purple Martin *Progne subis*

Completely dark-coloured martin, easily confused with the Galápagos Martin. However, the Purple Martin is larger, 19 cm as opposed to 15 cm for the Galápagos Martin. Males are all dark with a steely-blue sheen; the female is duller and with a grey forehead and greyish underparts. The immature bird is grey-brown above and on the head, with pale underparts. Not known to breed in Galápagos.
Best viewed: San Cristóbal; Española.

ⓜ Barn Swallow *Hirundo rustica*

A long-winged swallow with a deeply forked tail. Dark blue above and on the head. Underparts are pale buff, the forehead and throat a rich cinnamon, with a narrow blue chest band. The immature bird is less strikingly marked and lacks the chest band; the immature tail also lacks long outer feathers. Flight is fast and often close to the ground or water. It feeds on insects, always on the wing.
Best viewed: Widespread, but uncommon during northern winter.

Finches

There are 14 species of finch in the Galápagos, collectively known as 'Darwin's finches'. No other group of birds, indeed no other group of animals, has had such a profound impact on the development of human thought and our understanding of our place in our world, than these little brown and black birds. When Charles Darwin visited the Galápagos in 1835, he collected specimens of the animals and plants that he encountered. Surprisingly for someone normally so precise in his observations, he at first neglected to label his finch specimens on the first two islands that he visited, San Cristóbal and Española. When he returned home to England to examine and catalogue his collection, he started to appreciate that these little birds were something rather special. They were what we now know to be one of the finest examples of adaptive radiation. Fortunately for Darwin, he was not the only person collecting on the Beagle. Both Captain Fitzroy and his helper and assistant, Syms Covington, had collected finches and had labelled them carefully.

As Darwin gradually came to appreciate the significance of the finches, he could see clearly that all these little brown birds were essentially similar. This has since been confirmed by DNA testing. Each species was fitted into its own particular ecological niche: the small, medium and large seed eaters, the nectar eaters, the fruit and insect eaters and, most surprising of all, the tool-using bird. All had developed from a common ancestor as a result of isolation and a lack of pressure from predators.

Today, it is easy for us to see how the finches of Galápagos, Darwin's finches, help to explain how life has developed and evolved. What is extraordinary, was that Charles Darwin should see this over 150 years ago without the benefit of the technology and facilities that we have today. So when observing these finches, be sure to appreciate the role that they have played in the history of human thought.

The finches are mostly identifiable by beak size and shape, and location. However, recent research has shown that very significant and rapid changes in beak size can occur in line with variations in food abundance. The males are generally dark brown or black and the females mid-brown. While some species have adapted well to urban life, they have all been impacted by the arrival of mammalian predators, especially rats and cats. More recently the arrival of the parasitic fly *Philornis downsi*, which lays its eggs in the finch nests, has become a serious threat. This is particularly so with the Mangrove Finch, which is arguably the world's most threatened bird species. Preliminary results from a captive breeding programme started in 2014 are encouraging.

(e) Large Ground Finch *Geospiza magnirostris*

Much the largest (16.5 cm) of the ground finches, it is easily identified by its disproportionately large beak, which is as deep as it is long, and is ideally adapted for cracking large, hard seeds. It tends to be solitary in contrast to *G. fortis* which often feeds in small groups. The adult male is black with white or buff tips to undertail coverts. Female grey brown, paler underneath and streaked, especially on throat and breast.

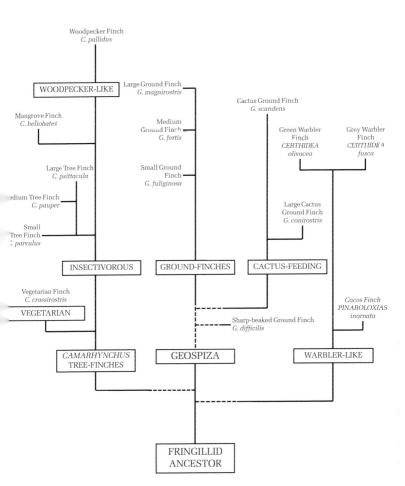

Woodpecker Finch
C. pallidus

WOODPECKER-LIKE

Mangrove Finch
C. heliobates

Large Ground Finch
G. magnirostris

Medium
Ground Finch
G. fortis

Small Ground
Finch
G. fuliginosa

Cactus Ground Finch
G. scandens

Green Warbler
Finch
*CERTHIDEA
olivacea*

Grey Warbler
Finch
*CERTHIDEA
fusca*

Large Tree Finch
C. psittacula

Medium Tree Finch
C. pauper

Small
Tree Finch
C. parvulus

Large Cactus
Ground Finch
G. conirostris

INSECTIVOROUS

GROUND-FINCHES

CACTUS-FEEDING

Vegetarian Finch
C. crassirostris

VEGETARIAN

*Cocos Finch
PINAROLOXIAS
inornata*

Sharp-beaked Ground Finch
G. difficilis

CAMARHYNCHUS
TREE-FINCHES

GEOSPIZA

WARBLER-LIKE

FRINGILLID
ANCESTOR

Finch family tree (after Lack).

(e) Medium Ground Finch
Geospiza fortis

Intermediate in size (12.5 cm)
between the Large and Small
Ground Finches, it has a heavy bill
but one that is much more pointed than
the Large. The beak size varies considerably,
even on the same island. The plumage is
virtually identical to that of the Large
Ground Finch. It tends to feed in flocks rather
than individually. This species also feeds on the
ectoparasites of tortoises and iguanas. Very well
adapted to urban areas.

(e) Small Ground Finch *Geospiza fuliginosa*

The smallest (11.5 cm) of the ground finches.
Very similar in plumage to the Large and the
Medium Ground Finches but with a short
stubby beak. Can be confused with the
Sharp-billed Ground Finch, but it is
much commoner. Has developed an interesting
relationship with the reptiles, feeding off their
ectoparasites. The tortoises and iguanas will often raise
themselves up to make it easier for the finches to clean
their legpits and undersides.

(e) Sharp-beaked Ground Finch *Geospiza difficilis*

Similar to Small Ground Finch but larger (12.5 cm) and
with a sharper more pointed beak, however, overlap
of species only occurs in the highlands of
Santiago, Fernandina and Pinta. On
Darwin and Wolf the species has
developed an interesting feeding habit,
probably in response to a relative paucity of food
and moisture. It feeds on the bird lice found in the
feathers of the Masked Boobies that nest there, and
also pecks at the base of the back feathers until it draws
blood, and then drinks the blood. They are also known to roll booby eggs
out of the nest to break them and consume the contents. The Sharp-billed
will also feed on the ectoparasites of tortoises and iguanas. Some think that
the separate populations represent distinct races.

(e) Cactus Ground Finch
Geospiza scandens

One of the more easily recognisable
finches (14 cm), it has a longer, more downcurved
beak than the other ground finches and is frequently
seen feeding on the flowers of the Opuntia cactus. This
often leaves it with a dusting of yellow pollen on the
head. It also nests in the Opuntia rather than in trees and
shrubs. The plumage is similar to the other ground finches.

(e) Large Cactus Ground Finch
Geospiza conirostris

The Large Cactus Ground Finch (15 cm) has two distinct races or subspecies, one found on Española, the other on the northern islands of Genovesa, Darwin and Wolf. It is not found on the same islands as its smaller cousin, *G. scandens,* and the southern population has a much heavier beak than *G. scandens,* while the northern population has a similar but straighter beak. It is less specialised in feeding on Opuntia than *G. Scandens.*

(e) Vegetarian Finch *Platyspiza crassirostris*

One of the largest finches (16 cm) with a distinctive plumage. The adult male is all black with a pale or yellowish belly. However, many individuals have only the head and back black. The female is brown above, with an olive rump and whitish or yellowish underparts, with dark streaking on breast and sides. Found mainly in transitional and humid zones. Beak short, deep and broad.

(e) Large Tree Finch *Camarhynchus psittacula*

The largest (15 cm) of the tree finches, the adult male has a black head, breast, neck and part of the back, the rest of the upperparts are grey/brown, the underparts pale tinged with yellow. The female is grey-brown above with underparts pale or yellowish. The beak is quite distinctive: stout and with strongly curved upper and lower surfaces giving it a parrot-like appearance. Found mainly in the humid zone.

(e) Medium Tree Finch *Camarhynchus pauper*

A smaller tree finch (12 cm) with a more pointed beak than Large Tree Finch, this species is found only in the humid zone on Floreana. The adult male has the head, neck and upper breast black; the back and tail is olive green. The undersides are pale or yellowish. The female is olive-green above and pale yellowish below.

(e) Small Tree Finch *Camarhynchus parvulus*

The smallest (11 cm) of the tree finches, the adult male has the head, neck and part of the back black. The rest of the upperparts are grey and the underparts pale yellowish. In common with other tree finches, the adult male plumage varies and some individuals have only a black head and neck. The female is grey brown with pale or yellowish underparts, sometimes with the suggestion of a pale eye ring and a stripe behind the eye. Found mainly in the Humid and Transitional Zones.

(e) Woodpecker Finch *Camarhynchus pallidus*

Quite a large finch (18 cm). The plumage of the sexes is similar with an olive or brown back and a rather paler underside. The beak is elongated but strong, curving down at the end quite sharply. This is very distinctive when birds are breeding as the beak usually turns black, which contrasts with the generally olive plumage. Possibly the best known of all the finches due to its habit of using a tool, generally a cactus spine or a twig to dig beetle larvae out of rotten wood. Found mainly in the Humid and Transitional Zones.

(e) Mangrove Finch *Cactospiza heliobates*

Very similar in appearance and size (14 cm) to the Woodpecker Finch, the Mangrove Finch is the most endangered of all the bird species in Galápagos, It is restricted to the mangrove swamps or forests of western Isabela which have been considerably reduced by man. The population is now down to some 30–40 pairs. The sexes are similar having brown upperparts with an olive rump and underparts pale with some spotting on the breast. The beak is similar to the Woodpecker Finch but less heavy. This species also uses tools to assist in its feeding.

(e) Warbler Finch *Certhidea* sp.

This, the smallest of the finches, has been split into two: Green Warbler Finch *C. olivacea* (left photo) found on Santiago, Rábida, Pinzon, Isabela, Fernandina and Santa Cruz; and Grey Warbler Finch *C. fusca* (right photo) found on the other islands. Plumages are similar though *C. fusca* is generally grey, while *C. olivacea* has a generally yellowish tinge to its plumage and breeding males develop an orangey throat patch; otherwise the sexes are similar. The beak is fine and warbler like. It can be confused with the Yellow Warbler but is smaller and lacks any yellow. It is the only finch with any real song.

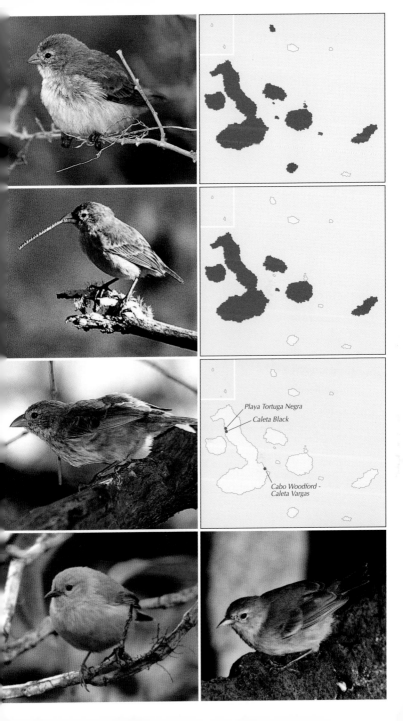

Playa Tortuga Negra
Caleta Black

Cabo Woodford -
Caleta Vargas

REPTILES

One of the most significant features of the wildlife of Galápagos is that the land animals are predominantly reptiles whereas in most of the rest of the world, mammals are dominant. Reptiles are dominant in Galápagos owing to the isolation of the islands. Apart from two bats the only native land mammals are the rice rats, which have been severely depleted by their larger cousin, *Rattus rattus*, the Black or Ship Rat, introduced by man. It is generally accepted that the islands have never been connected to the mainland of South America, so all the native animals have had to make a crossing of at least 1,000 km from the continent, to reach the islands. Reptiles are much better equipped than most mammals for such a journey, owing to their ability to survive long periods without water. As a result, until the arrival of man, the reptiles of Galápagos were unchallenged and developed into the fascinating varieties that we can see today.

One of the early visitors to Galápagos remarked that the loudest noise inland in the Galápagos is a hiss! This is almost true, as none of the reptiles found there – tortoises, iguanas, lizards, geckos and snakes – makes any appreciable noise. However, the mating male tortoise does emit a rhythmical snoring or grunting noise which can be heard from quite some distance. For the most part, identifying the reptiles is a fairly straightforward job. The particular species or subspecies will, as a rule, be identified by location as much as by any distinctive features.

Tortoises

The islands are named after the tortoises. *Galápago* is an old Spanish word for 'saddle' and several of the species, especially on the low-lying islands, have carapaces (shells) shaped very much like a Spanish saddle. When Charles Darwin visited the islands in 1835, the Vice Governor, an Englishman by the name of Lawson, told him that he was able to tell which island a tortoise came from by the shape of its shell. This is largely true and was a factor that helped Darwin in developing his theory of evolution. The Galápagos tortoise populations are a good example of 'adaptive radiation'.

The tortoises can be divided into two groups:

- the saddleback tortoises, which live on generally low islands, Pinta, Pinzón and Española;
- the dome-shaped tortoises, which live on the larger higher islands where there is an extensive moist area.

It is generally accepted that the saddleback shell evolved in species needing to reach high up into the vegetation to feed, while the dome-shaped animals evolved by remaining at or near ground level where there was plenty of suitable food. There is still disagreement as to whether the 10 existing tortoises and two extinct ones are distinct species, or sub-species: this argument is unlikely to be resolved any time soon. For simplicity this book will use the term species.

(e) Galápagos Giant Tortoise
Geochelone spp.

The Galápagos Giant Tortoise measures up to 1.5 m over the carapace and weighs up to 250 kg. The taxonomy of the species is currently under review, so that the current understanding of 11 extant species and three extinct ones (Floreana, Fernandina and Pinta) may change radically once the new research results are published. The current population is around 20,000 individuals and while some species populations are small, that of *G. vandenburghi* on Vulcán Alcedo, Isabela, numbers some 5,000 individuals.

The reproductive cycle is determined to a large extent by the climate. The dome-shaped tortoises inhabit islands with humid areas where they live for most of the year. Mating takes place towards the end of the warm season (March and April). Copulation, which may take several hours, is accompanied by loud snoring or grunting noises from the male. The sound of mating tortoises is familiar to many researchers and National Park wardens. It is often described as the

loudest noise in the Galápagos bush. The female then heads off to the lowlands where she locates a suitable area, generally with a reasonable depth of earth, digs a shallow pit up to 30-cm deep, and lays a clutch of up to 20 leathery eggs which look like large ping-pong balls. She then covers up the nest, urinates on it and tamps it down with her plastron as an additional protection.

Incubation takes between 120 and 140 days and after struggling to the surface, the young tortoises hastily locate the nearest cover to escape their potential predators. These include herons, snakes, owls, hawks and, if those were not enough, several species introduced by man, viz. cats, rats and dogs.

We do not know the full life-span of the Galápagos Giant Tortoise, though it is thought to be at least 150 years. Most species reach sexual maturity at the age of 20–25 years. We do know that their rate of

growth is controlled by the availability of food, wet years producing faster growth. This is traceable by means of the rings on the individual scutes (plates) of the tortoise carapace or shell. One Isabela tortoise at the CDRS put on 175 kg in 15 years!

Many of the populations of tortoises have been badly affected by the activities of man. The early buccaneers and whalers found them a handy source of fresh meat, as they would stay alive for long periods without water. They were also killed for the oil that is produced by rendering down their fat reserves. The taxonomy of the Galápagos Giant Tortoise is subject to considerable debate. The table below should help but may just confuse.

Best viewed: While there are still 11 species of Galápagos Giant Tortoise, visitors are only likely to see the Santa Cruz, San Cristóbal and Alcedo tortoises in the wild. You may see others at the tortoise breeding centres in Puerto Ayora (Santa Cruz) and Villamil (Isabela).

TORTOISE	LOCATION	ISABELA spp.	LOCATION
G. nigrita	Santa Cruz	G. vandenburghi	V. Alcedo
G. darwini	Santiago	G. vicina	V. Cerro Azul
G. ephippium	Pinzón	G. guntheri	V. Sierra Negra
G. chathamensis	San Cristóbal	G. microphyes	V. Darwin
G. hoodensis	Española	G. becki	V. Wolf
G. abingdoni	Pinta		

Isla Santa Cruz The population of dome-shaped tortoises *G. nigrita* on Santa Cruz is the second largest in the islands. They have managed to live in harmony with the farmers who now farm much of their moist and humid habitat. Some farmers charge visitors to come onto their land to view tortoises, an excellent example of sustainable use of natural resources. There are some 3,000 tortoises on Santa Cruz, divided into two populations by an area of farmland. The one in the west is appreciably larger than the one in the east. Dogs, and to a lesser extent pigs and cats, are a threat to this race.

G. nigrita

Isla Isabela There are five distinct species on the island of Isabela, each restricted to one of the five large-shield volcanoes. Each volcano is separated from the next by a lava flow, impassable to tortoises. This is an excellent example of species variation owing to topographical isolation. Since the volcanoes on Isabela have extensive moist areas, all the tortoises are essentially dome-shaped. There is, however, considerable variation and large elderly males may develop a more saddleback shape in some races.

The species *G. vandenburghi* is found only on Volcan Alcedo, the middle and lowest volcano on Isabela. The tortoise is dome-shaped and this is the largest single population of tortoises in the islands, with over 5,000 individuals. The tortoises are found largely on the southern rim of

the caldera, especially around an area of fumarolic activity where there are a number of shallow pools. Goats arrived on Alcedo in 1968, either by crossing Perry Isthmus to the south, or by human agents, and by 2000 there were well in excess of 150,000 goats on Alcedo, Darwin and Wolf volcanoes, doing irreparable damage to the vegetation and severely threatening the survival of the tortoises, especially on Alcedo. Between 2003 and 2006, Operation Isabela effectively eliminated the entire goat and donkey population on northern Isabela.

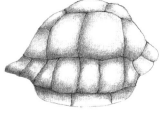

G. vandenburghi

Found only on Volcan Cerro Azul, the main population of *G. vicina* near Caleta Iguana, was virtually exterminated in the 1950s and 1960s owing to its living near to the coast. Since 1979, they have been bred in captivity by the CDRS. Numbers are now thought to be in the region of 1100–1200. Four were killed in the volcanic eruption of June 1998. Feral pigs and dogs are their main threat.

G. vicina

G. guntheri is found only on Volcan Sierra Negra and was previously one of the most numerous in the islands, but was reduced to perhaps 100–200 individuals by whalers around the end of the nineteenth century. The population has now recovered to over 700. Sierra Negra is the only inhabited volcano on Isabela and farmland divides the population into two. Feral pigs, dogs and cats are the main threat.

Volcan Darwin is a rather drier volcano than the others on Isabela because of the fact that it is lower than most and in the rain shadow of Volcan Alcedo. It is not surprising that the population of *G. microphyes* is smaller than on the other volcanoes, numbering

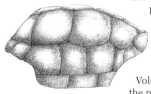

G. guntheri

around 1,000 individuals. Cats are the major threat.

Being appreciably higher than its neighbour Darwin, to the south, Volcan Wolf has a rather larger moist and humid area than its neighbour to the south and the population size of *G. becki* is uncertain. However, it may be in the region of 1,200 to 1,500 individuals. Owing to the nesting areas being close to the coast at Punta Albermarle and Puerto Brava in Banks Bay, this species is still suffering the predations of man. Cats are probably a lesser threat.

G. microphyes

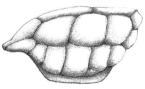

G. beckl

Isla Santiago The Santiago population of *G. darwini*, which now stands at 1,200 tortoises, is one that was seriously depleted by man; Porter in 1815 recorded taking 14 tons (about 500 individuals) on one visit! The Santiago race is of intermediate dome–saddleback shell shape, with some of the large males having quite saddlebacked carapaces. Until recently, their breeding success has been limited owing to the presence of feral pigs and goats. These invasive species were removed as part of Operation Isabela and the population should now thrive, though the presence of Black Rats, *Rattus rattus*, is cause for concern.

G. darwini

Isla Pinzón This small island has very rough terrain and virtually no moist or humid region. The population of the species *G. ephippium* was reduced to only 120 old individuals by the 1950s, having failed to reproduce for many years owing to predation on the eggs and hatchlings by black rats introduced to the island. Captive breeding was started by the CDRS in 1965 and the population is now some 500. Rats were eradicated from the island in 2012, in an operation that involved removing all Galápagos Hawks to an aviary while the operation was in process.

G. ephippium

Isla San Cristóbal The original population of *G. chatamensis*, which inhabited the southern end of San Cristóbal, is now extinct. There is a

G. chatamensis

second population of saddlebacks at the northern end, numbering up to 1,800 individuals. This may in fact be a separate race as it appears to be morphologically distinct from the specimen found at the south end of the island, by which the species was first described. Feral dogs and goats are its main threat.

Isla Española The Española race *G. hoodensis* has a very pronounced saddleback carapace. The survival of this race is a great conservation success. In 1964, the entire population consisted of only three males and twelve females. These were taken to the CDRS in 1965 and were the first Galápagos tortoises to be bred in captivity. The programme has now returned over 2,000 captive bred individuals to the island and some of those have started breeding. With goats eradicated, their future seems secure.

G. hoodensis

Isla Pinta
On June 24th 2012, Lonesome George, the last surviving Pinta tortoise died at the Charles Darwin Research Station on Santa Cruz. Project Pinta, the ecological restoration of Pinta, has started to repopulate Pinta, initially with non-breeding tortoises, but eventually with a breeding population, possibly of Wolf/Pinta hybrids, or with surplus Española tortoises. Tortoises are an important part of the ecosystem.

Lonesome George.

G. abingdoni

Turtles

(r) (es?) Galápagos Green Turtle *Chelonia mydas agassizii*

Much the commonest species of turtle found in the Galápagos and the only one to breed in the islands. It is a subspecies of the Pacific Green or Black Turtle. They spend most of their lives in shallow lagoons and waters around the islands, though they are frequently spotted in the open sea between the islands. The shell is generally dark green to black, but it does vary and can be an attractive yellow tortoiseshell colour.

The Green Turtle is almost entirely herbivorous. However, little work has been done on the Galápagos subspecies to confirm its feeding habits. Mating normally takes place in November and December and it is common to see a mating couple bobbing about offshore, the smaller male clinging to the larger female while another male waits his turn. The females come ashore at night, on sandy beaches from December to June, and having excavated a large pit with a smaller egg chamber at the bottom lay some 50–80 eggs at a time. The eggs are then covered up and left to incubate for about 60 days. A female may come ashore up to eight times over a two-week period. The temperature within the nest determines the sex of the hatchlings. Over 30°C, the young tend to be females; below 30°C they are more likely to be males.

Within the nest, the eggs may be attacked by a beetle, *Trox suberosus*. Once hatched, the young turtles are prey to everything from ghost crabs to sharks. They normally emerge at night; if they emerge during the day, few survive to make it to the water. Frigate birds, in particular, spot them as they come out of the nest, and pick them up with amazing precision.

(ro) Hawksbill Turtle *Eretmochelys imbricata bissa*

Appreciably smaller than the Galápagos Green Turtle, but with a much more amber-brown carapace, the source of 'tortoiseshell'. The plastron or underside of the turtle is yellow. Not common, but seen regularly. It is not easy to distinguish unless a good view is obtained. Size and colour are good indicators. The Hawksbill is omnivorous and its diet consists largely of seaweed, crabs, shellfish and jellyfish.

(oo) Olive Ridley Turtle *Lepidochelys olivacea*

The smallest turtle found in Galápagos, the Olive Ridley grows to little more than 75 cm in length and has an olive-green carapace. These are its two most distinctive features. Like all marine turtles, it is found throughout the tropics, but is not known to breed in Galápagos.

(oo) Leatherback Turtle *Dermochelys coriacea*

The largest turtle in the world, an average adult is 1.5m–1.8-m long and weighs up to 500 kg. The largest specimens are up to 2 m or more and weigh 600–700 kg. It can have a 'flipper span' of up to 3 m. In contrast to the other marine turtles, the Leatherback does not have a hard bony carapace but has tough leathery skin, characterised by longitudinal ridges. It is dark brown with white or yellow spotting, especially on the sides and flippers. Its size, ridges and carapace make it relatively easy to identify. It prefers the open sea more than other turtle species and feeds largely on jellyfish and other soft-bodied marine animals.

Lizards

(e) Marine Iguana *Amblyrhynchus cristatus*

The Galápagos Marine Iguana is the world's only sea-going lizard, and is found on all of the main islands. There are seven races or subspecies which vary considerably in size and colour from island to island. The ones on Española are the most brightly coloured. Northern Isabela boasts the largest (up to 1.3 m in length) and Genovesa the smallest (up to 75 cm in length). The males are larger and more brightly and distinctively coloured than the females. They are largely black or dark grey. However, the males take on a red or red-green tinge during the mating season. This is particularly evident in the Española race. Some races look to have lichens growing on them, such are the variations in their skin colour. Marine Iguanas have a pronounced crest which is most prominent on the head but runs all the way down their back and tail.

Because it is ectothermic, or cold-blooded, and yet feeds in the cool waters of the Humboldt and Cromwell currents, it must warm up by basking in the sun on the black lava rocks, both before and after feeding trips. To avoid overheating, which would occur if its body temperature exceeded 35°C, it varies its position in relation to the sun, often facing directly into it to reduce its exposure.

The Marine Iguana lives largely on land but feeds inshore and in the intertidal zone at depths of up to about 10 m. It feeds almost entirely on red and green algae but is also known to consume its own faeces as well as those of sea lions and crabs. This diet results in a high intake of salt. To eliminate this excess of salt, they spit out brine through their nostrils. This snorting is the only noise that they make.

The Marine Iguana can remain submerged for 10 minutes or more. It does not generally venture more than 50 m offshore. During a strong El Niño, when its food supply is severely affected, the population can suffer a very severe drop.

The timing of the mating season varies on different islands but generally starts in December to January, with egg-laying towards the end of the warm season, March and April. The female excavates a nest in the sand, a burrow up to 1-m long, then lays a clutch of up to four leathery elongated eggs, which take between three and four months to incubate. The young are 10-cm long when they emerge and almost entirely black. They are very vulnerable to predation by frigatebirds, herons, hawks and snakes as well as feral cats and dogs on land, and by moray eels and other predators in the water. Survival is quite an achievement. Once they are mature, their only real enemies are hawks and feral cats and dogs. *Best viewed:* Common throughout the islands on rocky coasts and cliffs.

1	2
3	4
5	6
7 8	9
10	11

SUBSPECIES	ISLANDS	CHARACTERISTICS
A. c. cristatus (1, 3, 4)	Fernandina	The first three races form a closely related group in the central and western islands
A. c. hassi (2)	Santa Cruz	
A. c. albemarlensis (5, 6)	Isabela	Largest in size
A. c. mertensi (7)	San Cristóbal; Santiago	
A. c. sielmanni	Pinta	
A. c. venustissimus (8, 9)	Española	Most brightly coloured
A. c. nanus (10, 11)	Genovesa	Very small, dark colour

Note: numbers relate to photograph positions as indicated by the symbol on the left.

ⓔ Land Iguana *Conolophus subcristatus*

This is the most widespread of the land iguanas, numbering between 5,000 and 10,000 individuals and measuring up to 1 m in length and 13 kg in weight. Land iguanas live in small colonies, in marked contrast to when Darwin visited the islands and had trouble pitching his tent due to the number of iguana burrows! The reduction in population is due to predation by man and introduced predators such as dogs, pigs, cats and rats. Land iguanas vary in size and coloration but are generally a pale to dark yellow, occasionally coming close to ochre. On some islands their colonies are restricted to suitable isolated habitats such as Cerro Dragon, an old tuff cone on Santa Cruz where it is easy for the iguana to excavate burrows for egg-laying. Elsewhere they are more widespread. On some islands such as Fernandina the females make long journeys to the nesting zones, some of which are within the caldera and constitute a major challenge for the hatchlings when they appear. The colony on Seymour Norte was introduced from Baltra in the 1930s. The Baltra population subsequently became extinct but recently individuals have been reintroduced to Baltra from Seymour Norte.

Adult land iguanas feed mainly on pads and fruit from the Opuntia cactus, as well as other plants and insects. Young iguanas feed mainly on insects and other arthropods, becoming largely vegetarian as they mature. They have even been observed taking finch nestlings. Normal lifespan is uncertain; in Seymour Norte it would appear to be more than 60 years.

Mating takes place towards the end of the year, with egg-laying from January to March. Mating is a fairly violent affair, with the male seizing a receptive female by the back of the neck prior to copulation. The young face the same formidable range of predators as the marine iguana on land, but do not have the added threat of the marine predators.

Best viewed: South Plaza; Santa Cruz – Cerro Dragon; Seymour Norte

ⓔ Santa Fé Land Iguana *Conolophus pallidus*

This species is found only on the island of Santa Fé. It is similar to *C. subcristatus*, though the males tend to be dullish yellow, occasionally with darker patches; the spine extends further down the back.
Best viewed: Santa Fe – Barrington Bay

ⓔ Pink Iguana *Conolophus marthae*

Although Pink Iguanas were first observed in 1986, it was not until 2008 that the existence of this new species was verified; it was described in 2009. There are thought to be only around 100 individuals, all found high up on Volcán Wolf, the northernmost volcano on Isabela. They have pink bodies with irregular black bands across their backs and largely black tails. There is little specific information available about them, and most visitors will have no chance of seeing this species.
Best viewed: Isabela – Volcán Wolf

ⓔ Hybrid Iguana

Marine and land iguana do hybridise occasionally; markings vary but hybrids are generally rather dark with irregular pale bands across the back. The crest is small and the head resembles the marine iguana, but hybrids are terrestrial in habit and probably sterile.

Best viewed: South Plaza

(e) Lava Lizard *Microlophus* spp.

There are seven species of the genus *Microlophus* in the Galápagos.
They are found on all the major islands apart from Genovesa.
M. albemarlensis is found on ten islands in the centre and west of the
archipelago, while the six other species are island specific and apart
from *M. duncanensis* on Pinzón, are found on the outer and eastern
islands.

Identifying a Lava Lizard is straightforward. The only possible
confusion would be with a very young Marine or Land Iguana or a
gecko. Iguanas are more heavily built, especially around the head.
Marine Iguanas are much darker than most Lava Lizards, except for
those on Fernandina, and Land Iguanas are much paler than almost all
Lava Lizards. The palest Lava Lizards are much smaller than recently
hatched Land Iguanas. The native geckos are smaller than adult Lava
Lizards, paler in colour and are nocturnal. The introduced geckos are
a similar size to Lava Lizards, but paler and with wider and flatter
heads. They are also nocturnal.

Male and female Lava Lizards are quite distinct. The male is
generally much larger (15–20-cm, exceptionally 30-cm, long) and has
rougher and more patterned skin, with a very distinct spinal crest. He
has a clearly visible black or reddish throat. The female is smaller
(12–18-cm long) and smoother with a less patterned skin and a red or
orange throat; this is often very bright and distinctive. Males in
particular are often to be seen displaying (doing 'push-ups') on the top
of rocks or National Park trail markers! You can, however, note
considerable variations in the size and colour of *M. albemarlensis* on
the ten islands it inhabits. This may be associated with the local
geology and vegetation. Those on Fernandina (black lava) tend to be
darker than those on Santa Cruz (where there is little black lava).

Lava Lizards are omnivorous, eating mainly insects and some plant
food, especially in the dry season. On Bartolomé, the flowers of
Tiquila are an important source of food. Cannibalism is not unknown.
Their chief predators are hawks, snakes, herons, centipedes and
mockingbirds.

Breeding takes place mainly in the warm season with clutches of
three to six eggs being laid in deep burrows. Several females may use
the same area and each female may lay several clutches three or four
weeks apart. The eggs take about three months to hatch and the young
are only 3–4-cm long. They are very hard to find. Females take only
nine months to reach sexual maturity, while males take three years.
Best viewed: On all major islands, except Genovesa, mainly in the
lowlands.

1	2
3	4
5	6
7	8
9	10
11	12

SPECIES	LOCATION
M. albemarlensis (3, 4, 5, 6)	Isabela, Santa Cruz, Fernandina, Santiago, Baltra, Santa Fé, Rábida, Seymour, Daphne Major and Plaza Sur
M. bivittatus (7, 8, 10)	San Cristóbal
M. grayi (1, 2, 12)	Floreana
M. habellii	Marchena
M. delanonis (9, 11)	Española
M. duncanensis	Pinzón
M. pacificus	Pinta

Note: numbers relate to photograph positions as indicated by the symbol on the left.

Geckos

There are five endemic species of gecko in Galápagos, one native and three introduced species. The endemic species can be identified by location, though *P. leei* has been identified at Villamil on Isabela. The introduced species are all larger than the endemic species.

ⓔ Galápagos Leaf-toed Gecko *Phyllodactylus galapagoensis*

Grows to 50 mm. Pale creamy brown with darker blotches and markings. Often seen without a tail which can be regenerated. Geckos have pads on their toes covered in microscopic hairs, which enable then to climb vertical surfaces, even glass, or walk on the ceiling. They are nocturnal and largely insectivorous, though they do eat their own discarded skin. Widespread but infrequently seen except in inhabited areas where they are often found in houses.

ⓔ San Cristóbal Leaf-toed Gecko *Phyllodactylus leei*

Darker than *P. galapagoensis* and smaller; found only on San Cristóbal. Breeding in both species is in October and November. A single egg is laid under a rock or dead tree, sometimes in a tree. The same nest may be used by several females on different occasions. The young have to fend for themselves from hatching.

ⓘ *Phyllodactylus reissi*

This species is a native of Ecuador and is widespread in the coastal areas in and around Guayaquil from where most freight for Galápagos originates. It was first reported in Puerto Ayora in 1979. It is a pale greyish colour with indistinct, irregular and diffuse darker spots or blotches. The belly is pale yellow or whitish. At 75 mm, it is much larger than the native and endemic geckos. Anecdotal evidence points to it spreading and supplanting the endemic *P. galapagoensis*, at least in Puerto Ayora.

ⓘ *Lepidodactylus lugubris*

Originally from South-East Asia, this species arrived in Galápagos via Ecuador. It is similar in size to the native and endemic species and has been reported from both Santa Cruz and San Cristóbal.

ⓘ *Gonatodes caudiscutatus*

A native of western Ecuador, this recently arrived gecko has so far been reported only from Puerto Baquerizo Moreno on San Cristóbal.

GECKO	STATUS	LOCATION
P. leei	Endemic	San Cristóbal
P. gilberti	Endemic	Wolf
P. barringtonensis	Endemic	Santa Fé
P. galapagoensis	Endemic	Isabela, Santa Cruz, Fernandina, Santiago
P. bauri	Endemic	Floreana, Pinta
P. tuberculosus	Native	San Cristóbal
P. reissi	Introduced	Santa Cruz
L. lugubris	Introduced	Santa Cruz, San Cristóbal
G. caudiscutatus	Introduced	San Cristóbal

Snakes

There are four species of snake found in Galápagos. They are all endemic and are found in the Coastal and Arid Zones. They feed on Lava Lizards, geckos, grasshoppers, young iguanas, mice and rats. They also prey on finch and mockingbird nestlings. They are constrictors and only mildly poisonous and are not at all aggressive. Although there is considerable disagreement about the classification of Galápagos snakes, it is likely that there will be significant changes agreed in the future.

(e) Hood Racer *Philodryas hoodensis*

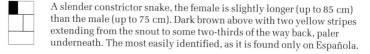

A slender constrictor snake, the female is slightly longer (up to 85 cm) than the male (up to 75 cm). Dark brown above with two yellow stripes extending from the snout to some two-thirds of the way back, paler underneath. The most easily identified, as it is found only on Española.

(e) Banded Galápagos Snake *Alsophis slevini*

Clearly identifiable as it is banded rather than striped, with bands of dark brown and pale creamy-yellow virtually the whole length of the body. The smallest snake in the islands with males up to 52 cm and females up to 42 cm. Found only on Fernandina, Isabela and Pinzón.
Best viewed: Fernandina – Punta Espinosa; Isabela – Punta Moreno, Tagus Cove, Urvina Bay; Pinzón.

(e) Striped Galápagos Snake *Alsophis steindachneri*

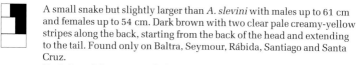

A small snake but slightly larger than *A. slevini* with males up to 61 cm and females up to 54 cm. Dark brown with two clear pale creamy-yellow stripes along the back, starting from the back of the head and extending to the tail. Found only on Baltra, Seymour, Rábida, Santiago and Santa Cruz.
Best viewed: Seymour; Rábida; Santiago – Sullivan Bay, Puerto Egas; Santa Cruz – Tortuga Bay.

(e) Galápagos Racer *Alsophis biseralis*

This species is divided into three subspecies. They are all appreciably longer than the other three endemic snakes and are generally dark brown with usually a striped pattern, but are often also spotted. They can be distinguished by location:

Eastern Galápagos Racer *A. b. biseralis*: male to 80 cm, female to 85 cm, found only on Gardner by Floreana and San Cristóbal.

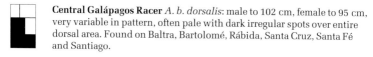

Central Galápagos Racer *A. b. dorsalis*: male to 102 cm, female to 95 cm, very variable in pattern, often pale with dark irregular spots over entire dorsal area. Found on Baltra, Bartolomé, Rábida, Santa Cruz, Santa Fé and Santiago.

Western Galápagos Racer *A. b. occidentalis*: the longest snake in Galápagos with males up to 125 cm and females to 110 cm. Much darker than the other two subspecies and spotted or almost banded in appearance. Found only on Isabela and Fernandina.

MARINE MAMMALS

In common with other isolated islands such as Hawaii and New Zealand, the Galápagos have very few mammal species, the majority of these being marine mammals. This is simply due to land-based mammals being ill-equipped to cross large expanses of water on their own. The marine mammals that are resident in Galápagos are two seals, two whales and two dolphins. Many other species of whale and dolphin are seen either regularly or occasionally. These are largely migratory and cannot be considered as residents. Nevertheless, the most enduring image that many visitors take home with them is of the Galápagos Sea Lion, which is found throughout the archipelago and has adapted well to the influx of visitors.

(e) Galápagos Sea Lion *Zalophus wollebacki*

1	2
3	
4	5
6	

1 Male
2 Female
3 Harem
4 Group resting
5 Female and pup
6 Pup suckling

The Galápagos Sea Lion is the largest animal found on land in the islands. While the normal population is estimated to be around 50,000, this can be severely reduced by a major El Niño event which seriously affects their food supply. The species also suffers from a virus known as 'sea lion pox', which is thought to be transmitted by mosquitoes. An epidemic of this pox erupts from time to time but does not appear to be a real threat to the species. They live very largely on fish and can be found out to sea, anywhere around the islands. As a rule they prefer sandy beaches. They are very well adapted to humans and frequently have to be removed from the small landing stages and docks found at many visiting sites or in the island ports. Male or bull sea lions, which are easily distinguished from the females by their larger size (up to 250 kg) and distinctive bump on the head, have well-defined territories that they guard jealously, especially during the mating season.

The mating season varies from island to island but is generally between June and September. A dominant bull will have a territory often consisting of a beach or bay, which will include a group of cows, immature sea lions and pups, loosely referred to as a 'harem'. While sea lions are generally very approachable, care should be taken with the bulls, which are naturally more aggressive than the cows and which should definitely be avoided during the mating season. It is not for nothing that they are referred to as 'beachmasters'. Successful males guard their territory jealously from other males, fights are frequent and can be quite bloody. The harem may consist of only a few cows or may be very much larger, up to thirty or so. The barking of the patrolling bull sea lion is one of the enduring sounds of Galápagos.

Mating normally takes place in the water and within four weeks of the cow giving birth, but owing to 'delayed implantation' the egg is not actually implanted in the womb for two months, thus allowing for an annual cycle. Gestation takes about nine months and the single pup grows rapidly on a diet of the mother's very rich milk. The pups start fishing for themselves at about five months; in the meantime they stay in the nursery with the other young and are only allowed to swim and play in the shallow water, often with human visitors. They show a total lack of fear of humans, often climbing into dinghies or onto a ship's boarding platform, or even onto the deck.

Identifying features: Unmistakable large dark seal. Male is much larger than the female and has a distinctive bump on the head. Larger than a fur seal and has a longer snout.

Best viewed: Widespread on the coast throughout the archipelago.

(e) Galápagos Fur Seal *Arctocephalus galapagoensis*

1	
2	
3	

1 Male
2 Female
3 Sleeping

The Galápagos Fur Seal, like the Galápagos Sea Lion is not a true seal (family Phocidae). It is technically a 'fur sea lion'. Both the fur seal and the sea lion have small but visible ears and use their front flippers for swimming. Indeed, they seem to 'fly' through the water using their flippers like a bird uses its wings. The fur seal is easily distinguished from the sea lion by its smaller size, large prominent eyes and much shorter snout, giving their head a rather bear like appearance, hence its Latin name, *Arcto* = bear, *cephalus* = head.

The exact population of fur seals is unknown, in part because they are far more difficult to count than sea lions owing to their preferred resting places, but it is thought to number about 25,000. They are found almost entirely on rocky shores where there is deep water immediately offshore. Sea lions on the other hand, owing to their size, coat and diet, enjoy sandy beaches and shallower water. Fur seals being appreciably smaller than sea lions are much more able to clamber up steep rocky shores. The very bulk of adult sea lions makes this much more difficult. The thick coat of fur seals means that they prefer to lie in the shade rather than the full sun. Their feeding requirements also dictate a different location. Squid are found in deeper waters, so fur seals are generally found around the outer shores of the archipelago rather than in the middle.

Fur seals feed on fish and squid, diving to depths of up to 100 m. They hunt mainly at night. This is partly because it is the time when the squid come closer to the surface and partly because they are less likely to be attacked by sharks at night. Fur seals fish much less when the moon is full; this is, again, thought to be linked to the availability of food and the likelihood of attack from sharks. It is quite common to see scars from shark attacks on both sea lions and fur seals.

The breeding season is from August to November with mating taking place during this period. The cow will mate immediately after giving birth, but owing to 'delayed implantation', fertilisation of the egg will not take place for another couple of months. Pups are suckled for two or three years and cows generally manage to raise at best one pup every two years. This is in part due to competition with older siblings, especially in times of food shortage during an El Niño period. In contrast, sea lions frequently raise a pup each year.

Fur seals were hunted almost to extinction during the nineteenth century because of their valuable fur. They have made a remarkable comeback and are now a great deal more common than even thirty years ago. They are not currently under threat but would be if their food source were to be overfished.

Identifying features: Smaller than the sea lion and with a shorter snout, and larger eyes. The head is bear-like and the ears tend to stick out.
Best viewed: Always on rocky costs, never on sandy beaches. Seymour, Santiago – Puerto Egas; Cousins Island; Genovesa.

CETACEANS – Whales and Dolphins

Cetaceans, an order of entirely aquatic mammals, is divided into two major groups. The baleen whales include most of the larger species and feed on plankton and other small marine animals. The toothed whales, which include the large Sperm Whale, Orca and all the dolphins and porpoises, feed on fish, squid, other cetaceans and marine mammals, such as sea lions and fur seals.

Some 24 species of whale and dolphin have been recorded in Galápagos, and it is almost certain that other species are present from time to time, but identification is difficult and often impossible. Most visitors will see at least one species, the Bottlenose Dolphin, and if you are observant, especially on the longer passages between islands, and to the west of Isabela, you may well see other species. The best identifier for the larger baleen whales is the shape of their 'spout' or 'blow', and species such as the Humpback, Sperm and the Orca, have distinctive features that make identification relatively easy. The illustrations here should help you if you are fortunate enough to get a good view. The precise status within the islands of most species is uncertain, and so they are marked with the periodicity of viewing. None is known, or likely, to be endemic. Sperm, Bryde's, Orca, and Common and Bottlenose Dolphins are present year round; Blue and Humpback are seasonal.

Baleen Whales

ⓄⓄ Sei Whale *Balaenoptera borealis*

A very large baleen whale. It has a dark steel grey back with the pleated throat and chest being appreciably paler. The Sei (pronounced 'say') feeds quite close to the surface and when it 'blows' it does not arch its back appreciably or show its flukes, giving the whale a very gentle appearance and disappearance. Most easily confused with the Blue and Bryde's Whales. It is much smaller than the Blue, has a single distinct ridge on its head, and does not arch its back as much as Bryde's.
Size: Males 15–18 m; females 16–20 m.
Weight: 12–29 tons.
Identifying features: Notice the slow, gentle blow, with gently arched back, no roll and flukes never shown. The spout is an inverted cone up to 3-m high. It has a single ridge on the head, and a uniformly dark appearance. The fin is up to 60-cm high and strongly hooked.

ⓇⓄ Bryde's Whale *Balaenoptera edeni*

Also known as the Tropical Whale. Very similar in shape and form to the Sei, Bryde's (pronounced *bree-dahs*) is smaller and less muscular. It is a deep diver and often shows the head on surfacing, followed by a distinctly arched roll of the back. The head has three distinctive ridges and the back is blue-grey compared to the Sei's steel grey back and single head ridge. This whale is known to approach boats and is the baleen whale that you are most likely to see.
Size: Males 12–14 m; females 13–15 m.
Weight: 12–20 tons.
Identifying features: Faster blow with a distinctly arched back. The flukes are rarely shown, but it has a tendency to roll on re-entry. The fin is up to 45-cm long and quite pointed. The spout is narrow, up to 4-m high. Three ridges on the head are diagnostic if you get a good view.

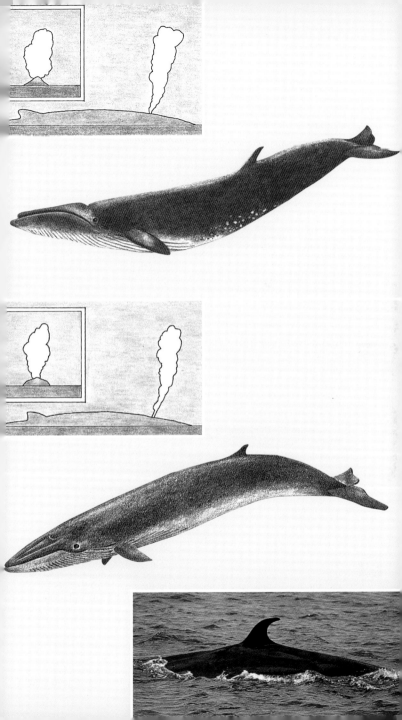

ⓞⓞ Minke Whale *Balaenoptera acutorostrata*

Also known as the Piked Whale. The Minke is the smallest of the rorqual, or baleen whales and is easily confused with Bryde's. It is less streamlined than its larger relative with a laterally flattened and pointed head, and distinct white patches on the flippers. The fin is slightly hooked and appears at the same time as the rather indistinct spout, which is only some 2-m high, possibly because it starts to blow before surfacing. The back is very strongly arched when blowing and the flukes are never seen except when it breaches. Like Bryde's Whale, the Minke often approaches ships.
Size: Males 8–9.5 m; females 8–10.2 m. *Weight:* 6–9 tons.
Identifying features: Small size and pointed head with one central ridge. The fin appears at the same time as a minimal spout. White patches on the flippers. Back strongly arched when diving; fins and flukes never show except when breaching.

ⓞⓞ Humpback Whale *Megaptera novaeangliae*

Easily identified with its broad rounded head and a string of fleshy tubercles or knobs in place of the median ridge; the edges of the jaws also have rows of hairy knobs. The body is blackish with white throat grooves. It is heavily built and narrows rapidly to the tail. The flippers are very large, up to 5-m long, mottled black on top and white underneath, and are heavily scalloped along the trailing edge. The spout is distinctively a broad bushy balloon up to 3-m high. The fin is short and squared and appears only as the body humps up to dive. The tail flukes, which are white underneath, are also heavily scalloped on the trailing edge, and are often raised clear of the water on sounding or diving. The Humpback also frequently breaches, leaping clear of the water, and also 'spyhops' or stands on its tail. It does not normally approach ships, but does not appear to object to being approached by ships or small boats.
Size: Males 14.5–17.5 m; females 15–19 m. *Weight:* 30–48 tons.
Identifying features: Knobbly head, humped back, square fin, long flippers with white undersides. Shows flukes when diving. Spout, broad and bushy to a height of 3 m.

ⓡⓞ Blue Whale *Balaenoptera musculus*

The Blue Whale is the largest animal known to have lived on the Earth. It is a regular visitor to Galápagos and is similar in general appearance to the Sei Whale, but is noticeably larger. The skin is blue-grey and somewhat mottled with paler spots giving them a shiny or silvery appearance when seen from a distance. When it surfaces and blows it has a very tall spout of 10 m or more coming from a double blowhole, a long rolling back that appears after the head has submerged, followed by a small stubby apology for a dorsal fin. Like all baleen whales, Blue's are seasonal feeders, feeding on copepods, such as krill, and plankton. They travel at speeds of up to 25 knots, which helped them to survive until the arrival of the steam-powered whale catchers.
Size: Females, 25–30 m; males smaller. *Weight:* Over 150 tons (largest weighed was 29 m in length and weighed 174 tons).
Identifying features: Huge size, very tall spout, long gently arching, mottled blue-grey back, very small stubby dorsal fin. Large tail up to 7.5 m wide.

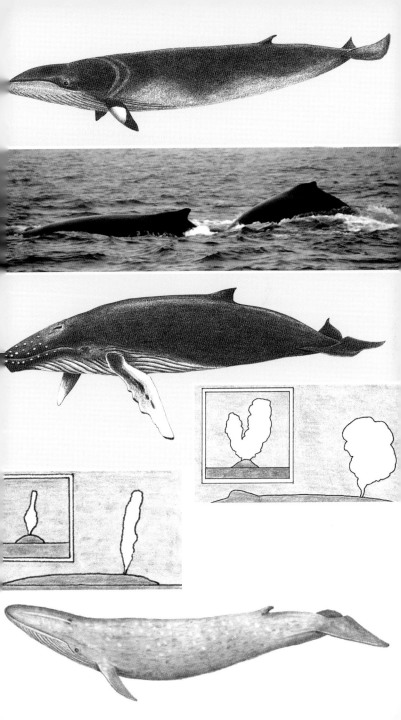

Toothed Whales

(ro) Sperm Whale *Physeter macrocephalus*

The Sperm Whale has an unmistakable profile with an enormous square-ended head which emerges first from the water. The body is dark steely-grey and the skin corrugated. The head is often covered with large circular scars from the Giant Squid which is the whale's main food source. The dorsal fin is almost non-existent and is more of a low rounded hump followed by four or five smaller lumps. The flippers are very small but the tail is large and always thrown clear of the water as the whale dives or sounds. The spout is 3–5 m in height and is directed forward at an angle of 45° and to the left as the blowhole is located on the front of the head and is offset from the median line.

Size: Males 15–20 m; females 11–17 m.
Weight: Males 36–38 tons; females 20–30 tons.
Identifying features: Large square head, angled spout, minimal dorsal fin, humped back and flukes clear of water on sounding.

(ro) (pr) Orca *Orcinus orca*

The most frequently viewed large toothed whale in Galápagos, the Orca, also known as the Killer Whale, has a blunt, rounded head and is clearly identifiable by its jet-black and white coloration. The back, apart from a grey saddle behind the dorsal fin, flanks and under-tail area is black, while the throat and belly are white extending onto the flank behind the dorsal fin. The flippers are large and paddle-shaped. There is a conspicuous white patch around and behind the eyes. The other identifiable feature is the dorsal fin. In the adult male, this can be 2-m tall and may appear to lean in front of any other whale. It is larger than in any other whale. In the female, it is smaller and curved backwards, but is still large. Orcas generally travel in family groups and are easily approached. They commonly spyhop and porpoise.

Size: Males 8–10 m; females 7–8.5 m.
Weight: Males up to 7 tons; females up to 4.5 tons.
Identifiable features: Black-and-white coloration; large dorsal fin.

(ro) (pr) Shortfin Pilot Whale *Globicephala macrorhynchus*

Also known as Pacific Pilot Whale. Often seen in groups of up to 30 or 40 individuals cruising on the surface, this is the only pilot whale found in Galápagos. Shorter and much slimmer than the Orca, it is almost all black apart from a grey anchor-shaped blaze on the belly which is hard to see. The head is round and melon-shaped and is clearly visible every time the whale breathes. The dorsal fin is long, rounded and back-curving. They are indifferent to ships and are often seen in the same area as Bottlenose or Common Dolphins.

Size: Male 5.5–6.75 m; females 4.25–5 m.
Weight: Male up to 3 tons; females up to 1.5 tons.
Identifying features: All black, rounded head, long back-curving dorsal fin; travel in large groups often cruising on the surface.

ⓡⓞ ⓟⓡ Bottlenose Dolphin *Tursiops truncatus*

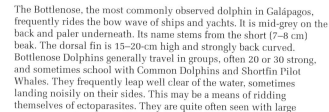

The Bottlenose, the most commonly observed dolphin in Galápagos, frequently rides the bow wave of ships and yachts. It is mid-grey on the back and paler underneath. Its name stems from the short (7–8 cm) beak. The dorsal fin is 15–20-cm high and strongly back curved. Bottlenose Dolphins generally travel in groups, often 20 or 30 strong, and sometimes school with Common Dolphins and Shortfin Pilot Whales. They frequently leap well clear of the water, sometimes landing noisily on their sides. This may be a means of ridding themselves of ectoparasites. They are quite often seen with large remora or sucker fish attached to their flanks.
Size: 3–4.2 m. Males slightly larger than females.
Weight: 200–300 kg. Exceptionally to 650 kg.
Identifying features: Colouring, short beak, large back-curved dorsal fin and habit of playing around ships and riding the bow wave.

ⓡⓞ Common Dolphin *Delphinus delphis*

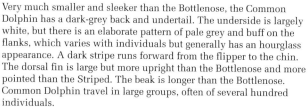

Very much smaller and sleeker than the Bottlenose, the Common Dolphin has a dark-grey back and undertail. The underside is largely white, but there is an elaborate pattern of pale grey and buff on the flanks, which varies with individuals but generally has an hourglass appearance. A dark stripe runs forward from the flipper to the chin. The dorsal fin is large but more upright than the Bottlenose and more pointed than the Striped. The beak is longer than the Bottlenose. Common Dolphin travel in large groups, often of several hundred individuals.
Size: 2.1–2.6 m.
Weight: 80–135 kg.
Identifying features: Buff and grey flank markings, long beak, upright dorsal fin, small size, speed and manoeuvrability.

ⓡⓞ Striped Dolphin *Stenella coeruleoalba*

Slightly larger than the Common Dolphin, but smaller than the Bottlenose. The Striped Dolphin is the least common of the three and rarely bow-rides. It is darkish brown on the back with very varied flank markings, but always has a dark line from the eye, along the flank to the anus. The underside is largely white. The beak is shorter than that of Bottlenose and Common Dolphins, but in both species it is always dark. It is best distinguished from the Common by its more rounded dorsal fin and the fact that the dark line running forward from the flipper is to the eye and not the chin. Unlike the Bottlenose, it rarely bow-rides.
Size: 2.4–3 m.
Weight: 100–130 kg.
Identifying features: Rounded dorsal fin, black lateral line, black line from eye to flipper and short beak.

ⓡⓞ Risso's Dolphin *Grampus griseus*

Mid-grey above and with a bulging forehead and short head. It has a tall slightly curved dorsal fin. The skin is distinctively scratched and scarred.
Size: 2.6–3.8 m
Weight: 300–500 kg.
Identifying features: Grey scarred skin, bulging forehead and tall dorsal fin.

LAND MAMMALS
Rodents

Rice rats and bats are the only native land mammals in Galápagos and they suffered significantly from the arrival of their larger cousins, the Black Rat and the Brown Rat, as well as humans. There is considerable debate about the number of species and sub-species of rice rat, so until this is clarified we will stick with the structure we accepted in 2000.

(ip) Black or Ship Rat *Rattus rattus*

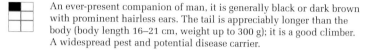

An ever-present companion of man, it is generally black or dark brown with prominent hairless ears. The tail is appreciably longer than the body (body length 16–21 cm, weight up to 300 g); it is a good climber. A widespread pest and potential disease carrier.

(ip) Brown Rat *Rattus norvegicus*

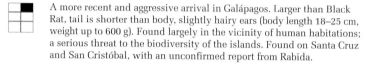

A more recent and aggressive arrival in Galápagos. Larger than Black Rat, tail is shorter than body, slightly hairy ears (body length 18–25 cm, weight up to 600 g). Found largely in the vicinity of human habitations; a serious threat to the biodiversity of the islands. Found on Santa Cruz and San Cristóbal, with an unconfirmed report from Rabida.

(ip) House Mouse *Mus musculus*

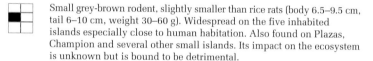

Small grey-brown rodent, slightly smaller than rice rats (body 6.5–9.5 cm, tail 6–10 cm, weight 30–60 g). Widespread on the five inhabited islands especially close to human habitation. Also found on Plazas, Champion and several other small islands. Its impact on the ecosystem is unknown but is bound to be detrimental.

(e) Galápagos Rice Rat *Aegialomys galapagoensis bauri*

Small (10 cm), long, brown rat with black bulging eyes and bat-shaped ears. Fearless and easily observed. The population has burgeoned since the goats were removed from Santa Fé in the late 1960s. They live mainly in holes, under rocks, and also in the giant Opuntia cacti. Omnivorous, feeding on seeds and small insects, probably also on carrion. Breeding is generally restricted to the warm season. Up to four young are raised. Found only on Santa Fé.

(e) Fernandina Rice Rat *Nesoryzomys fernandinae*

Larger than *A. galapogoensis*, rather greyer body and distinguished from *N. fernandinae* by its larger size (16 cm) and whitish feet. Like other rice rats it is largely nocturnal. Easily identified as found only on Fernandina.

(e) Darwin's Rice Rat *Nesoryzomys narboroughii*

Originally identified from bones found in owl pellets, confirmation of its existence was made in 1995. It is smaller (12 cm) than *N. fernandinae* with brown fur and feet, and is widespread and found at all elevations on Fernandina.

Santiago Rice Rat *Oryzomys swarthi*

Thought to be extinct until 1997. Similar in size to *N. narboroughii* but darker with pale underside and light brown feet. Body and tail equal length. Only rice rat to have survived competition with Black Rat. Females smaller and possibly less able to compete.

Bats

(e) Galápagos Bat *Lasiurus brachyotis*

Closely related to the Red Bat (*L. borealis*) of South America; locally abundant on Santa Cruz and San Cristóbal, found in all areas. It roosts in mangroves or dense scrub during the daytime. Smaller than the Hoary Bat. Insectivorous, it feeds within 8 m of the ground. Further distribution and biology unknown.
Best viewed: Santa Cruz – Puerto Ayora; San Cristóbal – Puerto Baquerizo.

(n) Hoary Bat *Lasiurus cinerius*

Widespread in North America. Attractive red-brown fur with white tips and buff-coloured throat. Roosts in mangroves or caves. Insectivorous, but feeds over 8 m above the ground. No breeding records but probably does.
Best viewed: Santa Cruz – Puerto Ayora; San Cristóbal – Puerto Baquerizo.

UNDERWATER WILDLIFE

Galápagos underwater is even more amazing and varied than on land;
there is less endemism than on land, but there is a huge variety of species
of both tropical and temperate families. All underwater species are
protected and should not be approached closely or disturbed. Some
species are potentially dangerous if they are provoked or feel threatened.
Indicated sizes given are the maximum; most will be significantly smaller.
Remember that underwater everything is magnified significantly.

Sharks

Most sharks are potentially dangerous, especially if they detect blood.

Whale Shark *Rhincodon typus*

Huge (to 14 m) unmistakable fish, greyish brown with a bold pattern of
white spots. Feeds on plankton, small fry and pelagic crustaceans. May
be seen anywhere in archipelago but more common around the northern
islands, especially Wolf and Darwin. The world's largest fish.

Galápagos Bullhead Shark *Heterodontus quoyi*

Distinctive (to 1 m) bottom-dwelling shark. Grey-brown above, with
large, irregular dark spots; white underneath. Has a short spine at the
front of each dorsal fin and blunt head. Uncommon, mainly western isles.

Scalloped Hammerhead *Sphyrna lewini*

Large (to 4.3 m), unmistakable shark with eyes at ends of laterally
flattened head, tall, vertical dorsal fin. Silver-grey above, white
underneath. Abundant around Darwin and Wolf, occasional elsewhere.
Smooth Hammerhead *S. zygaena* seen occasionally has smooth rather
than scalloped front to head. Feeds on fish and squid.

Blacktip Shark *Carcharhinus limbatus*

Medium-sized (to 2.5 m) silver-grey shark with black tip to dorsal,
pectoral and ventral fins, and lower tail lobe. Pale or white anal fin and
tall, distinctly rounded, dorsal fin. Widespread but uncommon in
inshore waters and lagoons. Feeds on reef fish.

Galápagos Shark *Carcharhinus galapagensis*

Smallish (to 2.1 m) shark, uniform silver-grey above, white underneath.
Tall pointed or sharply rounded dorsal fin. Feeds on fish, sea lions, other
sharks and rays. Widespread but uncommon around rock reefs, boulder
slopes and walls.

White-tipped Reef Shark *Triaenodon obesus*

Rather small (to 2.1 m) brownish-grey shark, white underneath, with
distinctive white tip to dorsal fin and upper tail lobe. Often sleeps on
bottom in caves during day. Feeds on reef fish, octopus and crustaceans.
Widespread in inshore waters and lagoons, the shark most likely to be
seen by snorkellers.

Rays and Eels

Giant Manta Ray *Manta hamiltoni*
Very large ray (up to 7 m), black above, largely white below, tail long and thin. Feeds on plankton, small fry and crustaceans. Widespread throughout the archipelago. Makes spectacular aerial leaps.

Spinetail Mobula *Mobula japanica*
Smaller than Giant Manta (up to 5 m). Grey above, with dark band across head, white below appendages on side of mouth are cone-shaped rather than flattened. Tail very long and thin. Widespread but not common, occasionally in schools in shallower water.

Spotted Eagle Ray *Aetobatus narinari*
Large (up to 2.5 m) ray, uppersides dark with numerous white spots. Underside white, body deep with a distinctive beak, poisonous spines at base of tail. Feeds on barnacles and molluscs and crustaceans in sand. Widespread throughout the archipelago, commonly in schools.

Golden Cownose Ray *Rhinoptera steindachneri*
Small (to 1 m), dull yellow or mustard-coloured ray, white below with long, thin tail with spines at base. Feeds on molluscs and crustaceans. Widespread; most often in large schools in sheltered mangrove lagoons.

Marbled Ray *Taeniurops meyeni*
Almost circular ray (to 2 m) with marbled black and grey upperside, white underside, tail thick at base to single barb, then vertically flattened. Common on sandy bottoms throughout. Feeds on small fish, molluscs and crustaceans.

Diamond Stingray *Dasyatis brevis*
Quadrilateral shaped (to 2 m) ray with olive-brown to grey coloration. Tail is thick and round, shorter than body, becoming vertically flattened after the barb. Widespread, especially on sandy bottoms. Feeds on molluscs and crustaceans.

Fine Spotted Moray *Gymnothorax dovii*
Large (to 1.7 m) olive or dark brown to black moray with fine white speckles on body and dorsal fin. Feeds on fish, crustaceans and octopus. Inhabits holes and crevices on reefs and boulder slopes. Found throughout the archipelago.

Tiger Snake Eel *Myrichthys tigrinus*
Small (to 0.75 m) pale beige eel with two rows of large dark brown oval spots along each flank and very small pectoral fins. Nostrils tubular, eyes have golden iris. Feeds on small fish and crustaceans. Widespread but uncommon on sand flats and rocky areas.

Galápagos Garden Eel *Heteroconger klausewitzi*
Very small (to 0.25 m) eel, grey with white blotches and a row of white spots below dorsal fin. Lives in burrow in sand, extending upper portion of body to feed on passing plankton. Common in small to large colonies in southern and central islands.

Heavy-bodied Fish – Sea Bass

Bacalao *Mycteroperca olfax*

Large (to 920 mm), dark greyish-brown fish with a speckled, occasionally barred appearance, belly pale silver. Bright yellow morph commonly known as Golden Grouper or Bacalao Rey. Feeds on small fish. Widespread throughout the archipelago.

(e) Camotillo *Paralabrax albomaculatus*

Medium sized (to 500 mm) reef fish with dark body, yellowish above and silvery below, and distinctive row of large white spots along body. Head generally yellow, fins yellow.

Flag Cabrilla *Epinephelus labriformis*

Similar to Bacalao in shape but smaller (to 540 mm). Colour varies olive-green to red-brown, covered in irregular and varied white blotches and spots. Feeds on fish. Widespread.

Leather Bass *Dermatolepis dermatolepis*

Large (to 920 mm), very deep-bodied, cumbersome-looking fish. Body mid-grey with several darker vertical bands, covered in irregularly shaped white marks. Head lighter grey to olive, tips of fins yellow. Juvenile has black and grey barring. Widespread and common.

Pacific Creolefish *Paranthias colonus*

Small (up to 350 mm), pinkish-grey schooling fish with three to five white, or occasionally dark, spots on back, belly salmon-coloured, and reddish tail deeply forked. Intermediate salmon-coloured with dark blue-ringed spot on pectoral fins. Juvenile yellow with dark spots.

Snappers and Grunts

Amarillo Snapper *Lutjanus argentiventris*

Large (to 1.35 m) silvery schooling fish, rear body and tail yellow, large eyes and prominent lips. Juveniles have a broad dark band from snout through eyes to back, and blue line below eye. Widespread but uncommon.

Blue and Gold Snapper *Lutjanus viridis*

Small (to 300 mm), easily recognised yellow schooling fish with silvery belly and five blue or green-blue lateral stripes from snout to tail. Widespread throughout the archipelago.

(e) Black-striped Salema *Xenocys jessiae*

Small (to 150 mm) silvery schooling fish with seven dark lateral stripes, back has yellow or green tint. Forms large polarised schools on walls and over rocky slopes.

ⓔ Galápagos Grunt *Orthopristis forbesi*

Small (to 300mm), slightly elongated silvery schooling grunt with a fine wavy pattern formed by dark markings on the scales. Eye golden, distinctive dark edge to back of gills. Widespread and common throughout the archipelago apart from the far north on rocky reefs and boulder slopes.

Peruvian Grunt *Anisotremus scapularis*

Small (to 300 mm), silver-grey schooling grunt with darker tail, steep forehead and distinct lateral line often extending above large, pale eye. Widespread throughout the archipelago but uncommon, in open water above rocky reefs and slopes.

Yellow-tailed Grunt *Anisotremus interruptus*

Large (to 600 mm), silvery grunt with large, dark-centred scales. Yellow tail and fins, silver belly and yellow eye. Widespread and common throughout the archipelago above rocky reefs and slopes.

Silvery Fish – Jacks and Chubs

Blue-bronze Chub *Kyphosus analogus*

Elegantly shaped (to 450 mm) and patterned schooling fish. Body silvery blue with thin, wavy yellow-bronze longitudinal stripes, yellow-bronze stripe from mouth to gill cover and also under eye. Widespread but uncommon throughout archipelago in inshore waters.

Cortez Chub *Khyphosus elegans*

Small (to 250 mm), rather nondescript, round-bodied schooling fish, dark silver above, paler below with two rather indistinct white lines below the eye. Widespread throughout the archipelago.

ⓔ Dusky Chub *Girella freminvilli*

Small (to 300 mm), silvery-grey schooling fish with large lips and a white spot in front of each eye. Widespread over sandy bottoms throughout the archipelago but not common.

Steel Pompano *Trachinotus stilbe*

Small (to 250 mm), round-nosed silvery schooling fish with long, thin, deeply forked tail and white bar behind head down to and behind the pectoral fin. Widespread and common throughout the archipelago.

Yellow-tailed Mullet *Mugil cephalus*

(Not illustrated) Common (to 600 mm), surface-feeding schooling fish. Body silver with somewhat forked yellow tail. Pectoral, dorsal and anal fins yellow. Common throughout the archipelago. Feeds on the surface often with boobies and pelicans. Immatures may feed on algae on rocks and in sand. Also seen in mangrove lagoons.

Parrotfish, Hogfish and Wrasse

These large, often slow-swimming reef fish all have three phases, juvenile (JP), initial (IP) and terminal (TP). The latter is most colourful, but the fish may breed in the initial phase.

Parrotfish

There are five species of these coral-crunching fish in Galápagos. All have large, projecting, continuously growing, fused teeth to scrape algae off rocks and crush coral, which is passed through their bodies and contributes to the creation of sand – one parrotfish can create 90 kg of sand a year.

Bumphead Parrotfish *Scarus perrico*

Large (to 760 mm) parrotfish with large bump and very prominent fused teeth. TP blue-green body with blue fins, blue markings around eye and mouth; head bump develops with age. IP similar in coloration but smaller and lacks bump. Widespread, especially in areas where there are stony corals.

Bicolor Parrotfish *Scarus rubroviolaceus*

Large (to 600 mm), snub-nosed fish. TP largely blue or blue-green with paler blue or pinkish markings on chin. IP dark red-brown head, changing to greenish and then pale on rear body; snub nose less obvious. JP striped white and greenish brown with white blaze on base of tail. Widespread but not common on rocky reefs and slopes.

Blue Chin Parrotfish *Scarus ghobban*

Medium-sized (to 450 mm) parrotfish with pointed snout. TP largely blue-green to blue with some yellow on flanks and distinctive blue markings under chin; some pink on dorsal and anal fins. IP rather more yellow, with five irregular, pale blue vertical bars on body. Widespread and common on rocky reefs and slopes.

Loosetooth Parrotfish *Nicholsina denticulata*

The smallest (to 300 mm) parrotfish, with individual rather than fused teeth. TP generally green with a red tail. IP varies from dark green-brown to much lighter with broad lateral band. Widespread in shallow water; sometimes in small schools. Commonest in western islands.

Streamer Hogfish *Bodianus diplotaenia*

(Mexican Hogfish) Sizeable (to 760 mm) reef fish with large head bump and long streamers on dorsal, anal and tail fins. TP greyish green on tail, shading to pinkish brown on head, pale yellowish vertical bar on mid-body (left photo). Individual front teeth often visible; head bump develops with age. IP snout pointed, scales pale with reddish edges and two dark lateral stripes (right photo). JP largely yellow with two narrow, dark lateral stripes. Widespread and common on rocky reefs and slopes.

Wrasse

At least 15 different species of this family are found in Galápagos. Colours very variable in all species; individuals of some species can change sex. They feed on a wide variety of invertebrates. Found throughout the archipelago on rocky reefs and slopes. Wrasse is a corruption of the Cornish word *wragh*, meaning 'old woman' or 'hag'.

Cortez Rainbow Wrasse *Thalassoma lucasanum*

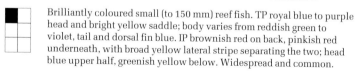

Brilliantly coloured small (to 150 mm) reef fish. TP royal blue to purple head and bright yellow saddle; body varies from reddish green to violet, tail and dorsal fin blue. IP brownish red on back, pinkish red underneath, with broad yellow lateral stripe separating the two; head blue upper half, greenish yellow below. Widespread and common.

Sunset Wrasse *Thalassoma grammaticum*

(Not illustrated) Small (to 200 mm) parrotfish-like reef fish. TP body green or blue-green, head violet to pink with a series of uneven green stripes. Young adults more yellow, head orangey. IP yellowish brown body with dark lateral stripe terminating in black spot. Commoner further north.

Chameleon Wrasse *Halichoeres dispilus*

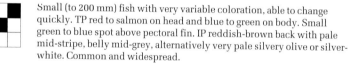

Small (to 200 mm) fish with very variable coloration, able to change quickly. TP red to salmon on head and blue to green on body. Small green to blue spot above pectoral fin. IP reddish-brown back with pale mid-stripe, belly mid-grey, alternatively very pale silvery olive or silver-white. Common and widespread.

Spinster Wrasse *Halichoeres nicholsi*

One of the larger (to 380 mm) wrasse. TP generally green to blue-green with distinctive irregular blue markings on head, yellow spot above and behind pectoral fins and vertical black bar behind spot. IP pale head and body, becoming yellow on tail and undertail, distinctive dark lateral stripe and vertical bar on back. JP yellow to brown with dark blotches and large, dark 'eye' on dorsal fin. Common and widespread.

Harlequin Wrasse *Bodianus eclancheri*

(Galápagos Hogfish) Large (to 620 mm) very variable reef fish, individuals having different colour patterns. TP white, orange and black, or alternatively black and yellow, with distinctive head bump. IP largely orange with wide, pale lateral bands and pointed snout. JP reddish to grey with broad, dark lateral bands and pointed snout. Widespread, commonest in south and west.

Boxfish and Triggerfish

These fish are also odd-shaped and have fused teeth for feeding on sea urchins, molluscs and hard-shelled crustaceans.

Pacific Boxfish *Ostracion meleagris*

(Spotted Trunkfish, Blue Boxfin) Small (to 150mm), distinctive box-shaped fish. Male has brown back with large, bright white spots and blue sides with marbled gold or black pattern. Female dark navy blue to black with large white spots over entire body. Mainly in northern islands, on rocky reefs, boulder slopes and walls.

Finescale Triggerfish *Balistes polylepis*

Large (to 770 mm), rather drab blue-grey to grey triggerfish, with prominent 'lips'. Body covered in fine scales, underside generally lighter, can change colour to suit surroundings. Widespread but uncommon on rocky reefs, boulder slopes and adjacent sandy areas.

Orangeside Triggerfish *Sufflamen verres*

Orange-bellied Triggerfish, Cachudo Panza Amarilla, Cochito Naranjo Medium-sized (to 440 mm), drab-coloured triggerfish. Mainly grey or olive-brown but with very broad yellowish-orange band along flank. White to yellow-orange stripe runs from mouth back to pectoral fin. Juvenile has mottled generally yellow undersides. Widespread on rocky reefs and boulder slopes.

Blunthead Triggerfish *Pseudobalistes naufragium*

(Stone Triggerfish) Large (to 900 mm), bluish-grey triggerfish, with three or four broad, dark bands on body and slightly concave snout. Widespread but not common on rocky reefs, boulder slopes and adjacent sandy areas.

Black Durgon *Melichthys niger*

(Black Triggerfish) Large (to 500 mm), distinctively patterned fish. Body blue-black, dorsal and anal fins black with pale blue lines along bases, black tip to tail. Widespread but commonest in northern islands on rocky reefs, boulder slopes and walls.

Big-eyed Reddish Fish

Bigscale Soldierfish *Myripristis berndti*

(Blotcheye Soldierfish) Medium-sized (to 300 mm), bright red-orange fish with large scales, black band on gills and white edges to top of rear dorsal, ventral, anal and tail fins. Nocturnal feeder on invertebrates. Commonest in northern islands, in cracks, crevices and caves.

Blacktip Cardinalfish *Apogon atradorsatus*

Very small (to 90 mm), copper-red fish with black spot on tip of rear dorsal fin; may also have dark tips to tail fin. Widespread and common.

Long, Thin and Odd-shaped Fish

Pelican Barracuda *Sphyraena idiastes*

Long (to 900 mm), thin silvery fish with slightly protruding lower jaw and protruding teeth, and dark barring on back. Found in large polarised schools in open water or over reefs throughout the archipelago, though not common.

Longfin Halfbeak *Hemiramphus saltator*

Very distinctive, small (to 300 mm), thin schooling fish with very long thin lower jaw. Body silver with scales giving a ribbed impression, tail deeply forked. Found throughout the archipelago, often jumps when pursued by predators. Ribbon Halfbeak (*Euleptorhamphus viridis*) is similar with long pectoral, anal and dorsal fins.

Reef Cornetfish *Fistularia commersonii*

Very long (to 1.2 m), thin fish with long filament-like tail and eye set well back from mouth. Body is silvery but with blue or green tint on back, belly silver-white. Widespread.

Trumpetfish *Aulostomus chinensis*

Long (to 750 mm), thin fish with hoover-like mouth, eyes set well back, and short tail with fan-like tail fin. Colour blue-grey to reddish brown with white spots close to tail. May be bright chrome-yellow; also a banded variant. Widespread, may be seen drifting in a vertical head-down position.

Mola Mola *Mola mola*

Very large (to 2.8 m), unmistakable fish with tall dorsal and anal fins but no tail. Greenish grey above silvery below. Dorsal fin often extends above water. Western islands only, mainly oceanic but comes into shallower waters to be cleaned by smaller fish.

Pacific Seahorse *Hippocampus ingens*

Unmistakable small (to 300 mm),upright swimming fish with horse-like head and long prehensile tail that it uses to hold on to coral, rocks and seaweed. Coloration variable, from red to orange, gold, yellow and brown. Widespread.

Pacific Beakfish *Oplegnathus insignis*

Large (to 600 mm), distinctively marked fish with beak-shaped mouth and large tail. Dark grey with large, irregular white spots all over. Mainly around western and southern islands.

Yellow-tailed Goatfish *Mulloidichthys dentatus*

Medium-sized (to 300 mm), mullet-like schooling fish. Body silvery with blue-green tint on back, prominent wide yellow lateral stripe from snout to tail. Two barbels under chin. Widespread and common.

Colourful Disc-shaped and Oval Fish

Thin-bodied, oval or rounded reef fish, surgeonfish have two razor-sharp spines located at the base of the tail. They feed mainly on algae. Butterflyfish feed on worms, polyps and other invertebrates, while angelfish feed mainly on sponges.

Yellow-tailed Surgeonfish *Prionurus laticlavius*

(Razor Surgeonfish) Round (to 450 mm), grey schooling reef fish with protruding snout, two dark vertical bands on head and yellow tail. Widespread and common throughout the archipelago on rocky reefs.

Goldrim Surgeonfish *Acanthurus nigricans*

(Whitecheek Surgeonfish) Small (to 200 mm), disc-shaped fish with deep blue body. Dorsal and anal fins are black with yellow base. Tail white, white patch under eye and white band under mouth. Found on reefs, mainly in the northern islands: rare or absent elsewhere.

Convict Surgeonfish *Acanthurus triostegus*

(Convict Tang) Small (to 150 mm) silvery fish, darker above than below. Six irregular dark vertical bands on body. Found in open water by reefs and walls. Commonest in the northern islands.

Barberfish *Johnrandallia nigrirostris*

(Blacknose Butterflyfish) Small (to 150 mm), almost circular, silver-yellow, schooling reef fish. Snout pointed with dark band over the top, eye dark with a black eye-ring, broad black band along the base of dorsal fin to tail, pectoral fins yellow. Widespread and common throughout archipelago.

Three-banded Butterflyfish *Chaetodon humeralis*

Small (to 150 mm), rectangular-looking silvery fish with a protruding snout and three broad black vertical bands on body, black edges to dorsal and anal fins, and black bands on tail. Widespread and common throughout archipelago in rocky areas; often in pairs.

Moorish Idol *Zanclus cornutus*

Distinctively-shaped (to 450 mm) schooling reef fish with protruding snout. Body has broad black and white vertical bands, tall, elongated dorsal fin and yellow on snout and rear upper body. Widespread throughout the archipelago over rocky areas and walls.

King Angelfish *Holacanthus passer*

Very colourful, almost circular (to 380 mm) schooling reef fish. Head and body dark with blue scale centres, dorsal and anal fins tinged orange, and tail and pectoral fins yellow. Broad white vertical band on forebody. Juvenile greenish with snout, tail and pectoral fins yellow, blue markings and broad orange band on forebody. Widespread and common throughout the archipelago over rocky areas. Often cleans other fish.

Small Oval Fish – Damselfish and Chromis

Damselfish and chromis are small, rather oval reef fish, often quite aggressive when defending their territory. Damselfish eat algae while chromis feed on zooplankton.

Scissortail Chromis *Chromis atrilobata*

Small (up to 130 mm), rather inconspicuous, deep-bodied schooling reef fish. Body dark greenish brown, belly paler, white spot close to rear end of dorsal fin, tail deeply indented. Widespread, sometimes common, feeds on plankton, in open water and over rocky reefs and slopes.

Giant Damselfish *Microspathodon dorsalis*

Large (to 300 mm), deep-bodied reef fish with long, trailing dorsal and anal fins with white or pale blue borders. Body blue but can darken or lighten, tail indent is U-shaped. Breeding male has grey on head. Juvenile bright blue with iridescent blue spots. Feeds on algae and when guarding nest can be very territorial. On rocky reefs and boulder slopes throughout the archipelago.

Bumphead Damselfish *Microspathadon bairdii*

Similar to Giant Damselfish, but dark brown with slight bump on head and triangular ends to dorsal and anal fins. Eyes bright blue. Juvenile blue-black with orange or yellow underside. Widespread and common on rocky reefs and slopes throughout the archipelago.

Galápagos Ringtail Damselfish *Stegastes beebei*

Small (to 150mm), round-bodied fish with very large dorsal fin. Adult dark greyish brown, broad white to indistinct band at base of tail. Pectoral fins have yellow tip and white edge. Intermediate blue on head and orange on back; juvenile redder on back and lack yellow on fins. Widespread throughout the islands; very territorial on rocky reefs and slopes.

Yellowtail Damselfish *Stegastes arcifrons*

Small (to 150 mm) reef fish with yellow lips, white head and yellow tail. Body mid-brown, eyes blue. Juvenile body green-blue with blue edges to dorsal, ventral and anal fins. Widespread throughout the islands on rocky reefs and boulder slopes; very territorial.

Panamic Sergeant Major *Abudefduf troschelii*

Distinctive small (to 230 mm) reef fish with five or six broad black vertical bands. Body silvery, eyes and back yellow. Breeding males develop an overall blue coloration and can be aggressive in guarding their nests. Widespread and common throughout archipelago apart from the western islands, where it is uncommon on rocky reefs and slopes.

Small and Odd-shaped Bottom-dwellers

Large-banded Blenny *Oiphioblennius steindachneri*
Small (to 250 mm) olive to brown fish with broad, pale bands on body, dark spot with pale surround behind eye and irregular cream-coloured markings on head. Widespread and common.

(e) Galápagos Barnacle Blenny *Acanthemblemaria castroi*
Very small (to 60 mm) goggle-eyed reef fish, which inhabits old barnacle shells. Orange-red with large white spots in two rows on back and side, many very small blue spots on head.

(e) Bravo Clinid *Gobioclinus dendriticus*
Small (to 150 mm) very vari-coloured reef fish, which blends with surroundings. Adult spotted and blotched with distinctive spot on gill cover; breeding males white with black vertical bands, yellow on head. Juveniles largely reddish. First three spines on dorsal fin longer than the rest. Widespread and common.

Red-lipped Batfish *Ogcocephalus darwinii*
Odd-shaped small (to 150 mm) fish with distinctive unicorn-like spike on head and red lips. Pectoral and ventral fins look like legs, grey-brown above and pale underneath. Widespread and common.

Coral Hawkfish *Cirrhitichthys oxycephalus*
Very small (to 80 mm) colourful reef fish. Whitish body covered in large red-orange splodges. Yellow tassels on tips of dorsal spines. Widespread and common.

Calico Lizardfish *Synodus lacertinus*
Medium-sized (to 250 mm) colourful fish with pointed, lizard-shaped head. Colours are very variable, red or brown on white base. May have several darker bands; can change colour quickly. Widespread but not common.

Stone Scorpionfish *Scorpaena mystes*
Large (to 500 mm), odd-looking, inelegant, camouflaged fish with large pectoral fins and numerous barbels under mouth. Mottled appearance with large blotches and skin flaps from grey-brown to red. Able to blend with surroundings. Dorsal spines poisonous. Widespread and common.

Hieroglyphic Hawkfish *Cirrhitus rivulatus*
Large (to 550 mm), dark blue-grey fish with irregular green markings outlined in blue and two pale or white spots on side below rear dorsal fin. Widespread and common.

Pacific Leopard Flounder *Bothus leopardinus*
Medium-sized (to 250 mm), oval-shaped, mottled brown flatfish. Lies on right side with left eye most obvious. Can change colour to blend with background. Widespread.

Odd-shaped Swimmers
Porcupinefish and Puffers

This group of oddly shaped shallow-water and reef fish can draw in water to inflate their body as a defence mechanism. Porcupinefish have spines that lie flat except when the body is inflated, burrfish have spines that are always erect, and smooth puffers lack spines but may use poison as part of their defence. All have fused teeth to help crush hard-shelled invertebrates, including barnacles.

Balloon Fish *Diodon holocanthus*

(Barred Porcupinefish, Longspined Porcupinefish) Large (to 510 mm), sausage-shaped, slow-swimming, spiny fish, pale brown to olive with irregular dark markings and scattered small, dark spots. Long spines on head, smaller further back. Fins rounded, iris yellow, pupil dark with blue-green flecks. Widespread in recesses on rocky reefs and boulder slopes. May inflate if attacked.

Porcupinefish *Diodon hystrix*

(Spotted Porcupinefish) Large (to 510 mm) sausage-shaped fish, with small spines all over and small dark spots, including fins. Colour varies olive to brown or dark grey. Widespread but uncommon in similar habitats to Balloon Fish. May inflate if attacked.

Spotfin Burrfish *Chilomycterus reticulatus*

(Spotted Burrfish, Pacific Burrfish) Similar to porcupinefish in size and shape, but light tan with larger, more prominent black spots all over, especially on fins. White underneath, small spines on body. Widespread but uncommon. May inflate if attacked.

Bullseye Puffer *Sphoeroides annulatus*

(Concentric Puffer) Medium-sized (to 400 mm), oddly shaped fish with concentric olive and ivory rings on back and flanks and large number of evenly spaced, small black spots; underside white. Widespread and common in coastal waters, often seen from boats. Some parts poisonous.

Guineafowl Puffer *Arothron meleagris*

(Yellow phase: Tamboril Amarillo, Botete Amarillo) Smaller (to 300 mm). Very distinctive puffer with two colour phases: spotted phase is dark purplish black with evenly spaced white spots; yellow phase is chrome-yellow with irregular dark blotches. Intermediate phase has white underneath. Widespread and common on rocky reefs, boulder slopes and walls.

(e) Galápagos Puffer *Sphoeroides angusticeps*

(Narrow-headed Puffer) Medium-sized (to 300 mm), puffer with mottled olive to pale purplish-brown head and body, long snout and small mouth. Prominent eyes have green pupil and orangey iris. Two small patches of black cirri (hair-like structures) on back. Widespread but not common, in areas of sand and small rocks.

INVERTEBRATES

The Galápagos, being oceanic islands, have relatively few species of higher animals. The same is true of the invertebrates. We have a reasonable degree of knowledge about the higher animals, albeit with some surprising gaps, but our knowledge of the invertebrate life of the islands is very patchy indeed, much of it derived from the various large expeditions that visited the islands at the end of the nineteenth and in the first part of the twentieth century. It is only now that the Charles Darwin Research Station is working on producing more comprehensive papers on the various families of invertebrates found in Galápagos.

Pirates, whalers and explorers were the first source of introduced species in Galápagos.

By their very nature, being very small, you will not see many invertebrates unless they bite or annoy you. There are, for example, 202 species of oribatid mites currently known to exist in Galápagos (Schatz 1998), but you are unlikely to see any of them unless you have a microscope with you. This guide will not therefore seek to attempt to illustrate more than a very small percentage of the nearly 2,500 known species of terrestrial and freshwater invertebrates found in Galápagos. There are many more species to be discovered here. It is sadly true that many species have already become extinct, largely due to the activities of humans, and more will follow. This is a particularly damaging loss as probably more than 50 per cent of all invertebrate species found in the islands are endemic.

INSECTS

Two-thirds of invertebrates found in Galápagos are insects (over 1,700 species). However, only a small percentage of these are likely to be seen, and fewer still will be identified by the casual visitor. Many of the species

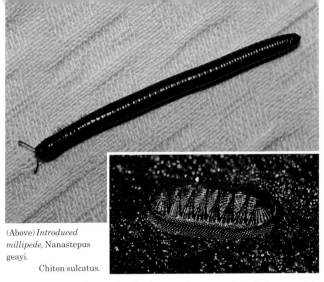

(Above) *Introduced millipede,* Nanastepus geayi.

Chiton sulcatus.

are present in numbers only after heavy rains, or at night. Others need to be searched for. Do not, therefore, be disappointed at not seeing as many insect species as you might have expected. This may also mean that you are visited by fewer mosquitoes!

Butterflies

These are probably the most easily seen and attractive insects that you are likely to see in Galápagos. There are ten species or subspecies resident in the islands, three of which are thought to be endemic, plus the *Actinote* sp. illustrated below, which is the only known record of this unidentified species. While recent research has increased our knowledge of the butterflies and moths, a great deal is still unknown. One of the ten species classed as resident, *Vanessa carye*, the Western Painted Lady, is known from only four records made in 1906, 1964 and 1995 on three widely separated islands. All observations should be noted and reported to the CDRS.

Actinote sp. photographed at 'Media Luna', Santa Cruz.

(n) Sulphur Butterfly *Phoebis sennae marcellina*

The most easily identified butterfly in the islands, lemon or sulphur-yellow with wingspan of 7 cm, frequently seen on Muyuyu and Parkinsonia. Caterpillars feed on Flat-fruited Senna *Senna pistaciifolia*. Small subspecies of the species that occurs throughout the western hemisphere.
Best viewed: Found on all the main islands up to 900 m.

(es) Galápagos Silver Fritillary *Agraulis vanillae galapagensis*

Slow-flying butterfly with a wingspan of 4–6 cm. Black and orange with silver spots on the underside of wing. Found in all zones, principally after rain. Caterpillars frequently found on Passion Flower *Passiflora foetida*.
Best viewed: Widespread but uncommon.

(n) Painted Lady *Vanessa virginensis*

A pan-American species with distinctive orange and brown mottled coloration and four distinct circular markings on rear wings. The two blue-centred spots on the rear underwing distinguish it from the Western Painted Lady *V. carye*, which is only rarely recorded in Galápagos.
Best viewed: Widespread in all areas especially after rain.

(n) Monarch Butterfly *Danaus plexippus*

The largest of the Galápagos butterflies with a wingspan of 10 cm, the wings are a rich red-brown, with a heavy black-veined pattern and black edging. It became established in the islands after the introduction of Milkweed *Asclepias curassavica*. First recorded by William Beebe in 1923.
Best viewed: Widespread, but not common, after rain.

(n) Queen Butterfly *Danaus gilippus thersippus*

Slightly smaller (7–8 cm) than Monarch; similar coloration but less dramatic markings, especially on the upper sides of the wings, which lack the large black veins and black border separating the fore and hind wings.
Best viewed: Arid zones to 400 m on all the southern islands except Isabela.

(e) Galápagos Blue Butterfly *Leptodes parrhasioides*

An unmistakable very small (1.6–2.5 cm), blue butterfly. Male has violet-bluish upper surfaces to the wings, dark brown below. Female has greyer upper surfaces with blue dusting especially near the body; undersides similar to male. Both sexes have two to four dark spots, often ringed with blue, at the rear inner edge of the hind wings.
Best viewed: Arid zone on virtually all main islands especially after rain.

(e) Large-tailed Skipper *Urbanus dorantes galapagensis*

Small brown 'tailed' butterfly. Wings brown with a greenish-olive gloss with whitish-yellow spots on the forewings. Dark brown line around edge of wings; rear wings have distinct 'tails' which are slightly darker than rest of wings. Sexes similar, female 5 cm, male 4.5 cm, female tail 6 mm, male 5 mm. Canna Skipper *Calpodes ethlius* is a recent arrival; it lacks a tail; row of four spots on hind wing. Found only on Isabela and Santa Cruz.
Best viewed: Widespread on all main islands at all elevations.

Moths

The fact that we have more information of the moths than of the butterflies of Galápagos, is probably due to their being largely nocturnal and being attracted to lights. Even so we have very little knowledge of the distribution, biology and life cycle of most species and there is a great deal of work to be done in this area. Of the more than 300 species of lepidoptera known to exist in Galápagos, the vast majority are moths. Around 30 per cent of moth species are endemic and a further 15 per cent are likely to be endemic subspecies.

(es) Green Hawkmoth *Eumorpha labruscae*

A large bright-green hawkmoth (sphinx moth), one of 12 species of this family in Galápagos. It is frequently attracted to lights, and can be seen feeding hummingbird-like on the nectar of many plants in the settlements. It is widespread, even being attracted to the lights of ships at sea.

(es) Galápagos Hawkmoth *Manduca rustica galapagensis*

A fairly common hawkmoth with a wingspan of 9 cm. It shows considerable variation in basic colouring from dark brown to gold and even to white, but with an overall mottled appearance. The forewings have a number of longitudinal bands running in from the wingtips across them. The hindwings are darker in colour and hairy at the thorax ends. Most commonly seen at night when attracted to lights.

(n) Fringed Noctuid *Ascalapha odorata*

This is the largest of 84 species of noctuid moth recorded in Galápagos. The largest moth in the islands, it has a wingspan of up to 15 cm. It has a varied brown and white coloration giving excellent camouflage on rocks and lichen-covered trees. Widespread, generally appearing around dusk.

(n) Crimson Speckled Footman Moth *Utethesia ornatrix*

An attractive day-flying moth with grey-white forewings and reddish or orange underwings. Frequently seen in the highlands where they can be quite numerous. At rest the wings are folded close to the body. Larvae probably feed on *Crotalaria*. There are three other species of this genus in Galápagos and they are hard to distinguish in the field.
Best viewed: Widespread in the Humid Zone.

(n) Sphinx Moth *Erinnyis* sp.

A widespread genus of moths found throughout the Americas; little is known about the species found in Galápagos.
Best viewed: Humid zones on main islands.

(e) Indefatigable Hawkmoth *Xylophanes norfolki*

A small brown hawkmoth with a wingspan of 6–7 cm. Found only in the highlands of Santa Cruz. The forewing pattern distinguishes it from *X. tersa*, a native species found on San Cristóbal and Santiago.
Best viewed: Santa Cruz – Los Gemelos.

Ants, Flies and Bees

ⓘⓟ Little Red Fire Ant *Wasmannia auropunctata*

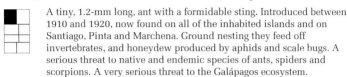

A tiny, 1.2-mm long, ant with a formidable sting. Introduced between 1910 and 1920, now found on all of the inhabited islands and on Santiago, Pinta and Marchena. Ground nesting they feed off invertebrates, and honeydew produced by aphids and scale bugs. A serious threat to native and endemic species of ants, spiders and scorpions. A very serious threat to the Galápagos ecosystem.

ⓘⓟ Tropical Fire Ant *Solenopsis geminata*

Similar to *W. auropunctata*, larger and less widespread but equally aggressive and the only ant able to compete successfully with it. It may affect the reproductive success of the Giant Tortoise, Land Iguana and birds. Large numbers of their stings can kill animals as large as black rats and can cause illness in humans.

ⓘ Longhorn Ant *Paratrechina longicornis*

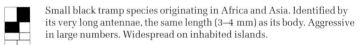

Small black tramp species originating in Africa and Asia. Identified by its very long antennae, the same length (3–4 mm) as its body. Aggressive in large numbers. Widespread on inhabited islands.

ⓔ Galápagos Carpenter Ant *Camponotus macilentus*

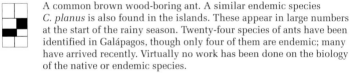

A common brown wood-boring ant. A similar endemic species *C. planus* is also found in the islands. These appear in large numbers at the start of the rainy season. Twenty-four species of ants have been identified in Galápagos, though only four of them are endemic; many have arrived recently. Virtually no work has been done on the biology of the native or endemic species.

ⓔ Galápagos Green-eyed Horsefly *Tabanus vittiger*

Largest fly in Galápagos (12 mm) with bright iridescent green eyes. Body is dark with reddish longitudinal lines, wings are translucent. Female feeds on the blood of iguanas, tortoises and sea turtles as well as humans. Male feeds on pollen, nectar and plant sap. Larvae live in the mud of lagoons and brackish ponds. You are likely to feel this species before you see it!

ⓘⓟ Biting Blackfly *Simulium bipunctatum*

Introduced to San Cristóbal in 1989, this biting fly causes large painful welts in humans. Found on other islands but needs running water to complete the breeding cycle, so may not be able to establish permanently.

ⓔ Galápagos Carpenter Bee *Xylocopa darwini*

The only bee in Galápagos. It is solitary. Female black (25 mm) and quite common. Male yellow-brown (about 18 mm) and less common. Feeds on plant nectar and is an important pollinator. With some flowers it bores a hole through the base to get at the nectar. Nests in dead wood, boring a 1-cm wide tunnel. Single egg is laid and larva is fed on nectar by female until it pupates. Widespread and common except in northern islands.

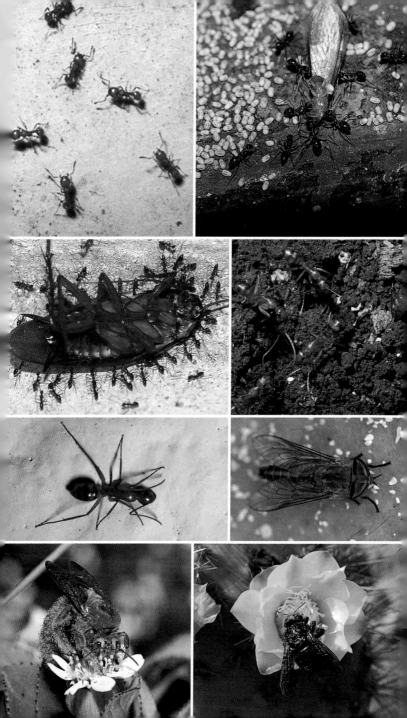

Wasps, Bugs, Beetles and Cockroaches

ⓘ Yellow Paper Wasp *Polistes versicolor*

Clearly identified by its yellow-and-black banded abdomen, this 25 mm long, delicately built aggressive wasp builds small ball-shaped 'paper' nests. Feeds on butterfly and moth larvae and other insects. First recorded in 1988, now found on all the inhabited islands. It has a nasty sting and is commoner on the coast than in the highlands.

ⓘⓟ Dark Paper Wasp *Brachygastra lecheguana*

First reported in 1994, this small, 12-mm long wasp has a pale brown-and-black banded abdomen. Feeds on butterfly and moth larvae and other insects. Nests are larger than *P. versicolor* and contain many females. Frequently swarms in large numbers.

There are a small number of endemic wasps in the Galápagos. These are rarely seen and are likely to have been affected by the presence of the two recently introduced species.

ⓔ Spotless Ladybug *Cyloneda sanguinea*

A bright-red spotless ladybug found on most of the major islands. It is an important predator and lives on a wide range of soft-bodied insects such as aphids and scale bugs.

ⓘⓟ Cottony Cushion Scale *Icerya purchasi*

A white almost circular insect with a rather furry appearance. It feeds off plant juices and is potentially a serious threat to the native flora. It has been found on 44 different species of plant, 15 of them endemic, on nine different islands. Its rapid dispersal since its introduction in 1982 is only partly accounted for by human agents, as it has probably spread to uninhabited islands by wind dispersal.

ⓝ Giant Long-horn Beetle *Stenodontes molarius*

The largest beetle in Galápagos, growing to some 6 cm in length with a fearsome pair of mandibles or pincers, over 1-cm long. Wing cases covering the abdomen are almost black. Eggs are laid in dead wood. The larvae bore long tunnels in the wood. The adults probably feed on fruit, plant sap, nectar and pollen. The pincers are larger in the male than the female and are used in both sexes for digging into trees and plants, and in the males for fighting other males for females.

ⓘ ⓔ Cockroaches

There are at least 18 species of cockroach in Galápagos. Eleven are recent introductions and five are endemic including two blind (*Chorisoneura* spp.) and three flightless species (*Ischnoptera* spp.). The endemic species are from the family Blattellidae. Many of the species are found in and around human habitation; they have a particular liking for ships. There is no evidence that the introduced species have displaced the native and endemic species, or that they have had any impact on other invertebrates.
They feed on litter and detritus and are food for birds and invertebrates.

Dragonflies, Grasshoppers and Crickets

(n) Spot-winged Glider *Pantala hymenaea*

Large (8–9 cm) dragonfly with reddish abdomen, often with a dark tip. Wings translucent with large brown spot on inner end of the hindwing. Nymphs develop in fresh or brackish water and often in as little as five weeks. A strong flier it is known to migrate long distances. It feeds on other insects and is frequently seen darting about over ponds and lagoons as it hunts its prey. This is one of eight species of dragonfly and damselfly found in Galápagos. Only one, *Aeshna galapagoensis* is endemic.

(e) Galápagos Field Cricket *Gryllus abditus*

Large (up to 5 cm) dark-coloured cricket, the long sharp rear end is not a stinging organ, but an ovipositor. This is lacking in the male. The head is shiny black and the hindlegs are dark brown. The wings extend beyond the end of the abdomen. There are eight species of *Gryllus* in the islands, *G. abditus* is the commonest. *G. galapageius* is similar with reddish brown hindlegs. Both are winged, the others are all flightless.
Best viewed:

G. abditus	Isabela, Santiago, San Cristóbal, Española, Floreana, Santa Cruz
G. galapageius	Santa Cruz, Santa Fé
G. isabela	Isabela and Fernandina
G. genovesa	Genovesa

(e) Large Painted Locust *Schistocerca melanocera*

Large (up to 8 cm) colourful grasshopper, particularly abundant after heavy rains. Head and thorax have irregular yellow markings, wings have reddish veins. Hindlegs are red above, yellow below and black on the sides. The immature or nymph stages are bright green, turning brown and then multicoloured. *S. melanocera* is more widespread than *S. literosa*. *Best viewed:* All islands except Española.

(e) Small Painted Locust *Schistocerca literosa*

Smaller than *S. melanocera*, up to 5 cm long and less colourful. It is pale brown with darker brown splotches making it well camouflaged. *Best viewed:* All islands.

(e) Galápagos Flightless Grasshopper *Halemus robustus*

One of four flightless species of this genus. A rather dumpy looking grasshopper due to the lack of wings. You will need to look carefully for these as they are well camouflaged with the brown coloration.

(n) Squeak Bug *Eburia lanigera*

Common beetle that gets its name from its ability to squeak or 'stridulate' when picked up. This is a defence mechanism to protect it from being eaten by birds. Body is about 25 mm long but with very long antennae and long legs. Fairly uniform grey in colour with yellowish spots. Attracted to lights and often found in considerable numbers.

SPIDERS, SCORPIONS, CENTIPEDES, MILLIPEDES

(n) Giant Huntsman *Heteropoda venatoria*

A common inhabitant of houses in Galápagos, this large spider does not weave a web, but hunts for prey, largely at night. Female is larger than male with leg span of up to 9 cm. The male may mate with several females; the female carries the egg sac underneath her abdomen.

(e) Galápagos Black Widow *Latrodectus apicalis*

A small dark grey or black spider with a bulbous abdomen and red markings on the underside. Lives in crevices in the rocks or under logs, and spins a web in front of its lair. There are no records of anyone being bitten, but as a relative of the Black Widow it is best avoided! It is widespread in the lowlands on all the major islands.

(e) Zig-zag Spider *Neoscona cooksoni*

A web-building spider with a habit of building its web across trails. The spider normally sits in the centre of the web but sometimes waits under a leaf or branch close by. It has a brownish back with an attractive cream-coloured pattern down the middle of it. It is found on all the major islands, most commonly in the Arid Zone.

(n) Silver Argiope *Argiope argentata*

A common web-building spider. It has a round abdomen and long legs and it sits in the middle of the web with its legs paired in an X. It spins four lines of white featherstitching in line with its legs. The purpose of these is uncertain.

(n) Star Spider *Gasteracantha servillei*

A web builder with a remarkable black-and-yellow, shell-like abdomen with six pointed spines. Most commonly found in the Coastal Zone, among mangroves and other shore vegetation.

(e) Galápagos Centipede *Scolopendra galapagensis*

This large centipede has a dark brown body, reddish legs and an impressive pair of fangs with which it poisons its prey. It grows up to 30 cm long. Found in the Arid Zone and is largely nocturnal. It preys on other invertebrates, lizards and even small birds. It is a favoured food of the Galápagos Hawk *Buteo galapagoensis*. There are at least eight species of centipede in Galápagos, the others are all very much smaller.

(es) Galápagos Scorpion *Hadruroides maculatus galapagoensis*

A small scorpion (up to 10 cm), common in the Coastal and Arid Zones. This species is a yellowy-brown colour with quite heavy pincers; the endemic *Centruroides exsul* is darker brown and has finer pincers. Feeds largely on other invertebrates. A favoured food of Lava Lizards.

MOLLUSCS

(e) Land Snails

The Galápagos land snails represent one of the more remarkable examples of speciation not just in Galápagos, but worldwide. There are 69 species from nine different genera, all of which are endemic. They are found in all vegetation zones on all of the major islands. Of the 69 species, 54 are from the genus *Bulimulus* which has an additional 12 subspecies. They are from 10–25 mm in length, with considerable variation in shape and coloration. Many of the species are probably extinct as a result of habitat loss from land clearance or feral goats and from predation by introduced species such as the Black Rat *Rattus rattus* and the Little Red Fire Ant *Wasmannia auropunctata*. (Left photo: *Succinea sp.* Right photo: *Bulimulus sp.*)

Marine Molluscs

1	2
3	4
5	6
7	

1 Horse Conch
2 Chief Rocksnail
3 Slender Triton
4 Cowries
5 Crowned Cone
6 Grinning Tun
7 Zebra Auger

Cowries – *Cypraea*
1 *C. teresa*
2 *C. nigropunctata*
3 *C. cervinetta*
4 *C. isabellamexicana*
5/6 *C. moneta*
7 *C. robertsi?*
8 *C. arabica*
9 *C. albuginosa*

Shells numbered left to right, top to bottom.

Some 800 species of intertidal and shallow water molluscs have been identified in Galápagos of which some 18 per cent are endemic. You may be able to identify some intertidal molluscs whilst walking along the coast, in particular the **Giant** or **Rippled Galápagos Chiton** *Chiton goodallii* (see photo p.115) is quite common. This is a large black-shelled mollusc that grows up to 15 cm long with a segmented shell. It makes an excellent meal and is therefore uncommon anywhere near inhabited areas. You may also come across the **Wide-mouthed Purpura** *Plicopurpura patula pansa* which is also found on intertidal rocks and has an attractive orange and white aperture. This shell is named from the purple dye that used to be extracted from it and was used to dye the purple robes of Roman emperors.

On the beach you will often come across cone shells; two common ones are the **Diadem** or **Crowned Cone** *Conus diadema* and **Woods Brown Cone** *Conus brunneus*. The former is plain chestnut brown, the latter is generally slightly darker and with white markings around the middle of the shell. Live cones are extremely poisonous, and they inject their poison through a harpoon-like organ. Watch out also for cowrie shells with their unmistakable double-lipped opening. The spotted **Little Deer Cowrie** *Cypraea cervinetta* is one of the commonest.

You may also find on the beach, or see while snorkelling or diving, the **Chief Rocksnail** *Hexaplex princeps* (up to 25 cm). It is whitish with reddish purple lines, with a series of large blunt spines. It is often entirely covered with soft corals and algal growth. It feeds on molluscs and barnacles, and drills holes through the shells to kill them. If you come across a long slender shell with zebra-like markings, it is the **Zebra Auger** *Terebra strigata*, a member of the *Terebridae* family (up to 12 cm). They are best seen in sandy bays; Santa Fé is probably the best location.

The two largest shells that you are likely to see in the islands are the **Grinning Tun** *Malea ringens* and the **Galápagos Horse Conch** *Pleuroploca princeps*. The former grows up to 24 cm long and is barrel-shaped. It lives on sandy bottoms in fairly shallow water, up to 8 m. The latter is longer, up to 40 cm, and more slender with a long orange opening. The animal is an amazing crimson colour with iridescent blue-purple spots.

The **Slender Triton** *Cymatium pileare macrodon* is another quite common shell found on beaches. The live shell is covered with a coarse hair. The shell is quite elongated and grows up to 11 cm in length and is characterised by three ribs or thickenings of the shell, which run up it longitudinally.

CRABS

ⓝ Sally Lightfoot Crab *Grapsus grapsus*

A dramatic scarlet and orange crab growing up to 20 cm across, often seen in large numbers. The underside is white, often bluish; juveniles are much darker, starting almost black, with small orange spots, becoming redder with each successive change of shell. They are predators and scavengers. Juveniles feed largely on algae and animal detritus, while adults feed on other crabs, including their own species, and small crustaceans. Their common name comes from their ability to 'walk on water' as they scurry from one rock to another.

ⓝ Hairy Rock Crab *Geograpsus lividus*

A fairly common rock crab with a dull orange carapace and hairy legs. A voracious predator which feeds on the small fish that inhabit the tide pools. Widespread but tends to hide in cracks or algae.
Best viewed: On rocky shorelines where there are tide pools.

ⓝ Velvet-fingered Ozius *Ozius verreauxi*

A neat, compact, blue-grey crab with a very smooth carapace up to 85 mm across. Claws of different size, one to hold its main prey, snails, the other to eat the flesh. Not uncommon but hides in cracks in the rocks.

ⓝ Fiddler Crab *Uca helleri*

Small, reddish brown crab up to 8 cm across. It has one very large claw, and one very small one. The male waves this large claw about during the courtship ritual, a little like a violinist's bow. It lives colonially in burrows amongst the roots of mangroves and feeds on algae and bacteria found on and around the roots.

ⓝ Ghost Crab *Ocypode gaudichaudii*

The commonest of a number of species of ghost crab. A small (10 cm) flesh-coloured crab. The eyes are on stalks which are raised when in the open, and lowered into the carapace in their burrows. Lives in the sand in the intertidal zone. They are omnivorous. They leave large numbers of little balls of sand that they have searched through for algal and animal detritus.

ⓝ Semi-terrestrial Hermit Crab *Coenobita compressus*

Hermit crabs have no hard carapace, but inhabit mollusc shells. As they grow they move to a larger shell. This species is light brown. Its external parts, head, claws and legs are laterally compressed. A common scavenger of the beach and in the littoral zone.

ⓔ Galápagos Hermit Crab *Calcinus explorator*

A small dark brown-to-black hermit crab with red-edged appendages. Another scavenger which is widely distributed and found mainly on rocks in the intertidal zone.

SEA URCHINS AND SEA STARS

Sea urchins and sea stars are echinoderms, or 'spiny skinned', which have radial symmetry. Sea urchins have hard globular-shaped shells covered with spines. Sea stars are flattened and have a generally softer exterior covered with spikes or bristles rather than spines.

(n) Pencil-spined Sea Urchin *Eucidaris thouarsii*

A distinctive sea urchin with stout, purple spines 5-mm thick and 5-cm long. It feeds on algae and corals and as with all echinoderms, has its mouth at the centre of the underside. The spines and segments of the shell are major constituents of many Galápagos beaches.

(e) Green Sea Urchin *Lytechinus semituberculatus*

A small sea urchin to 6 cm in diameter, with lime-green spines up to 15-mm long. Found mainly below the low-tide mark, but also in tidal pools. Frequently found washed up on sandy beaches.

Crowned Sea Urchin *Centrostephanus coronatus*

Black urchin with very long (12 cm), very sharp, spines, which break off easily and are slightly poisonous. A nocturnal carnivorous species found throughout the islands, best seen at very low tide or while snorkelling.

(n) White Sea Urchin *Tripneustes depressus*

A medium-sized urchin growing up to 10 cm in diameter with short, white or pale brown spines to 1 cm. They are normally found below the low-tide level, but can be seen during spring tides grazing, often in large numbers, on algae on exposed rocks.

(es) Sand Dollar *Micropora galapagensis*

An almost flat urchin, growing to 15 cm in diameter and up to 2-cm thick. It is pale-cream coloured to match its sandy habitat and has a clearly marked five-arm pattern on its upper surface. The spines are virtually non-existent. Often found washed up on beaches.

(n) Chocolate Chip Sea Star *Nidorellia armata*

Also known as the Spiny Sunstar, this five-armed starfish is common on rocky coastlines. It grows to 15 cm in diameter and is a generally orange-yellow coloration with a regular pattern of dark-brown short sturdy spines. It normally lives below the low-tide mark.

(n) Sea Cucumber *Holothuria* spp.

A soft-bodied relative of the starfish, it is a dark brown-to-black sausage-shaped animal, growing up to 20 cm in length. The largest member of the family in Galápagos, the Giant Sea Cucumber *Isostichopus fuscus* which is covered in yellow-brown bumps, has been the object of a commercial fishery since 1993 and its numbers have decreased substantially. It feeds on small gastropods and invertebrates as well as general detritus.

VEGETATION ZONES

There are seven generally accepted vegetation zones in Galápagos, all of them quite distinct:

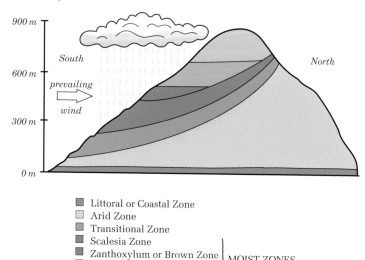

- Littoral or Coastal Zone
- Arid Zone
- Transitional Zone
- Scalesia Zone
- Zanthoxylum or Brown Zone
- Miconia Zone
- Pampa or Fern-sedge Zone

} MOIST ZONES

These zones are defined by their altitude and position on each island. Generally, the higher up, the wetter the climate. In addition, the south sides of the islands are very much wetter than the north. This is because the prevailing wind for much of the year comes from the south-east which results in the north side of the islands being in a rain shadow. Not all the large islands have quite the same vegetation zones owing to a variety of factors, in particular their height and location in relation to other islands. Isla Isabela is a very interesting case in point, because while it consists of five large shield volcanoes with heights varying from 1,123 m (3,650 ft) on Volcán Alcedo in the middle to 1,704 m (5,540 ft) on Volcán Cerro Azul in the south, each volcano has quite distinct vegetation. On Alcedo, there is virtually no bare lava. It is covered largely in volcanic ash and pumice and has only the lower five zones as it is itself relatively low. The two volcanoes to the north, Darwin and Wolf, have relatively smaller moist zones as they lie in the rain shadow of the rest of the islands. Cerro Azul, which is the extreme south-west of the islands, has the Transitional Zone on the coast and an Arid Zone on the rim which rises above the clouds and so receives only a small amount of precipitation in the garua season.

There are also very distinct differences between the flora of the islands Isabela and Fernandina and the rest of the archipelago. These are the younger islands and are thought to have less well-developed soils than the older islands such as Santa Cruz, Santiago and San Cristóbal. For the purpose of describing the vegetation zones, Santa Cruz has been used as the guide. While farming has damaged many of the zones, some irrevocably, it is still possible to see aspects of all of the zones quite clearly and, in addition, it is the island most likely to be visited by all visitors. It is also the one where visitors are most likely to explore the interior.

The Littoral or Coastal Zone

As its name suggests, this zone is immediately along the shore line and may extend 50 m to 100 m inland. The plants found here are not so much dependent upon the climate as on their ability to tolerate salt and to live on the edge of the sea. Many of the plants in this zone are evergreen, such as the several species of mangrove, and are characterised by heavy waxy, or fleshy succulent leaves.

Not many of the plants here are endemic and all will probably have arrived on the ocean currents.

The Arid Zone

This is the area that most visitors will become most accustomed to as it is also the habitat and breeding area for several of the animal species. On the south side of the islands, this may extend up to less than 100 m in altitude, while on the north side of the larger islands, it may extend up to an altitude of over 500 m. The smaller and lower islands are entirely in the Arid Zone. The most characteristic plants in the zone are the native Palo Santo tree (*Bursera graveolens*) whose silver-coloured bark contributes to the characteristic greyness of the zone, and the endemic Opuntia cactus (*Opuntia* spp.) which varies from a low cluster of pads to 10-m high brown-barked trees. You will also find a number of evergreen shrubs such as *Croton scouleri* and other drought-resistant plants. When the annual 'El Niño' rains come, the zone turns green very quickly, and many of the plant species of the zone, which are annuals, suddenly appear, flower and die within a period of six to eight weeks.

Brackish pool in Arid Zone.

The Transitional Zone

This is the zone between the dry and moist zones and is found at a much lower altitude (80–100 m) on the southern slopes of the larger islands than on the northern sides, and even at sea level in south-western Isabela. On some medium-sized islands such as Pinzón, Rábida and Pinta and Marchena, it is the only zone apart from the Littoral and Arid Zones. It is dominated by larger endemic deciduous trees such as Guayabillo (*Psidium galapageium*), Pega-pega (*Pisonia floribunda*)

Transitional Zone.

and the amazing native hardwood Matazarno (*Piscidia cathagenensis*). With no canopy to shut out light, there are a number of shrubs in this zone, some of which are evergreen. Many lichens and mosses attach themselves to the trees. While no species is dominant in this zone, all the species found here are also found in either the Arid Zone below or in the Scalesia Zone above. It has the greatest diversity of species of any of the vegetation zones.

The Scalesia Zone

Starting at around 180–200 m, this, the first of four moist zones, is a lush cloud forest and is characterised by the largest of the 20 members of the *Scalesia* genus found in the Galápagos, *Scalesia pedunculata*. While *S. pedunculata* is dominant on Santa Cruz, San Cristóbal, Floreana and Santiago, it is replaced on Isabela and Fernandina by *Scalesia cordata* and *Scalesia microcephala*, another good example of inter-island variation, possibly related to soil and climate differences. Scalesia form dense stands with trees up to 15 or even 20 m in height; from afar, they appear like a bright-green hummocky bog. Underneath the canopy the trunks and branches are encrusted with epiphytes: mosses, liverworts, ferns, bromeliads and orchids. Epiphytes (plants which grow on another plant, but do not parasitise them) are characteristic of

Scalesia Zone.

the moist zones of the Galápagos as a result of the long periods when the upper reaches of the higher islands are shrouded in cloud and mist. Many species of vine also flourish with the Scalesia forests. Much of this zone has been destroyed on the inhabited islands. It is the best area for agriculture, being well watered by the garua during the cool season. There is still a good area of Scalesia forest at the western end of Santa Cruz close to the airport road by the pit craters knows as Los Gemelos (The Twins).

The Miconia Zone

Starting at between 400 and 500 m, this zone is found only on Santa Cruz and San Cristóbal, on the southern, windward, slopes. It is dominated by *Miconia robinsoniana*, a shrub growing up to 5-m high. It forms a dense thicket which provides a perfect nesting area for the Galápagos Petrel. Unfortunately, the area has been invaded on Santa Cruz by the imported Quinine Tree *Cinchona succirubra*, a serious threat to the whole zone. On San Cristóbal, the stands of *Miconia* are less dense and are interspersed with other shrubs, while on Isabela and Fernandina, *Miconia* is entirely absent and replaced by a variety of other shrubs such as *Baccharis*, *Darwiniothamnus*, *Hyptis* and *Dodonea*.

Miconia Zone.

Bog pond in Pampa Zone, Santa Cruz.

The Pampa or Fern-sedge Zone

The highest zone of all is the Pampa Zone. Like upland moorlands worldwide, the vegetation here is almost entirely composed of mosses, grasses and ferns, most of which are no more than 30-cm high. One exception is the Galápagos Tree Fern, *Cyathea weatherbyana*, which grows up to 3-m tall but is generally found in gullies and ravines or inside small craters and potholes, where there is better water retention during the dry season. There are four species of orchid in this zone. Lichens are also abundant in this area, brightening it up with their varying shades of green, grey, yellow, orange and red.

SOILS

Given the importance of soil in determining the plants that will thrive in any area, it is surprising that very little work has been done on the soils of the islands. Laruelle (1966) worked on Santa Cruz and identified five different zones, which correspond approximately to the vegetation zones. The soils in the lower zones are neutral or moderately basic, and those above increasingly more acidic. Soil zones 1 and 2 are identified with the Coastal to Transitional Zones. Soil zones 3 and 4 are found with the Scalesia and Zanthoxylum Zones, and soil zone 5, where the increasingly acidic soils are found, with the Miconia and Pampas Zones.

This is an area where further research is needed – understanding all aspects of the biology of the islands is an essential prerequisite to being able to preserve them.

ECOLOGICAL ZONES

While the vegetation divides up into seven zones, there are three basic ecological zones in Galápagos. The first is the Coastal Zone, characterised by animals and plants which depend on the proximity of the sea. The Arid and Transitional Zones are characterised by long periods of drought and a relative lack of moisture. The animals and plants found here can survive long periods without water. Thirdly there is the Humid Uplands Zone, where there may be periods of drought, but as a general rule the plants and animals here are adapted to a relative abundance of water.

PLANTS

This guide will not attempt to provide you with an exhaustive list of the plants found in Galápagos, but it will help you to identify the commoner species that you are likely to see whilst visiting the islands. It will also help you to appreciate that while the differences between the plants on the various islands are not always as dramatic or well publicised as those in the Animal Kingdom, they are equally important in helping us to understand the very special nature of the Galápagos.

In the first instance, the very paucity of species is important. There are only some 600 Native species, subspecies, and varieties (taxa) of vascular plant in Galápagos; this compares with over 20,000 in mainland Ecuador. This lack of species is simply due to the isolation of the islands. Within this relative paucity of species, some 250 are Endemic, in other words found nowhere else. This is a remarkably high proportion. These endemic species have 'developed' or evolved from an original 110 species that arrived here by natural means. Most of these plants are closely related to ones found on the mainland.

'Adaptive radiation' is a term often used in relation to the development of the 13 species of Darwin's finch, or the 12 species of giant tortoise. Adaptive radiation is, however, equally evident in the plant world. There are 20 taxa of the genus *Scalesia*, a member of the daisy family, and 14 taxa of the genus *Opuntia*, a widely distributed member of the cactus family. The average visitor to Galápagos will get a better chance to see and identify several different plant taxa from the same genus than they will different animal taxa from the same genus. Keep your eyes open and look out for the differences that Darwin noted and that helped him to reach his revolutionary conclusions.

Coastal (Littoral) Zone Plants

The plants found in this zone need to be very tolerant of salt. Many of them are at times entirely or partially covered by sea water. To cope with this, they have special glands in the leaves which excrete the salt. You can often see or taste this.

(n) Red Mangrove *Rhizophora mangle*

The commonest of the four mangroves found in Galápagos, it is easily recognised by its thick, dark green, waxy leaves and often delicate stilt or prop roots. These external roots support the tree so that the main trunk itself is generally not in the water. With prop roots, the main trunk gradually diminishes in size the closer it gets to the water or beach. The flowers are individual, have four petals and are on short stalks. These develop into 15–25-cm long fruits or seedlings which fall off and float away to develop elsewhere. Found on sheltered beaches and in coves and lagoons throughout the islands, it normally grows up to 7-m high, but on Isabela, either side of the Perry Isthmus, it can grow to 15 or 20 m.
Best viewed: Santa Cruz – Puerto Ayora, Tortuga Bay, Turtle Cove and Caleta Negra; Isabela – Elizabeth Bay, Punta Garcia and Puerto Villamil; Fernandina – Punta Espinosa; Genovesa – Darwin Bay; Bartolomé.

(n) Black Mangrove *Avicennia germinans*

The largest mangrove in the islands, reaching heights of up to 25 m. It is slightly less common than the red mangrove, but is found throughout the islands. It takes its English name from the grey, at times almost black, bark. It is also found on beaches and lagoons but has a conventional root system sending out finger-like breathing roots (pneumatophores) which stick up out of the sand or mud and help to anchor the beach. These pneumatophores help to provide the plant with oxygen, as the soil is often waterlogged. It has smaller, more pointed leaves than the red mangrove. They have a grey tinge, darker above than underneath. The leaves often have a thin layer of salt on them, excreted by glands which help the mangrove to cope with the salt water. The black mangrove has clusters of small white flowers with 5 petals which develop into flattened drop-shaped fruit and which, like those of the red mangrove, are dispersed by the sea.
Best viewed: Santa Cruz – Puerto Ayora, Tortuga Bay, Las Bachas; Santiago – Espumilla Beach; Floreana – Punta Cormoran; Fernandina; Isabela – Elizabeth Bay; Rábida.

(n) White Mangrove *Laguncularia racemosa*

This species is best identified by its paler oval leaves with dots on the underside. Its flowers, which have five petals, form inconspicuous small greenish-white clusters. The fruits are pale green and flask-shaped. It grows as a shrub or tree up to 10 m in height. Though not common it is often found together with red mangroves in lagoons or brackish-water swamps but not on beaches.
Best viewed: Santa Cruz – Puerto Ayora, Tortuga Bay, Turtle Cove; Santiago – Espumilla Beach, Sullivan Bay; Fernandina – Punta Espinosa; Bartolomé; Isabela – Elizabeth Bay, Puerto Villamil, Punta Garcia, Punta Moreno.

(n) Button Mangrove *Conocarpus erectus*

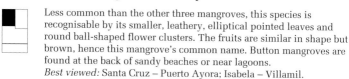

Less common than the other three mangroves, this species is recognisable by its smaller, leathery, elliptical pointed leaves and round ball-shaped flower clusters. The fruits are similar in shape but brown, hence this mangrove's common name. Button mangroves are found at the back of sandy beaches or near lagoons.
Best viewed: Santa Cruz – Puerto Ayora; Isabela – Villamil.

(n) Leatherleaf *Maytenus octogona*

An often prostrate shrubby evergreen tree, it grows to a maximum height of 8 m, but is normally 3–5 m. The leaves are thick and waxy with small, very inconspicuous, green flowers with five petals. The fruit is a red berry that develops within a three-sided capsule. The bark is highly fissured and the tree is found some way inland as well as on the coast. It is well adapted to dry conditions, as most of its leaves grow in a vertical plane to reduce exposure to the sun. The Spanish name, Rompe Ollas, is best translated as 'pot-breaker', and comes from the fact that it produces a lot of heat when burned and tends to break clay cooking pots unless used with care.
Best viewed: Santa Cruz – Puerto Ayora; Baltra; Rábida; Santa Fé; Seymour; Santiago – Espumilla, Puerto Egas; Floreana – Punta Cormoran; Bartolomé; South Plaza.

(n) Saltbush *Cryptocarpus pyriformis*

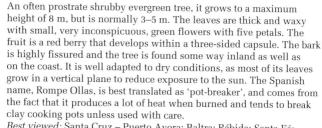

This low, creeping evergreen shrub behaves rather like a bramble and forms impenetrable thickets close to the beach, hence its local Spanish name 'bejuco' that translates idiomatically as 'the grape vine'. It has thick waxy leaves and inconspicuous small green flowers which produce a five-segmented fruit. You will see this in many places. It is frequently used as a nesting area for frigate birds and pelicans and can be seen on the walk from the Charles Darwin Research Station to the village in Academy Bay on Santa Cruz.
Best viewed: Santa Cruz – Puerto Ayora, Tortuga Bay; Española – Punta Suarez, Gardner Bay; North Seymour; Genovesa – Darwin Bay; Floreana – Punta Cormoran and Post Office Bay; Rábida; Santiago - Espumilla Beach and Sullivan Bay; Bartolomé; Isabela – Tagus Cove; Rábida; Santa Fé.

ⓝ Saltwort *Batis maritima*

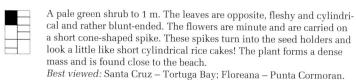

A pale green shrub to 1 m. The leaves are opposite, fleshy and cylindrical and rather blunt-ended. The flowers are minute and are carried on a short cone-shaped spike. These spikes turn into the seed holders and look a little like short cylindrical rice cakes! The plant forms a dense mass and is found close to the beach.
Best viewed: Santa Cruz – Tortuga Bay; Floreana – Punta Cormoran.

ⓝ Scorpion Weed *Heliotropium curassavicum*

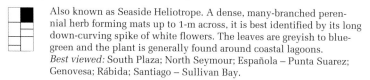

Also known as Seaside Heliotrope. A dense, many-branched perennial herb forming mats up to 1-m across, it is best identified by its long down-curving spike of white flowers. The leaves are greyish to blue-green and the plant is generally found around coastal lagoons.
Best viewed: South Plaza; North Seymour; Española – Punta Suarez; Genovesa; Rábida; Santiago – Sullivan Bay.

ⓝ Salt Sage *Atriplex peruviana*

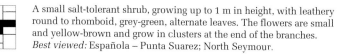

A small salt-tolerant shrub, growing up to 1 m in height, with leathery round to rhomboid, grey-green, alternate leaves. The flowers are small and yellow-brown and grow in clusters at the end of the branches.
Best viewed: Española – Punta Suarez; North Seymour.

ⓝ Sea Grass *Sporobolus virginicus*

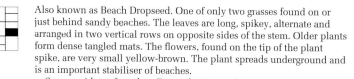

Also known as Beach Dropseed. One of only two grasses found on or just behind sandy beaches. The leaves are long, spikey, alternate and arranged in two vertical rows on opposite sides of the stem. Older plants form dense tangled mats. The flowers, found on the tip of the plant spike, are very small yellow-brown. The plant spreads underground and is an important stabiliser of beaches.

    *S. pyramidatus,*found on Española, Fernandina and Isabela, does not creep and the leaves are not arranged so precisely.
Best viewed: Santa Cruz – Puerto Ayora, Las Bachas, Tortuga Bay; Floreana – Post Office Bay, Punta Cormoran; Santiago – Sullivan Bay; Genovesa; Española – Gardner Bay.

ⓝ Desert Plum *Grabowskia boerhaaviaefolia*

Low shrub growing to 2.5 m, bark whitish on new growth, turning brown with age. The branches are often thickly encrusted with lichens. Pale-green slightly elongated leaves. Small white trumpet-shaped flowers 3–5-mm long, produced in clusters at the branch ends producing a small red-orange berry.
Best viewed: South Plaza; Española – Punta Suarez.

ⓔ Galápagos Clubleaf *Nolana galapagensis*

A low shrub to 1.5 m. The dense clusters of short, pale-green sometimes yellowish, fleshy, club-shaped leaves, give the plant the appearance of a succulent. The flowers are small, white and bell-shaped. Found very close to the shore at a number of visiting sites.
Best viewed: San Cristóbal – Punta Pitt; Santa Cruz – Tortuga Bay; Floreana – Punta Cormoran.

(n) Ink Berry *Scaevola plumieri*

Also known as Sea Grape. A compact but spreading shrub, growing to about 1 m, found on or close to the beach. The leaves are alternate, waxy, almost circular. The flowers are white with long narrow petals. The fruit looks like a large blackcurrant but starts off green.
Best viewed: Floreana – Post Office Bay, Punta Cormoran; Santa Cruz – Tortuga Bay; Isabela – Villamil.

(e) Galápagos Carpetweed *Sesuvium edmonstonei*

A low-lying perennial herb with fat, fleshy cylindrical leaves, The flowers are small, white and star-shaped. The plants are green after rain but turn a spectacular orange-red during the dry or garua season. The seeds are black and contained in a small oval capsule.
Best viewed: South Plaza; Sombrero Chino; North Seymour; Española – Punta Suarez; Santiago – Sullivan Bay; Genovesa.

(n) Common Carpetweed *Sesuvium portulacastrum*

Also known as Sea Purslane. Very similar to the Galápagos Carpetweed *Sesuvium edmonstonei,* but with flatter rather more pointed leaves and a pink rather than white flower. This species also forms dense carpets and turns red in the garua season.
Best viewed: Santa Fé; North Seymour; Santa Cruz – Puerto Ayora, Tortuga Bay; Isabela – Punta Moreno.

(n) Beach Morning Glory *Ipomoea pes-caprae*

An unmistakable perennial with its long creepers stretching 10 m or more, found on sandy beaches and dunes. Leaves leathery and oval to elliptical. The attractive purple-mauve trumpet flower is typical of the genus, producing large oval seed-pods containing a number of hairy seeds. An important stabiliser of beaches and sand dunes.
Best viewed: Española – Gardner Bay; Genovesa; Santa Cruz – Puerto Ayora, Tortuga Bay; Bartolomé; Isabela – Elizabeth Bay, Punta Albemarle.

(e) Galápagos Shore Petunia *Exodeconus miersii*

This annual herb is easily identified by its large trumpet-shaped white flowers. It will only appear during the rainy season, when it forms dense mats. The leaves are large and oval with indented edges. The stems are hairy and sticky. The seed capsule is egg-shaped.
Best viewed: Española – Punta Suarez; Floreana – Post Office Bay, Punta Cormoran; Genovesa – Darwin Bay; Fernandina – Punta Espinosa; Isabela – Tagus Cove, Urvina Bay.

(n) Morning Glory *Ipomoea triloba*

A commonly seen vine in both the Arid and Transitional Zones after heavy rains. It has large (up to 10 cm) three-lobed leaves and attractive trumpet-shaped, pink, lavender or purple flowers (occasionally white).
Best viewed: Santa Cruz – inland from Puerto Ayora.

Arid and Transitional Zone Plants

There are no clear boundaries between the seven different vegetation zones. The Transitional Zone, by its very nature, includes plants from the Arid and the Humid Zones. Most visitors will see more of these two zones than any others. The zones as described exist only on the southern or windward slopes of the islands. On the northern slopes, which are in a rain shadow, the Arid and Transitional Zones extend much higher up. The best place to observe this is on the airport road on Santa Cruz, where in less than a kilometre, you move from the moist Scalesia Zone to the Arid Zone.

Cacti

The large family Cactaceae are succulents: plants with fleshy leaves or stems or both. Cacti are generally characterised by extremely sharp spines. These are actually the leaves and also their main defence against herbivorous predators. Galápagos cacti vary in size from the Lava Cactus, which rarely exceeds 60 cm in height, to the large Prickly Pear and Candelabra Cacti both of which can reach heights of 8–12 m.

(e) Lava Cactus *Brachycereus nesioticus*

The smallest of the Galápagos cacti, found exclusively on barren lava fields, it is usually one of the first plants to colonise a fresh lava flow. It consists of a number of short spiny cylinders or stems up to 60 cm in length. The individual stems do not branch, but it is easy to see how an individual stem may have grown in several stages. The younger stems and spines are a fresh greenish yellow, gradually turning grey to black with age. The individual plants or clumps may be as much as 2 m or more across. It flowers very briefly, the large creamy white flowers opening before dawn and shrivelling within a few hours. The fruits are dark brown up to 3.5-cm long and with yellow spines.

Best viewed: Santiago – Sullivan Bay; Bartolomé; Isabela – Punta Moreno; Fernandina – Punta Espinosa; Genovesa – Prince Philip's Steps; Sombero Chino.

(e) Candelabra Cactus *Jasminocereus thouarsii*

This large candelabra-shaped cactus grows up to 7 or 8 m high and is found mainly in the Arid Zone. The arms are made up of fluted, very spiny cylindrical sections, which become woodier with age. The red/orange coloured flowers open before dawn, these turn into reddish-purple globular-shaped fruit up to 50-cm long which are edible. When the plant or part of it dies, the hollow woody 'skeleton' is left behind. There are three varieties of this species:

J. thouarsii. var. *thouarsii*
Is found on San Cristóbal, Floreana and Corona del Diablo.
J. thouarsii. var. *delicatus*
Is found on Santa Cruz, South Plaza and Santiago
J. thouarsii var. *sclerocarpus*
Is found only on Isabela and Fernandina.

Best viewed: Santa Cruz – Puerto Ayora; Sombrero Chino; Floreana – Punta Cormoran, Corona del Diablo.

ⓔ Giant Prickly Pear Cactus *Opuntia* spp.

The most widely distributed and numerous of the islands' cacti, Opuntia are an excellent example of adaptive radiation, there being six different species divided into 14 different varieties. There are considerable variations from island to island. The tallest, *Opuntia echios* var. *gigantea* found on Santa Cruz may grow to 12 m; while on Santa Fé *O. echios* var. *barringtonensis* has a girth of up 2.60 m. On North Seymour, *O. echios* var. *zacana* and on Rábida *O. galapageia* var. *profusa* look like a heap of jumbled pads.

When young, the tree species have a trunk covered with a fearsome display of spines facing outwards and downwards. As they develop, the spines give way to a beautiful rich brown bark. However unlike *Jasminocereus*, opuntias do not become woody and if you find a fallen one you can see how the trunk is made up of layer upon layer of a fibrous honeycomb material. The pads (the spines are the leaves and the pads are the stem) also have a wonderfully delicate pattern. Both of these are sometimes used as decorative material.

While there is no conclusive evidence, it seems reasonable to suppose that the large, trunked species of *Opuntia* evolved in response to competition for light, and also as a protection from predators, mainly tortoises and Land Iguanas. It is certainly true that for the most part, where there are tall, trunked varieties, there are also tortoises, and islands such as Marchena and Rábida, which have no tortoises, have low or prostrate forms, often with virtually no spines, or only soft ones.

Opuntia spp. are very important in the Galápagos ecosystem. The pads and fruit provide an important part of the diet of tortoises and Land Iguanas. Doves and mockingbirds also enjoy the fruits which are from 4 to 7 cm long. The two Cactus finches, *Geospiza scandens* and *G. conirostris*, are dependent upon the cactus flowers, fruits and seeds, and even extract water from the pads. In an environment not noted for its flowering plants, the flowers are an important source of nectar for insects.

Opuntia may flower at any time of the year, the flowers are bright yellow and multi-petalled, and emerge from the end of the already formed, top-shaped fruit. In some species the flowers turn pinkish-orange with time.
Best viewed: Widespread throughout the Arid Zone and into the Transitional Zone on most islands.

O. echios var. *barringtonensis*
This is found only on the island of Santa Fé, and is distinguished by its immense trunks. The fruits of this variety are up to 7-cm long. Santa Fé has never had a tortoise population but does have its own species of Land Iguana which may have impacted on the evolution of this variety of cactus in the same way that tortoises are thought to have elsewhere.

O. echios var. *echios*
Found on Baltra, Daphne, South Plaza and the northern parts of Santa Cruz. On South Plaza the variety is tall and treelike, up to 4 m in height, but elsewhere the shrubby variety is found. The fruits are top-shaped. There are no tortoises on any of these islands apart from Santa Cruz, but Land Iguanas are found on South Plaza and northern Santa Cruz.

O. echios var. *gigantea*
The tallest of the *Opuntia* varieties, growing up to 12 m in height, it occurs only on Santa Cruz, noticeably around Puerto Ayora. Both tortoises and Land Iguanas were found here.

O. echios var. *inermis*
A tree-like variety found only on Volcán Sierra Negra on Isabela. It grows to a height of 6 m. The best place to see this variety is around the town of Villamil. Tortoises and Land Iguanas are found here.

O. echios var. *zacana*
A shrubby form 1–2 m in height, found only on North Seymour, often close to the Dwarf Palo Santo tree *Bursera macrophylla*. There have never been tortoises on this island and the Land Iguanas were introduced from Baltra in the 1930s.

Opuntia galapageia var. *galapageia*
A relatively short (to 4 m) trunked variety found on Pinta and Santiago. On Pinta in particular, the trunk often tapers quite markedly to a point about 2–3 m up where it branches into a dense mass of pads giving it the appearance of a giant mushroom. There are, or were, tortoises and Land Iguanas on both islands.

Opuntia galapageia var. *macrocarpa*
A trunked variety found only on Pinzón. This is another island with its own tortoise population but no Land Iguanas.

Opuntia galapageia var. *profusa*
A shrubby variety found only on Rábida. It has soft spines and produces a very large number of fruit, hence its scientific name. This island has never had a tortoise or Land Iguana population.

Opuntia helleri
A low-growing shrubby species found on the northern islands of Darwin, Wolf, Marchena and Genovesa. None of these islands has had a tortoise or Land Iguana population. The spines are often soft and wavy.

Opuntia insularis
A short-trunked and sometimes shrubby variety, found on Fernandina and Isabela. It cohabits on Cerro Azul with *O. saxicola* and on Sierra Negra with *O. echios inermis*. It differs from the latter in being rather taller, up to 6 m and having longer spines, 5–8 cm and top-shaped fruits. There are, or were, tortoise and Land Iguana populations on both islands.

Opuntia saxicola
A rare trunked variety found only on Volcán Cerro Azul, Isabela, an island with both tortoise and Land Iguana populations.

Opuntia megasperma var. *megasperma*
This trunked variety is found only on Floreana and the Corona del Diablo. This species has the largest seeds of any of the species, up to 13-mm long. Floreana has had both tortoise and iguana populations in the past.

O. megasperma var. *orientalis*
Another very thick and heavily tapering trunked variety found only on San Cristóbal and Española. Both islands have tortoise populations but there are no Land Iguanas on Española.

O. megasperma var. *mesophytica*
Found only on San Cristóbal and its offshore islands. This trunked variety is found at higher elevations and has a thinner trunk and smaller seeds than *O. m. orientalis*. San Cristóbal has both tortoise and Land Iguana populations.

Arid and Transitional Zone Trees

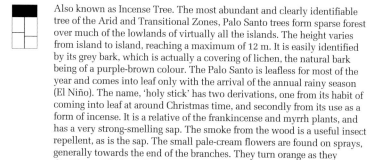 Palo Santo *Bursera graveolens*

Also known as Incense Tree. The most abundant and clearly identifiable tree of the Arid and Transitional Zones, Palo Santo trees form sparse forest over much of the lowlands of virtually all the islands. The height varies from island to island, reaching a maximum of 12 m. It is easily identified by its grey bark, which is actually a covering of lichen, the natural bark being of a purple-brown colour. The Palo Santo is leafless for most of the year and comes into leaf only with the arrival of the annual rainy season (El Niño). The name, 'holy stick' has two derivations, one from its habit of coming into leaf at around Christmas time, and secondly from its use as a form of incense. It is a relative of the frankincense and myrrh plants, and has a very strong-smelling sap. The smoke from the wood is a useful insect repellent, as is the sap. The small pale-cream flowers are found on sprays, generally towards the end of the branches. They turn orange as they die. The small cherry-like fruits are much favoured by Darwin's finches, endemic rats (where still surviving), and Land Iguanas.
Best viewed: Santa Cruz; Genovesa – Darwin Bay, Prince Philip's Steps; Floreana – Post Office Bay, Punta Cormoran; Isabela – Tagus Cove, Elizabeth Bay, Puerto Villamil, Punta Garcia, Punta Moreno, Urvina Bay, Volcán Alcedo; Baltra; Rábida; San Cristóbal – Frigatebird Hill; Santa Fé; Santiago – Espumilla Beach, Puerto Egas, Sullivan Bay.

Dwarf Palo Santo *Bursera graveolens malacophylla*

Also known as Galápagos Incense Tree. Very similar to *B. graveolens*, this is a short stubby form found only on Baltra, North Seymour, Daphne, and northern Santa Cruz. This is thought to be a subspecies of *B. graveolens* with quite variable differentiation from that species. Found on Santa Cruz, SE Santiago and Bainbridge Rocks.

Matazarno *Piscidia carthagenensis*

The tallest tree in the Transitional Zone, growing to over 15 m, recognisable by its large alternate, pinnate leaves, its sprays of pink to purplish flowers and when present, by its seeds which look a little like an old butter paddle with four 'wings'. It often has leaves in the dry season and so can be clearly seen from afar. The wood of this tree has long been used locally as it is very hard, virtually indestructible, and impervious to marine borers which makes it valuable for boats, mooring docks and piers. Most of the National Park marker posts are made of this wood.
Best viewed: Santa Cruz between Puerto Ayora and Bellavista and on the trail to Tortuga Bay; San Cristóbal.

Pega Pega *Pisonia floribunda*

A large many-branched Transitional Zone tree growing to 10–15 m in height, and frequently festooned with mosses and lichens. The flowers are in small inconspicuous clusters. They produce sticky fruit which helps their dispersal by birds. Hence the Spanish name *pega pega* which translates as 'sticky sticky'. It is a much broader tree than most in the zone and is recognisable by its shape as well as its fairly dense foliage.
Best viewed: Santa Cruz – between Puerto Ayora and Bellavista.

ⓔ Guayabillo *Psidium galapageium* var. *galapageium*

Also known as Galápagos Guava. An easily identifiable Transition Zone tree growing to 8–10 m with smooth reddish-grey bark. The branches are often quite crooked and covered in long hair-like lichen, especially higher up near the moist zones. It has thin elliptical, pale-green leaves, large white flowers 10–15 cm in diameter, which produce small apple-like fruit. Found also in the Scalesia Zone, the wood is used locally for fencing and buildings, but is not as hard or enduring as Matazarno *Piscidia carthagenensis*.
Best viewed: Santa Cruz, on Airport Road from Puerto Ayora to Baltra; Isabela – V. Sierra Negra; Santiago.

Psidium galapageium var. *howellii*
This rare variety is found only on San Cristóbal and Santa Cruz. It has slightly smaller flowers, up to 1-cm across, smaller petals, 4–9-mm long and flower buds that have five lobes at their tips.

ⓝ Poison Apple *Hippomane mancinella*

Also known as Manchineel. Large evergreen tree growing up to 10 m in height with small very shiny elliptical leaves. Not widespread in the islands, but locally common. The yellow/green flowers appear on a long (up to 10 cm) spike at the end of the branch. They produce small, highly alkaline, green apple-like fruit about 5 cm in diameter. The tree gets its English name from the milky sap which is poisonous and can burn the skin. Avoid contact with the tree or its fruit, and do not sit underneath it. The antidote to the sap, if you should get any on your skin, is lemon juice.
Best viewed: Santa Cruz – Puerto Ayora, Academy Bay; Santiago – Espumilla Beach; Isabela – Urvina, Punta Moreno.

ⓝ Flame Tree *Erythrina velutina*

Large spiny tree found throughout the islands. Spikes of large, flaming red flowers which appear before the leaves and following rain. The flowers are a favoured food of the finches. The seeds are red with a black line and are produced in a pod. *Erythrina* is found mainly in the Arid Zone and provides a welcome flash of colour in the often sombre vegetation.
Best viewed: Santa Cruz – Puerto Ayora.

ⓘⓟ Rose Apple *Syzygium jambos*

A tall tree up to 15 m with opposite, dark green, pointedly elliptical leaves. The flowers are greenish white and have four petals, but these are almost entirely obscured by the mass of long delicate stamens. The apple shaped fruit can be eaten raw or cooked.
Best viewed: in the inhabited and cultivated areas. .

ⓘⓟ Lead Tree *Leucaena leucocephala*

A small (to 3m) tree with the same delicate bipinnately compound leaves as the mimosa and acacia families, but with no spines. The flowers are a delicate white ball and the seeds are produced in long pods. Found mainly on rocky areas on San Cristóbal.
Best viewed: San Cristóbal – Puerto Baquerizo Moreno.

(n) Muyuyu *Cordia lutea*

Also known as Yellow Cordia or Glue Bush. An attractive shrub with rounded leaves growing to 8 m. The light-grey twigs appear dead during the garua season, but spring to life with the rains. The bright-yellow trumpet-shaped flowers produce translucent berries each containing one seed. The seed is surrounded by a sticky substance, which helps to ensure dispersion, and is also an excellent paper glue.

Best viewed: Santa Cruz – Puerto Ayora; Santa Fé; Española – Punta Suarez; Isabela – Tagus Cove; Rábida; North Seymour; Floreana – Puerto Velasco Ibarra, Post Office Bay.

(n) Parkinsonia *Parkinsonia aculeata*

Also known as Jerusalem Thorn or Palo Verde. A graceful spreading tree to 10 m. Leaves are long narrow spikes (17–45 cm) with 20 to 30 pairs of small oval leaflets along their length. Attractive yellow-orange flowers on a spike, which produce seedpods up to 20-cm long. Branches have many strong, hooked spines. The sap of the tree is food for small scale-insects (Coccidae) which are tended or farmed by ants who feed off their sugary liquid.

Best viewed: Baltra; Santa Cruz – Puerto Ayora; Floreana – Post Office Bay, Punta Cormoran; Española – Gardner Bay; Isabela – Puerto Villamil; San Cristóbal – Puerto Baquerizo Moreno; North Seymour.

(n) Acacia *Acacia* spp.

Also known as Thorn Tree. Large spreading tree with small yellow or orange ball-like flowers which produce long seedpods. The leaves are compound with small pairs of leaflets giving them a very delicate appearance. The branches are armed with fierce straight thorns up to 4 cm long.

A. rorudiana
5–30 pairs of leaflets. Each leaflet has 14–24 pairs of secondary leaflets, each less than 1-mm long.
A. macracantha
Slightly bigger secondary leaflets 1–3-mm long, sometimes viewed as variant of *A. rorudiana*.
A. insulae-iajobi
1–5 pairs of leaflets, 5–10 pairs of secondary leaflets, each 3–15-mm long.
A. nilotica (Nile Acacia) Introduced
3–16 pairs of leaflets, 10–30 pairs of secondary leaflets, each 3–15-mm long.

Best viewed: Santa Cruz – Puerto Ayora, Floreana; Santiago – Espumilla Beach, Post Office Bay.

(n) Mesquite *Prosopis juliflora*

A large tree very similar to the Acacia, but with a long cream flower-spike instead of a ball. The spines are shorter (1–2 cm) and are found at the base of the leaves. Similar seedpod and leaves to *A. insulae-iacobi* but with one or two pairs of leaflets with six to 20 secondary leaflets.

Best viewed: Floreana – Punta Cormoran, Post Office Bay; Española – Gardner Bay, Punta Suarez; Isabela – Elizabeth Bay; Santa Cruz – Tortuga Bay.

Arid and Transitional Zone Shrubs

(e) Galápagos Croton *Croton scouleri*

Slender shrub or tree to 6 m. Four varieties distinguishable largely by location. Bark grey, leaves grey-green varying in size according to location. Fruit round and divided into three segments. Flowers small, cream-coloured on spikes up to 10-cm long. The sap of the Croton is well known to stain clothes a dark brown.
Best viewed: Santa Fé; Santa Cruz; Genovesa; Isabela–Tagus Cove.

(e) Curl-leaf Cordia *Cordia resoluta*

Shrub to 4 m, slender upright branches, leaves alternate, blade-shaped, waxy with edges curled under. Flowers white, tubular, in small clusters, fruit bright red, ovoid, 4–6 mm. *C. leucophlyctis* to 2 m, lance-shaped, rough leaves, smaller white flowers. *C. anderssonii* and *C. scouleri* similar. Best viewed: Fernandina, Floreana Isabela, Santiago. Other species: Española, Santa Cruz, San Cristóbal, Pinzon, Pinta.

(e) Galápagos Lantana *Lantana peduncularis*

Small shrub up to 2 m. Branches four-sided, leaves pointed with serrated edges. White flowers have yellow centres, forming compact dome-shaped heads. Var. *peduncularis* is widespread, and var. *macrophylla* which has smaller leaves is found only on Genovesa and Gardner by Española.
Best viewed: Santa Cruz – Puerto Ayora; Santa Fé; Española – Punta Suarez; Isabela – Tagus Cove; Floreana – Post Office Bay, Punta Cormoran.

(n) Glorybower *Clerodendrum molle*

Deciduous shrub to 5 m, dark-green elliptical leaves. Long (to 3 cm), trumpet-shaped, white flowers with stamens extending 2 cm beyond petals. Fruits ball-shaped, less than 1 cm in diameter.
Best viewed: Santa Cruz – Puerto Ayora, Airport Road.

(n) Black Stick *Tournefortia psilostachya*

Spreading, vine-like shrub, leaves alternate, sage green, broad but pointed. Flowers brown and in scorpoid spikes. Seeds round and green. Older stems black, hence its common name.
Best viewed: Santa Cruz – Puerto Ayora.

(e) White-haired Tournefortia *Tournefortia pubescens*

Shrub up to 4 m in height. Young branches covered in white hairs. Leaves alternate, elliptical and pointed. White flowers in scorpoid sprays. Fruit is a white berry.
Best viewed: Santa Cruz – Airport Road.

(e) Red-haired Tournefortia *Tournefortia rufo-sericea*

Shrub to 5 m with reddish-brown bark, young branches having reddish hairs. Leaves alternate and have a corrugated appearance. White flowers in scorpoid sprays. Fruit is a white berry.
Best viewed: Santa Cruz – Airport Road.

ⓔ Spiny Bush *Scutia spicata* var. *pauciflora*

Also known as Thorn Shrub. Dark green, spiny bush up to 2.5 m. It appears to have few leaves, being elliptical and about 1 cm long. The spines are numerous and up to 6 cm long. Flowers are small and greenish, producing bright red to purple fleshy fruits, edible but sour, eaten by finches and Land Iguanas. Common near the shore but found inland also.
Best viewed: Widespread; present at most visiting sites.

ⓔ Bitterbush *Castela galapageia*

Spiny, many-branched, normally erect shrub to 2 m. Alternate leaves are small, dark green, waxy and oval. Plants either male or female; both produce small red or yellow flowers. The fruits are bright red.
Best viewed: Santiago – Puerto Egas; Española – Punta Suarez, South Plaza; Santa Cruz – Puerto Ayora; Floreana – Punta Cormoran.

ⓔ Desert Thorn *Lycium minimum*

Dense spiny shrub to 3 m. All twigs and branches end in a spine but no other spines. Leaves club-shaped in groups up to five. Flowers are numerous and white. The fruit is small (5–6 mm), egg-shaped and red-orange. Found mainly close to the coast.
Best viewed: Española – Punta Suarez.

ⓝ Spiny-headed Chaff Flower *Alternanthera echinocephala*

A low compact shrub with narrow pointed opposite leaves. The flowers are clearly identifiable with their white spiky tuft-like flowers, which are found either at the base of the leaves, or at the ends of the branches.
Best viewed: Santa Cruz – Puerto Ayora, Airport Road.

ⓝ Thread-leafed Chaff Flower *Alternanthera filifolia*

Low compact shrub, often dome-shaped, with a dense mass of thin green branches which turn brown during dry periods. Leaves are opposite, very narrow and relatively few in number. Flowers are like small green-white pincushions, petals may be yellowish.
Best viewed: Santa Cruz – Puerto Ayora, Airport Road.

ⓔ Pearl Berry *Vallesia glabra*

Shrub or small tree growing to 6 m. Leaves alternate, long and pointed, and droop down from the branch. Flowers white with five petals in small clusters, and grow upwards from the branch. Fruit, a white translucent elongated berry. Var. *pubescens* is endemic and has the leaves, stems and flowers covered in fine hairs. Var. *glabra* is native and lacks these hairs.
Best viewed: Floreana – Post Office Bay; Isabela – Villamil, Urvina; San Cristóbal – Puerto Baquerizo; Santiago – Espumilla; Santa Cruz – Airport Rd.

ⓔ Narrow-leafed Darwin Bush *Darwiniothamnus tenuifolius*

Thickly foliaged shrub growing to 3 m. The leaves are alternate, narrow, pointed and grow very close together. Flowers in small clusters at the branch tips are daisy-like with white petals and yellow stamens.
Best viewed: Isabela – Volcán Sierra Negra, Urvina, Punta Moreno.

(e) Floreana Daisy *Lecocarpus pinnatifidus*

Also known as Cutleaf Daisy. A small bushy evergreen shrub (found on bare lava or cinder) up to 2 m, but more commonly 1 m with a single stem and a bushy head of leaves and flowers. The flowers are yellow and daisy-like. One species of *Lecocarpus* found on each of San Cristóbal, Española and Floreana.
Best viewed: Floreana – Punta Cormoran.

Darwin's Daisy, *Lecocarpus darwinii,* is similar to *L. pinnatifidus,* but found only on San Cristóbal.

Fitzroy's Daisy, *Lecocarpus lecocarpoides,* again very similar to *L. pinnatifidus* but found only on Española.

(n) Galápagos Cotton *Gossypium barbadense* var. *darwinii*

A rather open shrub growing up to 3-m high. The leaves are large (15–20 cm) and three- to five-lobed. Easily identified by its spectacular large yellow (up to 16 cm) flower with a purple centre. The seeds are oval, up to 3-cm long, and break open to produce a white lint or cotton, which is commonly used by finches and other smaller birds for nest lining. Normally flowers only after heavy rains. Largest flower on any native or endemic plant in Galápagos.
Best viewed: Floreana – Post Office Bay; Isabela – Tagus Cove, Urvina Bay; San Cristóbal – Frigatebird Hill, Puerto Baquerizo Moreno; Santa Cruz – Airport Road.

(n) Waltheria *Waltheria ovata*

A small many-branched shrub with the twigs changing from reddish-brown to dark grey with age. As its name suggests, the leaves are 'ovate', which means egg-shaped, but with a broad rather flat base and slightly pointed tip. They are also slightly serrated along the edge. The small yellow flowers occur in small clusters at the branch ends.
Best viewed: Santa Cruz; Isabela – Urvina, Tagus Cove; Genovesa.

(e) Needle-leafed Daisy *Macraea laricifolia*

A bushy shrub growing up to 2.5 m in height. The leaves are short, very narrow with the edges down-turned and in clusters especially towards the ends of the branches. The flowers are composite, yellow and on stalks 2–3-cm long. The Spanish common name, *Romerillo,* refers to its resemblance to rosemary, although it is in fact a member of the sunflower family.
Best viewed: Floreana; Isabela; Rábida; San Cristóbal; Santa Cruz; Santiago.

ⓝ Flat-fruited Senna *Senna pistaciifolia*

This low shrub, previously known as *Cassia picta*, is common along roadsides and in quarries. The leaves are alternate and pinnate with rounded tips. The flowers which are on spikes, are yellow and pea-like. The seeds are held in flattened pods. Not to be confused with *S. bicapsularis* and *S. alata*, both recently introduced and found on Santa Cruz.
Best viewed: Santa Cruz – Airport Road, New and Old Quarries.

Arid and Transitional Zone Herbs and Vines

ⓘⓟ Sticky Caper *Cleome viscosa*

An annual herb growing to 1.6 m. The stems and seed-pods are covered with sticky hairs. The leaves are alternate with three lobes. The flowers are yellow with four petals. The fruit is a long (to 10 cm) pod containing many reddish-brown seeds. The sticky hairs have ensured the rapid spread of this plant, first recorded on Baltra in 1963 to Santa Cruz, Floreana, Seymour, Pinta and Santiago.
Best viewed: Santa Cruz – Airport Road; Seymour; Baltra.

ⓝ Dwarf Rattlebox *Crotalaria pumila*

An upright perennial herb growing to 1 m in height. The leaves are alternate, pinnate with three leaflets. Flowers are on long spikes, are yellow and pea-like. The seeds are held in short (to 2 cm) long pods. This species is similar to Fuzzy Rattlebox *C. incana*, which is rather larger.
Best viewed: Santa Cruz; San Cristóbal; Santiago.

ⓘ Poreleaf *Porophyllum ruderale* var. *macrocephalum*

An annual herb growing up to 1 m in height. The stems are purplish. The leaves are sage green, oval with slightly scalloped edges. Both stems and leaves have a waxy covering. The flowers are sunflower-shaped, 6–7-mm across, purplish with yellow flecks. The fruit capsule contains a single seed and is hairy.
Best viewed: Santa Cruz – Airport Road; Española; Floreana; Seymour; San Cristóbal.

ⓔ Galápagos Passion Flower *Passiflora foetida galapagensis*

A vine found covering rocks or shrubs. The leaves are large (6 cm) and ivy-shaped. It has long tendrils, which wrap around branches or stems of other plants and easily identifiable white flowers with a purple centre. The fruits are egg-shaped (up to 1.5-cm long), green becoming orange as they ripen, and wrapped in a protective mesh formed by the sepals. Found from near sea level up into the Scalesia and Miconia Zones.
Best viewed: Santa Cruz – Puerto Ayora; Floreana; Isabela.

(e) Grey Matplant *Tiquilia nesiotica*

Rarest of four species, found only in arid sandy locations. Small, grey-green leaves with very small white flowers hidden amongst them. Flowers are often eaten by the Lava Lizards which also eat flies or other insects visiting them.
Best viewed: Bartolomé; Santiago – Sullivan Bay.

Of the other three species, *T. darwinii* and *T. fusca* form spreading mats up to 1-m across. The third, *T. galapagoa* is a low spreading shrub up to 50 cm in height.
Best viewed: Bartolomé; Isabela; San Cristóbal; Floreana; Rábida; Santa Fé; Española; Plazas; Baltra; Daphne; Santiago – Sullivan Bay.

(e) Spurge *Chamaesyce* spp.

The ten Galápagos species of this genus show a considerable degree of adaptive radiation. They are varied, with both annual and perennial herbs, and small shrubs up to 1.5 m in height. All have the characteristic milky white latex-like sap and small white flowers.

C. amplexicaulis (middle left photo) Small shrub with round stemless leaves. Found on Bartolomé, Daphne and Genovesa.
C. punctulata Similar but with narrow pointed leaves. Found on Isabela and Santiago.
C. viminea Shrub to 1.5 m with long (to 4 cm) leaves with parallel edges occurring individually or in clusters. Found widely in the islands including Puerto Ayora, Genovesa, Isabela and Floreana.

(e) Galápagos Milkwort *Polygala* spp.

There are three species and four subspecies in Galápagos. *P. anderssonii* and *P. galapageia* are perennial growing to around 1 m in height, found on light sandy or ashy soils at low altitudes. *P. sancti-georgii* is an annual herb growing to 50 cm. Stems of all three are reddish yellow with alternate, pointed, sage-green elliptical leaves on *P. anderssonii* and *P. galapageia* but more rounded on *P. sancti-georgii*. The flowers are small and yellow in clusters at the end of the stems.
Best viewed: Isabela; Santiago; Santa Cruz; Floreana; San Cristóbal; Rábida.

(n) Horse Purslane *Trianthema portulacastrum*

Low perennial succulent herb with red stems. Oval leaves are opposite, of differing sizes. Flowers are individual purplish-white and have five petals. The seeds are held in a small dark egg-shaped capsule.
Best viewed: Baltra; Española – Punta Suarez; Floreana; Genovesa; Isabela; Rábida; San Cristóbal; Santa Cruz; Santa Fé; Seymour.

(e) Mollugo *Mollugo crockeri*

Perennial herb, normally low growing but occasionally erect. There are five species and seven subspecies of this genus in Galápagos. The flowers are white with five petals. *M. crockeri* is found only on Santiago. *M. flavescens* has reddish stems and small baseball bat-shaped leaves. One of the earliest colonisers of fresh lava.
Best viewed: Fernandina; Genovesa; Isabela – Punto Moreno; San Cristóbal – Frigatebird Hill; Santa Cruz; Santiago; Bartolomé.

(i) Cherry Tomato *Solanum pimpinellifolium*

Erect or often prostrate herb. Leaves alternate and pinnate with variable numbers of leaflets. Yellow flower with five pointed petals. Fruits small, orange-red and edible. The seeds have a low germination rate unless they pass through the gut of an animal. Easily confused with the endemic species *Solanum galapagense,* the Galápagos Tomato. The other endemic, *Solanum cheesemaniae,* the Hairy Galápagos Tomato, is easily identified by its hairy and slightly sticky stems.
Best viewed: Widespread after rain on all the major islands.

(n) Goat's Head *Tribulus cistoides*

Also known as Puncture Weed. Low creeping plant has pinnate leaves with six to eight pairs of leaflets. The bright-yellow flowers are simple with five well-separated petals. Seed is enclosed in a fearsome spiked casing which gives it its common name and which can penetrate all but the stoutest shoe soles.
Best viewed: Baltra; Bartolomé; Seymour; Santa Cruz; Daphne; Española – Gardner Bay, Punta Suarez; South Plaza; Santiago – Puerto Egas; Sombrero Chino.

(i) *T. terrestris,* an annual pan-tropical weed, is best distinguished by its larger and spikier seed casings, 2-cm across (1.5 cm in *T. cistoides*).
Best viewed: Near inhabited areas.

(n) Momordica *Momordica charantia*

Vine with five-lobed fig-leaf shaped leaves up to 8-cm across and long tendrils. Flowers large (4–5 cm) and pale yellow with five petals. Fruits are spiny, 5–10-cm long and turn orange red as they ripen, then burst open to reveal 20–30 bright red seeds each about 1-cm long. The seeds stick to the inside of the capsule even after it has burst open.
Best viewed: Isabela – Villamil; Santa Cruz – Puerto Ayora.

(n) Stickleaf *Mentzelia aspera*

An annual herb, generally spreading. Stems with barbed hairs. Leaves alternate, pointed with serrated edges. Flowers are yellow with five petals. Seed capsule is cone-shaped, 5–11-mm long and covered in barbed hairs. Extremely successful at sticking to any human or animal and is widespread in the islands.
Best viewed: Baltra; Española; Floreana; Genovesa; Isabela; Rábida; San Cristóbal; Santa Cruz; Santa Fé; Santiago.

(e) Galápagos Purslane *Portulaca howellii*

Fleshy-leaved perennial growing on lava close to the shore. In the dry season, it loses its leaves and is reduced to a clump of grey smooth stems. After rain it produces leaves and large yellow flowers up to 4-cm across. Now largely restricted to offshore islets due to goats, but its relative, *Portulaca oleracea* (Native) is found throughout the islands and in the Arid rather than Coastal Zone. It has smaller flowers and less fleshy leaves which used to be valued as a salad vegetable.
Best viewed: Santa Cruz – Puerto Ayora; Genovesa; Daphne; Santa Fé; Sombrero Chino; South Plaza; North Seymour.

(e) Arrow-leafed Morning Glory *Ipomoea linearifolia*

A perennial vine that climbs over vegetation or across bare lava. The leaves are alternate and distinctly arrow-shaped. The flowers are large white, occasionally pink, trumpets with a well-defined pink throat. The seeds are dark brown and held in an oval capsule.
Best viewed: Fernandina; Genovesa; Isabela; Rábida; Santa Cruz; Seymour.

(n) Hairy Morning Glory *Merremia aegyptica*

An annual vine with hairy stems that covers vegetation after heavy rains. Leaves alternate with five elliptical and slightly ribbed leaflets. Flowers are white and trumpet-shaped. They are only open in the early morning. The brown seeds are held in a brown capsule.
Best viewed: Disturbed sites and roadsides and on: Genovesa; Española; Isabela; Rábida; Santa Cruz; Santa Fé; Santiago; Seymour.

(n) Climbing Pea *Rhynchosia minima*

A perennial vine with purplish stems found especially on disturbed sites. The leaves are alternate and have three leaflets. The flowers are yellow and pea-shaped. The seeds are held in a short 1.5-cm long pod.
Best viewed: All major islands, but not on Volcán Sierra Negra, Isabela.

(n) Hairy Ground Cherry *Physalis pubescens*

Annual herb up to 1 m. Purplish stems are hairy and slightly sticky. Leaves are oval to elliptical and pointed with clearly visible veins. Flowers are bell-shaped, pale yellow to white. Fruit is a round berry, contained in a lantern-like capsule. Three other related species *P. galapagoensis* (endemic), *P. angulata,* and *P. peruviana* are found in Galápagos. This last is the cultivated Cape Gooseberry.
Best viewed: Baltra; Española; Fernandina; Genovesa; Rábida; Santa Cruz; Santiago; Seymour.

(n) Yellow Ground Mallow *Bastardia viscosa*

Annual herb growing to 1 m in height with slightly hairy stems. Leaves are an elongated heart-shape, pointed and with edges slightly serrated. Flowers are yellow with five rounded petals. Fruit has six or seven sections, each with a single seed.
Best viewed: Española; Floreana; Isabela; Rábida; San Cristóbal; Santa Cruz; Santiago; Seymour.

(e) Oily Pectis *Pectis tenuifolia*

A low perennial herb often forming a low tussock to 15 cm in height, frequently found on bare rock. The leaves are opposite, needle-like, with oily glands on the underside, and a purplish tinge, especially during dry periods. The five-petalled flowers are yellow with orange undersides, and are carried on short stems facing upwards. Two other similar species, *P. subsquarrosa* which is much less compact and lacks the purplish tinge, and *P. linifolia,* are also found in the islands.
Best viewed: Fernandina; Floreana – Post Office Bay; Genovesa; Isabela – Tagus Cove, Punta Moreno; San Cristóbal; Santa Cruz; Santa Fé; Bartolomé.

ⓔ Galápagos Bean *Phaseolus mollis*

Annual vine with stems to 3 m. Young stems are quite hairy. Leaves alternate with three shield-shaped leaflets. Flowers pea-shaped, pink or purplish in colour and on long racemes or sprays. The short (2.5–3 cm) pod holds between two and four seeds.
Best viewed: Fernandina; Isabela; Santa Cruz.

P. adenanthus a similar species found only on Española, has paler flowers, almost white, and a larger seed-pod, (7–12-cm long).
Best viewed: Española.

ⓘ Blue Morning Glory or Moonflower *Ipomoea nil*

A vine with slightly hairy stems up to 5-m long. It may be annual or perennial. The leaves are large, up to 18-cm long and like a three-lobed maple. The large (3–5 cm) flowers are blue to purplish with a white throat. The seeds are held in a small capsule.
Best viewed: Floreana; San Cristóbal; Santa Cruz; Santiago.

ⓝ Boerhaavia *Boerhaavia caribaea*

Annual herb, often prostrate. The stems are hairy and sticky. Leaves are opposite and have a wavy edge. Flowers are in clusters at the base of the leaves and are reddish purple. The seeds are sticky.
Best viewed: Española; Fernandina; Floreana; Genovesa; San Cristóbal; Santa Cruz; Santa Fé; Santiago.

ⓝ Wartclub *Commicarpus tuberosus*

Prostrate herb with green stems. The leaves are opposite and rounded and appear to grow around the stem. Flowers are small, up to 1-cm long, bell-shaped and pinkish purple. Seed has longitudinal grooves and small 'warts' near the top. These are very sticky and adhere to passing animals.
Best viewed: Floreana; Isabela; Rábida; San Cristóbal; Santa Cruz; Santiago.

ⓝ Heliotrope *Heliotropium angiospermum*

Upright perennial with woody lower stems. Leaves are alternate, rather pointed, and very heavily veined, sometimes almost corrugated. White flowers are on a backwards-curving spike which gives it its Spanish name, *Cola de escorpion* (Scorpion tail). Not to be confused with *H. andersonii*, a rare endemic which has pale-yellow flowers, found only on Santa Cruz.
Best viewed: Española; Fernandina; Floreana; Genovesa; Isabela; Rábida; San Cristóbal; Santa Cruz; Santa Fé; Seymour.

ⓘ Maple-leafed Mallow *Anoda acerifolia*

A herb which can grow to 70 cm in height. The alternate leaves are triangular when young, becoming maple-shaped as they develop. The flower is white with five petals and the fruit is an attractive five-pointed star. Found mainly along the roadsides in Santa Cruz.
Best viewed: Santa Cruz – Airport Road.

ⓔ Scalesia *Scalesia* spp.

Scalesia is a genus endemic to Galápagos and one of the best demonstrations of adaptive radiation to be found in the islands. The 15 species and six subspecies have adapted to different vegetation zones on different islands. They vary in size from under 1 m to over 15 m in height. Most species occur in the Arid and Transitional Zones, though the largest and most easily identified one, *S. pedunculata* is found in the zone that bears its name, where it is the dominant plant. Several species are threatened, thanks mainly to the grazing of feral goats. One species, *S. gordilloi,* was discovered as recently as 1985.

The Scalesias are members of the daisy family, one of the commonest plant families in Galápagos. The flowers are similar in having a flower head made up of a number of small flowers. In some species there are petals around the outside of the main flower disc. These are 'ray flowers' that are similar to the internal flowers but have one large petal on the outside. The following species are the most likely to be seen and identified by the visitor.

ⓔ Radiate-headed Scalesia *Scalesia affinis*

Found from sea level to around 600 m. A pioneer on barren lava and cinder slopes, a shrub normally growing to no more than 3-m high. The leaves are alternate, pointed with a serrated edge and up to 15-cm long. The single white daisy-like flowers appear at the ends of the branches. Three subspecies have been identified: *S. affinis affinis* on Floreana; *S. affinis brachyloba* on Santa Cruz; and *S. affinis gummifera* on Isabela and Fernandina.
Best viewed: Isabela – Villamil, Punta Moreno, Tagus Cove, Sierra Negra, Punta Albermarle; Santa Cruz.

ⓔ Heller's Scalesia *Scalesia helleri*

Low shrub growing to 2.5 m. Found mainly on cliffs and near the shore, this species appears to be favoured by feral goats. The leaves are alternate or opposite and, while being generally oval in shape to 10-cm long, are very heavily divided, giving a fuzzy appearance. Flower heads are up to 1.7-cm across and are made up of 30–100 individual flowers. There are two subspecies, *S. helleri helleri* found on Santa Cruz and Santa Fé (left photo), and *S. helleri santacruziana* found only on Santa Cruz (right photo).
Best viewed: Santa Cruz – Tortuga Bay; Santa Fé.

ⓔ Tree Scalesia *Scalesia pedunculata*

By far the largest member of the genus, with trees reaching 15 m or more. This is the dominant species in the Scalesia Zone on Santa Cruz, Santiago, San Cristóbal and Floreana. The tree has a largely unbranched trunk, often covered in a variety of mosses, with a dome of branches on top making it look rather like a calabrese flower head. When the trees grow close together, they provide a dense and uniform canopy. As the Scalesia Zone provides some of the best farming land, much of the zone has been destroyed. The leaves are alternate, elliptical/lanceolate, and slightly hairy. Flowers are white, in bunches at the ends of branches, up to 2-cm across and are made up of 50–150 individual flowers.
Best viewed: Santa Cruz – Los Gemelos, Airport Road; Floreana – highlands.

ⓔ Longhaired Scalesia *Scalesia villosa*

An open, rather untidy shrub up to 3 m with characteristically narrow hairy leaves which are alternate and found at the tip of the stems, often with a bunch of dead leaves beneath them. The flower heads which are large, white and almost thistle-like are up to 2-cm across and made up of 200–300 individual flowers. This species is found only on Floreana and its offshore islets.
Best viewed: Floreana – Punta Cormoran.

ⓔ Crocker's Scalesia *Scalesia crockeri*

left
page

A small, Arid Zone shrub to 1 m in height. The leaves are opposite, broadly elliptical, and are found at the end of the branches with a bunch of dead leaves beneath them. The flower heads are up to 2-cm across and are made up of 20–60 individual flowers.
Best viewed: Baltra; Santa Cruz; North East.

ⓔ Stewart's Scalesia *Scalesia stewartii*

left
page

A shrub growing to 3 m in height. The leaves are alternate, lanceolate, 6–10-cm long and with white hairs on the undersides. The flower head is around 15 mm in diameter with 35–90 individual flowers on each head.
Best viewed: Santiago – Sullivan Bay; Bartolomé.

ⓔ Heart-leafed Scalesia *Scalesia cordata*

right
page

A tree up to 10 m in height. The leaves are alternate, 4–9 cm in length and shaped like an elongated heart. The edges are sometimes serrated. The white flower heads consist of some 15–30 individual flowers.
Best viewed: Isabela – Sierra Negra.

ⓔ Cut-leafed Scalesia *Scalesia incisa*

right
page

Found only on San Cristóbal, *S. incisa* grows to some 4 m in height. The leaves are opposite and divided into lobes, the lobes themselves are divided or toothed. The flower head is up to 15-mm across and consists of up to 30–50 flowers, together with the occasional individual ray flowers.
Best viewed: San Cristóbal – Punta Pitt.

Scalesia species and their distribution

Species	Islands and zones	Types
S. affinis affinis	Floreana (W); Arid	Shrub, large flower
S. affinis brachyloba	Santa Cruz (S); Arid, Transitional	Shrub, large flower
S. affinis gummifera	Fernandina, Isabela; Arid	Shrub, large flower
S. aspera	Santa Cruz (NW); Arid, Transitional	Shrub, large flower
S. atractyloides atractyloides	Santiago; Transitional	Shrub, narrow hairy leaves
S. atractyloides darwinii	Santiago; Transitional	Shrub, narrow hairy leaves
S. baurii baurii	Pinta, Pinzón, Wolf; Arid	Shrub, divided leaves
S. baurii hopkinsii	Pinta, Wolf; Arid, Transitional	Shrub, divided leaves
S. cordata	Isabela; Arid	Tree to 10 m, small flower
S. crockeri	Baltra, Seymour, Santa Cruz (N); Arid	Shrub, large flower
S. divisa	San Cristóbal; Arid	Shrub, divided leaves
S. gordilloi	San Cristóbal; Arid	Shrub
S. helleri helleri	Santa Cruz (S), Santa Fé; Arid	Shrub, divided leaves
S. helleri santacruziana	Santa Cruz (S); Arid	Shrub, divided leaves
S. incisa	San Cristóbal (N); Arid	Shrub, large flower
S. microcephala microcephala	Fernandina, Isabela; Humid	Small tree, small flower
S. microcephala cordifolia	Isabela (N), Wolf; Transitional	Small tree, small flower
S. pedunculata	Floreana, Santa Cruz, Santiago, San Cristóbal	Tree to15 m, small flower
S. retroflexa	Santa Cruz (SE); Arid	Shrub, large flower
S. stewartii	Bartolomé, Santiago (E); Arid	Shrub, narrow leaves
S. villosa	Floreana and islets; Arid	Shrub, hairy leaves, large flower

Humid Zone Trees and Shrubs

There are up to four clearly defined humid or moist zones:
- The Scalesia Zone, named after the dominant tree.
- The Brown Zone, here the dominant trees and other shrubs are covered with epiphytes, giving the zone its brown colour.
- Miconia Zone, named after the dominant shrub, *Miconia robinsoniana*. This is found only on Santa Cruz and San Cristóbal.
- Pampa or Fern-sedge Zone which is open moorland.

The zones vary from island to island, more noticeable on the south sides of islands. Northern slopes are generally in a rain shadow and the transition from Pampas to the Arid Zone takes place over a short distance.

ⓘ️ Quinine Tree *Cinchona pubescens*

Trees growing to 12 m. Leaves opposite, large (to 20 cm) and glossy with distinct ribbing. Initially dark green, turning pink and then red with age. Flowers small and pink, fruit winged. Introduced to Galápagos in 1946 in response to a quinine shortage. No longer cultivated. Serious threat to all of the moist zones as it is taller than Miconia and has dense foliage, cutting out the light. Also a threat to the breeding success of Galápagos Petrel.
Best viewed: Santa Cruz – Media Luna.

ⓘ Common Coral Bean *Erythrina corallodendron*

One of several species of *Erythrina* introduced to the farming regions. Used as living fence posts growing to 5–6 m. Flowers bright red and on a long spike. Seeds are small red beans in a pod. Other introduced species include; *E. edulis*, *E. fusca* (palo prieto), *E. poeppigiana* (poro gigante) and *E. smithiana* (porotillo).
Best viewed: Santa Cruz, San Cristóbal, Floreana, Isabela.

ⓘ Balsa *Ochroma pyramidale*

Very large tree to 30 m. Trunk has buttresses at the base, bark is smooth and grey with white blotches. Leaves alternate, three-lobed and very large (30 cm). Flowers white with five petals. Fruit is a pod to 25 cm.
Best viewed: Farming zones; Isabela; Santa Cruz.

ⓘ️ Common Guava *Psidium guajava*

Very common shrub or tree to 8 m in height. Leaves are opposite, dark green, elliptical to 15-cm. Flower white with five petals and grows alone or in small axillary clusters with a large brush of stamens. Fruit is round, up to 5 cm and is edible. Forms dense thickets and is a major threat to the natural vegetation of the Humid Zones.
Best viewed: Floreana, Santa Cruz, Isabela and San Cristóbal.

ⓘ Brazilian Tea *Stachytarpheta cayennensis*

Also known as False Vervain. A much-branched shrub to 2.5 m. Leaves have a slightly purplish tinge, are opposite, elliptical, and have coarsely serrated edges. The bluish-purple flowers have a whitish throat, on long (to 35 cm) terminal spike.
Best viewed: Floreana; Isabela; San Cristóbal, Santa Cruz.

ⓔ Coscojo *Acnistus ellipticus*

A shrub or small tree growing up to 5 m, with large (10–15 cm), slightly waxy, alternate leaves. The attractive bell-shaped flowers are white and the tips of the petals often curl backwards. They grow directly out of the branch alone or in clusters of up to eight. The fruit are spherical (1–2 cm), green becoming black.
Best viewed: Highlands of Santa Cruz, Santiago, Floreana, San Cristóbal.

ⓘ Silky Inga *Inga schimpffii*

A tree growing to 10 m in height. The leaves are alternate, elliptical, dark green, waxy and clearly ribbed. The white flowers grow in axillary clusters and are tube-shaped, with the stamens extending beyond the petals. The seeds are held in a long pod and the white pulp surrounding them is very good to eat.
Best viewed: Farming zones on Isabela and Santa Cruz.

ⓘⓟ Cuban Cedar *Cedrela odorata*

A large tree with smooth brownish bark, growing to over 30 m in height. The leaves are alternate and pinnate with 10–20 leaflets. The pale greenish-yellow flowers are small and hard to see from the ground, even though they grow in clusters. The seeds are numerous and winged. The tree was introduced to provide wood for construction, furniture and shipbuilding. It is fast growing, light and adaptable. Owing to the winged seeds, it is a potential threat to the native vegetation as it now grows outside the farming zones.
Best viewed: Floreana; Isabela; San Cristóbal; Santa Cruz.

ⓔ Miconia *Miconia robinsoniana*

A shiny-leaved shrub up to 5 m in height, growing in dense almost impenetrable stands above the Scalesia Zone. The long (to 25 cm) slender pointed leaves turn reddish in periods of drought giving the whole zone a reddish tinge when seen from afar. The clusters of pink or purple flowers are produced at the end of the branches. The fruit is a small blue-black berry. It provides an excellent nesting habitat for the Dark-rumped or Hawaiian Petrel *Pterodroma phaeopygia,* which nests in this area during the garua season. This species is threatened both by agriculture and by invasive Guava *Psidium guajava* and Quinine *Cinchona succirubra* trees.
Best viewed: Santa Cruz; San Cristóbal.

ⓝ Cat's Claw *Zanthoxylum fagara*

Also known as 'Wait-a-Minute Bush', this shrub or small tree grows to a height of 10 m. It is the dominant plant in the Brown Zone and is frequently encrusted with a dense growth of epiphytic mosses, lichens and liverworts. The branches are armed with sharp hooked spines which give the plant its common name. The leaves are compound with five to eleven leaflets. The inconspicuous greenish-white flowers produce small dark berries.
Best viewed: Santa Cruz by Airport Road.

(e) Galápagos Mistletoe *Phoradendron henslowii*

Widespread parasitic shrub, growing on a variety of woody shrubs and trees in all zones. It is not alone in particularly liking attachment to Cat's Claw (*Zanthoxylum fagara*). The leaves are broadly elliptical and rather leathery. The small greenish flowers are on spikes which grow from the base of the leaves. The fruit are small (up to 6 mm) translucent berries.
Best viewed: Santa Cruz – highlands.

(ip) Multicoloured Lantana *Lantana camara*

A shrub to 3 m in height, the stems are hairy, often prickly. The leaves are opposite and ovoid with a serrated edge. The flowers which grow from the base of the leaves are clustered in bunches. Each flower is small, 3–4 mm, starting off yellow-orange but turning pinkish purple with time. This results in flowers of more than one colour on each head. This is a recent introduction which has spread out of people's gardens.
Best viewed: Santa Cruz – Puerto Ayora, Bellavista; San Cristóbal – Puerto Baquerizo; Floreana – Puerto Velasco Ibarra.

(ip) Mora *Rubus niveus*

Also known as Hill Raspberry. Climbing shrub or vine very similar to the Blackberry of Northern Hemisphere. Introduced to San Cristóbal; now also found on Santa Cruz in or close to the farming zone. It threatens to be a serious pest species forming dense thickets. Stems are 3 m or more in length and covered with sharp stout prickles. Leaves are alternate, pinnate with prickles on the underside; leaflets are up to 5-cm long. Flowers have five petals, dark pink, found in bunches at the end of the stems. Fruit are raspberry-like, red, turning black and edible.
Best viewed: Farming zones on Santa Cruz and San Cristóbal.

(i) Angel's Trumpet *Brugmansia candida*

A readily recognisable shrub growing to 7 m in height. The leaves are alternate, broad and oval with distinct veins. The flowers are large white trumpets, up to 20-cm long and 10–15-cm across. They hang vertically downwards. The seeds are held in a capsule 4–8-cm long. The leaves are poisonous as they contain the alkaloid hyoscine.
Best viewed: Inhabited and cultivated parts of Floreana, Isabela and Santa Cruz.

(i) White Valerian *Astrephia chaerophylloides*

Weak-stemmed herb growing with and over other plants. Leaves pinnate and feathery looking pinnae and leaflets heavily indented. Flowers white on long axillary stems, three flowers per stem.
Best viewed: Farming zone, Santa Cruz.

(e) Galápagos Dead Nettle *Pilea baurii*

Erect annual, or occasionally perennial herb, reddish stems and leaf stalks. Leaves opposite, oval to 10 cm, pale-green tending to yellow as they age, sometimes pinkish. Leaf edges serrated. Flowers green on axillary sprays. Seeds in tiny (0.4 mm) individual capsules.
Best viewed: Floreana; Isabela; San Cristóbal; Santa Cruz; Santiago.

Humid Zone Herbs and Vines

(e) Galápagos Peperomia *Peperomia galapagensis*

Small upright perennial herb to 20 cm, stems grow closely together. Slightly fleshy leaves in whorls of three or four, often with red edges and spatula shape. Flowers small and green, on short spikes. Two varieties of this plant: var. *galapagensis* is hairless, while var. *ramulosa* is found on Floreana, Isabela, Pinta and Santa Cruz.
Best viewed: Santa Cruz – Los Gemelos.

(e) Galápagos Orchid *Epidendrum spicatum*

Epiphytic perennial herb growing on trees, often hanging downwards. Leaves alternate, slightly fleshy, to 15-cm, encircling the stem at their base. Flowers whitish green on a spray at the end of stem, three petals in typical orchid form. Seeds are like a fine powder, in an elliptical capsule 2.5-cm long.
Best viewed: Santa Cruz – Los Gemelos.

(n) Ionopsis *Ionopsis utricularoides*

Small delicately flowered epiphytic orchid with strap-shaped leaves. Flowers white with reddish-purple stripes, pansy or viola-shaped in clusters on long stem. Seeds are dust-like in small brown capsules, to 2 cm.
Best viewed: Floreana, Isabela, Pinta, Pinzon, Rábida, Santa Cruz, Santiago. Arid lowlands to moist uplands.

(n) White Leadwort *Plumbago scandens*

Sprawling perennial herb, stems normally green, sometimes dark red, up to 6 m. Leaves are alternate, generally elliptical, often red. White flower has five petals and a long (2.5-cm) tube. Seed capsule, is covered with sticky hairs.
Best viewed: Highlands of Santa Cruz, Floreana, Isabela and San Cristóbal, common on roadside.

(n) Purple Vervain *Lippia strigulosa*

Dense low, perennial herb, the stems purplish towards the base. Leaves opposite, elliptical, surfaces are slightly hairy, edges serrated and often purplish. Flowers form clusters on the end of axillary stalks, white with yellow throat and purple bracts.
Best viewed: Isabela; San Cristóbal; Santa Cruz.

(e) Bromeliad *Racinea insularis*

An unmistakable plant, a member of the Pineapple Family. An epiphyte found throughout the humid zones, grows on trees, shrubs and rocks. Long pointed leaves up to 45-cm, green to reddish-green in colour. Flower spike can be 75-cm tall. Flowers themselves are small and whitish. Bromeliads are an important feature of the ecosystem as they collect water in their centres, which becomes a breeding place for mosquitoes and other invertebrates.
Best viewed: Santa Cruz.

(n) Verbena *Verbena litoralis*

An erect perennial herb growing up to 2 m in height. The leaves are opposite, long (to 10 cm) and narrow with serrated edges on the outer two-thirds. The flowers are a pale pinky violet colour and are on spikes at the end of the stems.
Best viewed: Floreana; Isabela; San Cristóbal; Santa Cruz.

(n) Purple Cuphea *Cuphea carthagenensis*

Annual upright herb to 50 cm, stems are reddish and slightly hairy. Leaves are opposite, elliptical and slightly hairy. Purple flowers in small axillary spray, have a long (1 cm) tube which is distinctly wider at the base and longitudinally striped. Six very narrow, well-separated petals.
Best viewed: Farming zones on San Cristóbal and Santa Cruz.

(i) Bush Violet *Browallia americana*

A straggling annual herb to 1 m in height. The leaves are alternate and narrowly egg-shaped. The purple flowers are tubular with a white lip to the throat and a yellow spot in the centre.
Best viewed: Farming zone of Santa Cruz.

(n) Blechum *Blechum pyramidatum*

Low perennial herb. Leaves are opposite, spear-shaped, and hairy, especially when young, at the growing points forming an unusual and distinctive pyramidal shape. Flowers pale purple, occasionally almost white, with five square-ended petals, grow on an upright spike.
Best viewed: Floreana; Isabela; San Cristóbal; Santa Cruz; Santiago.

(e) Galápagos Justicia *Justicia galapagana*

Untidy perennial herb with hairy stems, growing to 1 m height. Leaves opposite, hairy, especially when young, and spear-shaped with a distinct mid-rib. Flowers, pea-shaped with three lower lobes, are a bright purplish pink with a striking white pattern at the entrance to the throat.
Best viewed: Isabela; Santa Cruz; Santiago.

(n) Ageratum *Ageratum conyzoides*

Upright, annual herb with purplish stems growing to 1 m. Leaves opposite, oval with purple veins and edges, which are also serrated. The purplish pink flowers grow in multiple clusters at the ends of the stems. An identifying factor is its rather unpleasant smell.
Best viewed: Floreana; Isabela; San Cristóbal; Santa Cruz; Santiago.

(n) Germander *Teucrium vesicarium*

Upright, square-stemmed perennial herb growing to 1.2 m. Leaves are opposite, elliptical with serrated edges. The flowers, which are a mid-pink to near white, are tubular and grow on a densely packed spike.
Best viewed: Floreana; Isabela; San Cristóbal; Santa Cruz.

ⓘ False Mallow *Sida rhombifolia*

An upright perennial herb growing to 1.5 m in height. The older stems become woody. The leaves are alternate, elliptical, slightly rhomboid, with serrated edges towards the tip. The flower is yellow with five petals and a brownish-purplish ring around the stamens. The stiff straight woody stems are used to make brooms, hence the Spanish common name of *Escoba*. Eight other species of *Sida* occur in Galápagos. The plant is a favourite food of tortoises.
Best viewed: Floreana; Isabela; San Cristóbal; Santa Cruz.

ⓔ Galápagos Jaegeria *Jaegeria gracilis*

An annual herb found most frequently in the Humid Zone. The stems are purplish-brown, the leaves are opposite and oval to pointed. The flowers are yellow, daisy-like, and on long stalks at the ends of the shoots.
Best viewed: Fernandina; Floreana; Isabela; San Cristóbal; Santa Cruz; Santiago.

ⓔ Indefatigable Passion Flower *Passiflora colinvauxii*

Distinguished from *P. foetida* (p. 168) by its leaves which are shaped rather like a boomerang or a crescent moon, and its larger and more brightly coloured flower. A similar species, *P. suberosa,* is also found in the islands but is much less common.
Best viewed: The highlands Santa Cruz – Los Gemelos.

ⓘ Common or Greater Plantain *Plantago major*

A low, perennial, stemless herb. The leaves are a broad oval shape and all emanate from the central root. The small yellowish-green flowers are on long (to 40 cm) spikes. This common worldwide weed is a recent arrival and found in the towns, where it is sometimes cultivated, as well as highlands.
Best viewed: Floreana; Isabela; San Cristóbal; Santa Cruz; Santiago.

ⓝ Indian Heliotrope *Heliotropium indicum*

A bushy perennial herb growing to 1 m in height. The leaves are alternate, broadly elliptical and very crinkly, especially when young, with the veins clearly indented. The small purplish to bluish flowers have a white or sometimes yellowish throat and are on just one side of a backwards-curving spike.
Best viewed: Floreana; San Cristóbal; Santa Cruz.

ⓝ Beggar's Tick *Bidens pilosa*

Also known as Spanish Needle. An annual many-stemmed herb growing to 1 m in height. The leaves are opposite, with serrated edges. Some are simple, others pinnate with three leaflets, the central one being longer than the two lateral ones. The yellow daisy-like flowers are on a stalk, either individually or in a cluster.
Best viewed: Floreana; Isabela; San Cristóbal; Santa Cruz.

ⓘ Smooth Sow Thistle *Sonchus oleraceus*

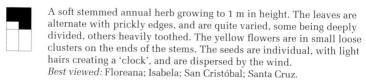

A soft stemmed annual herb growing to 1 m in height. The leaves are alternate with prickly edges, and are quite varied, some being deeply divided, others heavily toothed. The yellow flowers are in small loose clusters on the ends of the stems. The seeds are individual, with light hairs creating a 'clock', and are dispersed by the wind.
Best viewed: Floreana; Isabela; San Cristóbal; Santa Cruz.

ⓝ St John's Wort *Hypericum uliginosum* var. *pratense*

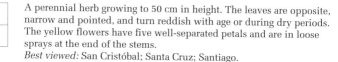

A perennial herb growing to 50 cm in height. The leaves are opposite, narrow and pointed, and turn reddish with age or during dry periods. The yellow flowers have five well-separated petals and are in loose sprays at the end of the stems.
Best viewed: San Cristóbal; Santa Cruz; Santiago.

ⓝ Clubmoss

There are at least six species of clubmoss in Galápagos. They are not mosses, but are related to ferns. The shortness of their yellowish-green leaves (less than 1 cm) gives them a furry look like mosses; the club shape of their seed capsules explains their English name. They are epiphytes, and may have individual branches up to 60-cm long.

Lycopodium cernuum An upright species looking like a miniature Christmas tree, found mainly in the Miconia Zone.
L. clavatum A terrestrial species growing close to the ground but with the ends of the branches turning upwards and producing candelabra-like flower spikes (bottom right photo).
L. dichotomum Generally found hanging from trees in the humid zones.
L. passerinoides Another species found hanging from trees and shrubs.
L. reflexum A species generally found growing on rocks, either upright or spreading with the tips turned upwards.
L. thyoides An upright terrestrial species found especially in shaded ravines.

Best viewed: Highlands of major islands.

Lichens

A lichen is not a higher plant but a fungus that can only exist by means of a symbiotic relationship with an alga. The alga provides the fungus with carbohydrate and in return gains protection. Some 300 species of lichen are found in Galápagos, mainly in the Arid and Transitional Zones where they are very much in evidence on trees, rocks and even tortoises. The Palo Santo tree, which is characteristic of the Arid Zone, derives its white colour from crustose lichens; the bark is actually a brown-purplish colour. In the Transitional Zone trees can be found that are almost completely hidden beneath festoons of long grey-green lichen. One of these, Dyers' Moss *Rocella babingtonii*, is well known to produce a purple dye. The lichens obtain their moisture from the garua, and also when close to the coast from the moist air off the sea. They come in a wide range of forms and colours and have been little studied. There are likely to be a number of endemic species that have yet to be described.

Grasses and Sedges

ⓝ Feather Fingergrass *Chloris virgata*

An erect annual herb growing to 80 cm in height. The leaves are alternate and narrow, 3–7-mm wide. The flowers are on short, 5–10 cm, spikelets which have numerous minute flowers and hairs giving the grass a feathery appearance. There are two other species of *Chloris* in Galápagos, *C. inflata* and *C. radiata*. *C.inflata* was first recorded in 1963 and is therefore almost certainly introduced; the status of the other two species is uncertain.
Best viewed: Baltra; Española; Floreana; San Cristóbal; Santa Cruz; Santa Fé; Seymour.

ⓘⓟ Elephant Grass *Pennisetum purpureum*

A perennial herb growing to 6 m, more commonly 2–3 m, forming dense clumps. The leaves are alternate, narrow (3–4 mm) and up to 120-cm long. The flowers are brown and produced on a spike 10–30 cm in length. A recent introduction for forage for cattle. *The Flora of the Galápagos* (Wiggins and Porter 1971) says 'There is no previous report of this species from Galápagos.' Now it is widespread in the farming zone and has spread outside it. A potentially very dangerous invasive species due to the denseness of its clumps which excludes all other species.
Best viewed: In and close to the farming zones on Floreana, Isabela, San Cristobál; Santa Cruz.

ⓔ Galápagos Sedge *Cyperus anderssonii*

A perennial herb with one or more upright triangular stems to 70 cm in height. The leaves are basal and of similar length, 2–6-mm wide. The brown flowers appear in a number of short spikes or sprays at the stem-ends. Found in most of the vegetation zones. There are 18 species of *Cyperus* found in Galápagos. Three of these are endemic.
Best viewed: Baltra; Fernandina; Floreana; Genovesa; Isabela; Rábida; San Cristóbal; Santa Fé; Santiago.

C. ligularis is similar to *C. anderssonii* but is generally taller, has wider leaves and is less widely distributed, being found in the coastal zone only, on Fernandina, Isabela, and Santa Cruz.

ⓘ Bermuda Grass *Cynodon dactylon*

A low creeping grass with alternate leaves and flowering spikes growing to 40 cm in height. The flowering spike divides into five or six spikelets, each with many small greenish flowers. Commonly used for lawns and pasture.
Best viewed: Floreana, Isabela, San Cristóbal, Santa Cruz.

Ferns

Ninety species found in Galápagos, largely in the humid zones. Most are terrestrial, others are epiphytes, most native with a few endemics. Ferns have no flowers but produce spores on the undersides of their leaves.

(e) Galápagos Tree Fern *Cyathea weatherbyana*

An unmistakable fern growing to 6 m. Older plants have a distinct trunk which may be up to 30 cm in diameter, topped by a luxuriant spray of typically fern-like fronds. Found in the Fern-sedge Zone but very often hidden in potholes or gullies or on the inside of small crater walls.
Best viewed: Santa Cruz – Los Gemelos, Mount Crocker.

(n) Bracken *Pteridium aquilinum* var. *arachnoideum*

Large branching fern to 3 m in height. Fronds bipinnately compound and up to 2 m in length The variety of bracken found in Galápagos is virtually indistinguishable from that found elsewhere in the world.
Best viewed: Santa Cruz; San Cristóbal; Isabela.

(n) Carolina Leaf Flower *Phyllanthus c. caroliniensis*

Annual or occasionally perennial herb up to 30 cm, found in open grassy areas in humid zones. Leaves alternate and oval in shape with a reddish-brown stem. Pale yellow-green flowers, individual or in pairs, grow from the axils; fruit small, dark reddish-black each containing 3–6 seeds.
Best viewed: Moist zone on Floreana, Santa Cruz, San Cristóbal, Isabela.

(n) Hart's-tongue Polypody *Polypodium phyllitidis*

A distinctive fern with broad (3–10-cm wide) shiny, yellow-green fronds. The symmetrically lanceolate fronds are 20–80-cm long. Not to be confused with the Lance-leafed Polypody *Polypodium lanceolatum* which is epiphytic and grows individual lance-shaped fronds from a long rhizome.
Best viewed: Santa Cruz – Los Gemelos.

(n) Hand Fern *Doryopteris pedata* var. *palmata*

Individual stems growing vertically upwards from the rhizome. The leaves lie horizontally and are broad but deeply indented, with three or five lobes, at times hand-shaped.
Best viewed: Floreana; Santa Cruz; San Cristóbal; Isabela.

(n) Golden Polypody *Polypodium aureum* var. *areolata*

A large fern with golden yellow-green, deeply indented, leathery fronds up to 1 m. Underside has a whitish bloom and clearly visible sporangia containing the spores.
Best viewed: Santa Cruz – Los Gemelos.

Bryophytes, Mosses and Liverworts

Over 110 species of liverwort and 90 species of moss have been described in Galápagos. As with ferns identification is very technical. *Frullania aculeata*, a liverwort, can be identified. It is the brown moss-like species that adorns many trees in the Scalesia and Brown Zones.

GEOLOGY AND VULCANOLOGY

The Galápagos lie in the eastern Pacific Ocean 1,000 km west of the mainland of South America and astride the Equator. Geologically they lie at the meeting point of two submarine ridges, the Carnegie Ridge running westward from South America and the Cocos Ridge running south from Central America. The meeting point of these two ridges is known as the Galápagos Hot Spot. The islands lie at the northern edge of the Nazca Plate which is moving eastward at a rate of 2 cm per year. This movement is responsible for the building of the Andes mountain range and for the continuing earthquake and volcanic activity along the western edge of South America. As the plate moves and the hot spot stays stationary, so a series of volcanic islands are formed. This explains why the oldest islands, Isabela & Fernandina at 0.7 million years, lie to the east and the youngest, Plazas at 4.2 my. and San Cristóbal at 2.4 my., to the west. Fernandina and Isabela, especially the former, are two very active volcanic islands. In 1968 there was a major event when the floor of the caldera on Fernandina fell over 300 m. This was accompanied by a large ash eruption which covered much of the northwestern slope of the volcano. There was a large eruption on the flank of Fernandina in 1995. On Isabela there was an eruption on the southern flank of Cerro Azul in 1998 and on the northern rim of Sierra Negra in 2005.

Blowhole on the basaltic shore of Española (Hood) Island.

The isthmus of Bartolomé and Pinnacle Rock, the remains of a tuff cone.

Fernadina, a large Shield Volcano.

For the most part the islands are the tips of large submarine volcanoes. However, most of the eastern islands, Santa Fé, Plazas, the north-eastern edge of Santa Cruz, Baltra and Seymour, are uplifted submarine lava. It is, however, clear that the sea level has varied considerably over the millennia because, underneath the submarine lava, are volcanic deposits which must have been laid down above water. Fernandina and Isabela are huge shield volcanoes, looking from a distance like upturned soup bowls. These all have large calderas measuring several kilometres across and up to 1,000 m deep.

Another feature which illustrates the continuing volcanic activity in the islands is the volcanic uplift which occurred in 1954 at Urvina Bay on the western coast of Isabela. Here some 5 km of coastline was uplifted by up to 4 m. In 1994, a further uplift of some 90 cm occurred at Punta Espinosa and Tagus Cove, making the landing docks unusable except at high tide.

There are two distinct types of lava. The Aa (pronounced 'Ah Ah') and Pahoehoe (pronounced 'Pahoyhoy'). The former is very rough and hard to walk over. Aa is Hawaiian for 'hurt'. The latter is smooth and ropy and is the result of the lava containing a lot of gas. Pahoehoe is Hawaiian for 'ropy'. You can see excellent Pahoehoe lava on Santiago opposite Isla Bartolomé or on Fernandina at Punta Espinosa. Most other fresh lava you encounter is likely to be Aa!

Sunken volcanic crater, Bartolomé.

Volcanic uplift – the white line is the old sea bed.

Caldera

A caldera develops as the top of a large shield or strato volcano starts to collapse back into the magma chamber, from whence came the lava that built it in the first place. The caldera in Fernandina is 1,000 m in depth.

Cinder Cones

These are normally found further inland than tuff cones, and on the flanks of the main volcano. They are often termed 'parasitic cones', and are frequently nearly perfect cone shapes. Cinder cones are the result of explosive eruptions, where there is a lot of gas in the magma, which expands rapidly as the magma comes to the surface. The liquid lava is thrown into the air in lava fountains and solidifies before touching the ground. The cinder or scoria is used on the inhabited islands to make roads, which are very dusty when dry.

Collapse or Pit Craters

These form when the roof of a large subterranean lava tube or magma chamber collapses. The best examples of these are Los Gemelos (the twins) on Santa Cruz. The road to the airport goes right between the two craters. Calderas are effectively huge collapse craters.

Hornito ('Little Oven')

A small cone on a lava flow, generally less than 50 cm in height formed by escaping gas or steam. The lava is often shiny and colourful due to the minerals in it. Generally found on Pahoehoe flows.

Fumaroles

Volcanic vents which emit gases, these very often contain sulphur dioxide and result not only in a foul smell, but also in yellow deposits of sulphur. The volcanoes of Alcedo and Sierra Negra on Isabela have accessible fumaroles.

Lava Bomb

A lava rock that has been ejected with explosive force during a volcanic eruption. Generally rounded in shape and often isolated and some distance away from its point of origin.

Lava Tubes

These are formed when a crust forms on a lava flow, insulating the hot core. When the lava stops flowing it leaves behind a tube which is often very nearly circular and up to 10 m or more in diameter running at times for several kilometres.

Lava Toes

Small extrusions of lava on a pahoehoe flow, which are forced out as the lava cools.

Magma

This is the molten volcanic material while it is still beneath the ground, hence 'magma chamber' where the molten magma is 'stored' before an eruption.

Pumice

This is the result of a very violent eruption involving water. In Galápagos it is found only on Isabela on Volcan Alcedo. However, because pumice floats, you may find it washed up on beaches around the islands, especially after the rainy season.

Driblet Cones

These are very small cones formed by rather glutinous lava which is thrown out in dollops, but which solidifies into smooth and often quite colourful cones which look as if they are made of melted toffee. Spatter cones are very much larger versions of driblet cones and may also be part cinder.

Tree Shapes or Moulds

With Pahoehoe lava, it is not uncommon to find the outline shapes of trees that were enveloped by the lava. When the lava cooled the wood burned away leaving a mould of the tree.

Tuff and Tuff Cones

Tuff is formed when water is present during an eruption and is a form of compacted volcanic ash. Tuff cones are generally found near the coast. The famous pinnacle rock on Bartolomé is made of tuff.

Volcanic Dyke

This is the result of molten lava being forced up into a crack in older material, often tuff. If the surrounding material is softer then the dyke is left standing proud as the surrounding material erodes more rapidly.

Volcanic Plug

Very often when a tuff or cinder cone ceases to be active, the magma tube or vent remains filled with magma which has not formed into tuff or cinder. As the cone is eroded away, the plug, which is made of much harder material, is left behind.

Aa Lava

Very rough, normally black, lava formed when there is very little gas. It is often clinker-like and very difficult to walk on. Most of the recent lava flows have been of Aa Lava. The name, pronounced 'Ah Ah' is Hawaiian for 'hurt'.

Pahoehoe Lava

Smooth or ropy lava, often forming amazing patterns. It is a result of the magma containing a large amount of gas. The name is pronounced 'pahoyhoy', which is the Hawaiian for 'ropy'.

HISTORY

The islands were discovered in 1535 by Fray Tomas de Berlanga, the Bishop of Panama, who drifted there while on a voyage from Panama to Lima, Peru. He noted the tortoises and iguanas, as well as the tameness of the animals. The islands soon became a useful base for pirates when raiding Spanish ports along the coast of South America. They became known as Las Encantadas or bewitched islands due to the strong currents, which not only made navigating difficult, but combined with the garua and mists, made it seem as though the islands themselves were moving rather than the ships.

The islands were named by Abraham Ortelier in 1574, after the giant tortoises. The shell of the saddle-back tortoises looks similar to a Spanish saddle or Galapago. Tortoises that could live for months without food or water were extremely valuable and tens of thousands of tortoises were taken to provide

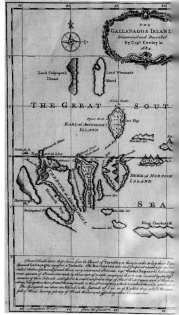

Early map of Galápagos by Ambrose Cowley.

fresh meat. Charles Darwin certainly enjoyed their flesh and the *Beagle* brought a number of small specimens back to England.

The first recorded resident of Galápagos was an Irishman named Patrick Watkins who was marooned on Floreana in 1807. Post Office Bay on Floreana had become a regular stopping place for whaling ships.

Pirate Cave, Floreana.

Ships arriving from Europe would leave letters, while those returning home would collect letters. The first post barrel was erected by Captain James Colnett in 1792. Ecuador annexed the islands in 1832, by which time there was a small settlement on San Cristóbal as well as on Floreana; the latter was soon turned into a penal settlement. The settlement at Villamil on Isabela dates from 1893 and Puerto Ayora on Santa Cruz was started by a group of Norwegians who had come out to set up a fish-processing plant at Post Office Bay in 1926. Floreana became known world-wide in the mid 1930s due to the antics of 'The Baroness', Eloise Bosquet-Wagner and her two companions, and Dr Friedrich Ritter and his companion Dore Strauch.

Post Office Bay, Floreana.

The first successful commercial venture in the islands was a sugar plantation and mill, built at Progreso in the highlands of San Cristóbal in the 1880's by Manuel Cobos. Cobos rapidly turned the island into a personal fiefdom but he was eventually murdered in 1904 by his own slaves. While fishing and farming initially formed the basis of the islands economy, it was not until international tourism started in the late 1960's that the islands started to develop commercially.

Ecuador recognised the scientific importance of the islands in 1934, passing unenforceable legislation to protect the fauna and flora. In 1942 following its entry into the Second World War, the United States built a military base on Baltra. Galápagos controlled the approaches to the Panama Canal and had acquired strategic importance. The one stone building left on Baltra was the officers' club and this can still clearly be seen near the centre of the island. The airstrip and dock are still those that were built for the base, though both have been extended and renovated by the Ecuadorian government.

Until 1968, the only way to get to Galápagos was by sea. An occasional flight used the airstrip at Baltra but there was no permanent base there. The trip out from Guayaquil by sea took 3–4 days and the return trip was shared with the cattle, coffee and dried fish that were the islands' principal exports. Tourism was possible using the supply vessel, but most visitors remained on the ship as there were no charter boats to take them around the islands.

In 1968 the first regular tourist flights started on a fortnightly basis, servicing the schooner, Golden Cachalot. This was increased in 1969 to two flights a week with the arrival of the first cruise ship, the 60 passenger 'Lina A'. Now there are at least five flights a day to either Baltra or San Cristóbal. The population was about 2,500 in 1968, and had increased to 25,000 in 2010. There are now over 100 vessels servicing the tourism industry.

Charles Darwin and Evolution

Charles Darwin's visit to the Galápagos in 1835 was the catalyst that ensured that he would be remembered, not only as the pre-eminent scientist of his time, but as one of the truly great scientists of all time. The idea of evolution was not a new one. Lucretius, writing in the first

Cobos grave.

century BC in his *De Rerum Natura* put forward the concept of evolution. Darwin's grandfather, Erasmus, put forward his own theory of evolution in his work entitled *Zoonomia*. In 1835 the most accepted theory was Lamarckism, named after the French scientist Jean Baptist Lamarck. What none of these earlier theories could provide was a realistic and credible mechanism for the process of evolution.

Darwin was born in Shrewsbury in England in 1809. In 1825 he went to Edinburgh to study medicine but in 1827 he left to study divinity at Cambridge. He was destined for the life of a country parson, when in 1831 he was invited by Captain Robert FitzRoy to be the naturalist on board *HMS Beagle* which was soon to depart on a five-year voyage, surveying the waters around the southern tip of South America. The voyage was without doubt the turning point in Darwin's life, and the visit to the Galápagos was the most significant single episode on that voyage.

On his return to England, he published *The Voyage of the Beagle* which established Darwin as an important figure in the scientific community of his day. His powers of observation were acute and he is credited with developing two new sciences, quite apart from his work on evolution. These were ethology (the study of animal behaviour in natural surroundings) and ecology (the study of the relationship between animals and their environment).

In 1859, after much hesitation, he finally published *On the Origin of Species*, a book that was to have a revolutionary impact on the way we view ourselves. The mechanism that Darwin had discovered, due in large part to his observations and collection of specimens in the Galápagos, he called natural selection: species that changed and adapted to their environment through a series of random genetic mutations would be the ones that would survive. Darwin was reluctant to publish his theory as he was aware of its implications, and was only persuaded to do so because Alfred Russell Wallace had come up with the same mechanism.

Before arriving in Galápagos, Darwin was chiefly interested in their geology, but it is quite clear from his diary that even after only a few days he started to realise that their zoology was most unusual, and by the time he left he was already starting to suspect their true significance.

Charles Darwin aged 40, painted by TH Maguire.

228

When I see these islands in sight of each other, and possessed of but a scanty stock of animals, tenanted by these birds, but slightly differing in structure and filling the same place in nature, I must suspect they are only varieties. ... If there is the slightest foundation for these remarks, the zoology of Archipelagoes will be well worth examining; for such facts would undermine the stability of species.

Large Ground Finch.

It was Darwin's genius that he not only observed the differences between species on the various islands, but that he was able to develop his theory of evolution using that visit in 1835, followed by years of painstaking research into barnacles, pigeons and other animals. These later studies gave him the necessary scientific data to develop his theory and to be able to defend it. Over 150 years later, it is still the accepted backbone of our understanding of the natural world and of our own origins. Since Darwin's visit, scientific research and observations have reinforced his conclusions that the Galápagos really are a laboratory of evolution. Darwin's finches, one of the key groups to alert him to the significance of the islands, have been the subject of frequent investigation. A 50-year study on Daphne that is still ongoing, is the longest and most detailed.

Evidence for evolution in Galápagos is evident in the many examples of adaptive radiation. There were at one time 66 species of land snails of the genus *Bulimulus*, all descended from one original species. There are seven, largely island-specific, species of cricket of the genus *Gryllus*. In the plant world, *Scalesia*, a member of the daisy family has 21 species and subspecies found in all vegetation zones.

So why did Galápagos become such a remarkable showcase for evolutionary development? It is not just that the islands are isolated both from South America and from each other. It is not just that the prevailing winds and currents come from the continent, nor the variation in the vegetation and climatic conditions. It is a combination of all of these factors. Additionally, the islands were, until recently, not attractive to human habitation. Herman Melville of *Moby Dick* fame 'doubted whether any other spot on earth can in desolateness furnish a parallel to this group'. This isolation has meant that in this small group of islands we have been able to study and observe the processes by which life has evolved everywhere on earth.

Scalesia crockerii.

OCEAN CURRENTS

The chief influences on the climate of the Galápagos are the ocean currents. Galápagos lie on the equator at the confluence of three major ocean currents, the Humboldt, the Cromwell and El Niño. The major influence is the Humboldt or Peru Coastal current, which brings cool, nutrient-rich water up from the southern oceans. This heads out westwards from the coast of Peru, becoming the South Equatorial current. It extends some 300 m below the surface. The deeper water is cooler and more saline subantarctic water, which upwells when it hits the Galápagos. It flows through the islands for eight to nine months of the year, and results in cooler, lower humidity air than might be expected on the equator.

The current is driven in part by the southeast trade winds, which blow towards the equator from May to December. When they retreat southwards, then so does the current. This then allows an influx of warmer water from the north bringing warm humid tropical air and heavy rains. This warmer water is known as El Niño and is a much shallower current extending to less than 100 m in depth.

The third current, the Cromwell or Equatorial Undercurrent, is a submarine current which flows eastward from the central Pacific. It is cool and saline and creates very cool water conditions around Fernandina

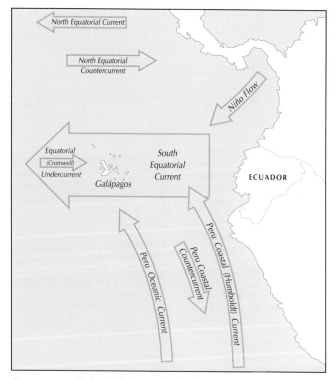

Ocean currents affecting the Galápagos, based on CDRS Museum exhibit.

and the western side of Isabela. This is a favoured area for whales and dolphins, as well as yellow fin tuna.

The Climate

The climate of Galápagos can be divided into two seasons, the garua or cool season lasting from June through November, and the warm season which runs from January through April. The months of May and December are changeover periods when the weather can vary considerably from year to year. On the coast the garua season is very dry: rainfall records in Academy Bay on the south (wetter) side of Santa Cruz show the average monthly rainfall in the months of August, September and October to be less than 10 mm while February to April the average is 50–70 mm. In the highlands it is much wetter during the garua season. The warm season may or may not include a rainy period, El Niño, which is normally of four to six weeks, exceptionally longer. Here again there is generally more rainfall in the humid zones than on the coast.

During the garua season, the cool water around the islands results in a temperature inversion, where the air close to the sea is cooler than that which is higher up. This results in the formation, between 500 and 1,000 m, of stratocumulus clouds which produce very light rain or drizzle, know locally as 'garua'.

During the Garua season, the stratocumulus clouds accumulate around the tops of the higher volcanoes producing a lush and in parts fertile, humid zone. The highest zones are so wet and fog enshrouded that they have become bogs and moorlands. This is a far cry from the arid lowlands which only receive any appreciable rain during the El Niño periods. The north sides of the islands are in a rain shadow and so receive almost no rain during the garua season. Here the arid zone stretches well above 500 m and the humid vegetation zones which are so evident on the south sides are compressed. The exception to this is on Cerro Azul on Isabela where, due to the height and steepness of the volcano, the moist zone extends almost to the coast while the rim is normally above the clouds which results in an arid zone on the rim.

El Niño

El Niño occurs every year along the coast of Ecuador and Peru. Its name in Spanish means 'The Child', after the Christ Child, because the warm water and the rains come in December every year. In Galápagos the rains come mainly between January and March, though in some years they do not come at all. The term El Niño, has been adopted by the international scientific community to refer to the major shift in the ocean currents that cause El Niño and result in major climatic changes throughout the Pacific region. The term La Niña, the girl child, refers to the opposite system and generally results in dry periods in Galápagos. Major El Niño events have very serious consequences for much Galápagos wildlife with boobies, sea lions and marine iguanas particularly affected. In contrast others such as finches and mockingbirds breed continuously.

The variations in rainfall can be dramatic. During the El Niño event of 1982–83, over an eight-month period, well over 3 m of rain was recorded in Puerto Ayora on Santa Cruz, and over 5.5 m was recorded at Santo Thomas in the highlands of Isabela. In contrast, the average annual rainfall in Academy Bay for the years 1965–70 was only 200 mm. These extreme variations exert considerable evolutionary pressures and yet the ecosystem as a whole recovers quite rapidly.

El Niño, Santiago vegetation.

Urvina Bay in an El Niño year.

Urvina Bay: the contrast with an El Niño year.

El Niño, Floreana

El Niño, Santiago.

Galápagos Sea Lion, a casualty of El Niño.

The cause of major El Niño events is unknown. There have been two in the last 20 years, in 1982–83 and 1997–98. Over the past hundred years the normal pattern has been to have a strong El Niño every three or four years. However, no events of the magnitude of 1982–83 or 1997–98 have previously been recorded. There is naturally a suspicion that global warming may be involved.

CONSERVATION

Oceanic islands normally have fewer species than continental land masses. As a rule there are also fewer predators, and the native species, while well adapted to their own ecological niches, do not have to fight particularly hard to retain those niches. On a continental land mass, species have many competitors and need to fight hard to survive. Introduced species are therefore a major threat to island ecosystems.

Charles Darwin was the first to draw attention to the remarkable biodiversity of the Galápagos. In 1935, on the centenary of Darwin's visit to the islands, the Ecuadorian government passed the first legislation to protect the animals and plants of the Galápagos. In 1959, the centenary of the publication of Darwin's *On the Origin of Species*, the Ecuadorian government passed new legislation, declaring the islands a National Park. In the same year the Charles Darwin Foundation for the Galápagos Islands (CDF) was established under the auspices of UNESCO. In 1960, the CDF established a research station in Puerto Ayora on Santa Cruz. Since its establishment, the Charles Darwin Research Station has been a key player in the conservation of Galápagos . In its early years it was the only agent of conservation in the islands. This programme was taken over by the Ecuadorian National Park Service (SPNG) which was set up in 1968. The two organisations have always worked closely, with the CDRS providing the information and the scientific basis for the conservation programme, which is carried out by the National Park.

Scientific research has focussed primarily on threatened species and obtaining a better understanding of the Galápagos ecosystem. Conservation work has focussed largely on removal of invasive alien species, such as goats, donkeys, rats and cats, while at the same time developing captive breeding programmes for those species under severe threat. Examples of

233

Park warden ringing a Galápagos Petrel.

successes are the removal of goats and donkeys from Isabela and goats and pigs from Santiago, the former being the largest such eradication ever attempted. Captive breeding programme successes include several tortoise species, notably the Espanola one, land iguanas and the mangrove finch.

More recently, the conservation programmes have taken into account the needs of the inhabitants of Galápagos. The population has grown rapidly, largely due to the success of tourism, from a level of 2,000 inhabitants in the early 1960s to around 25,000 in 2100 – a 1,250 per cent increase in 50 years. It rapidly became obvious that if the measures to protect the biodiversity of the islands are to succeed, that the people who live there need to be brought into the process, to help provide the answers to the problems, rather than being part of them. This can only be achieved by means of education and carefully crafted programmes to make full and sustainable use of the islands' economic resources.

Goat damage, Alcedo Rim, Isabéla.

Tourism is a classic example of a renewable resource. When the first 'Plan Maestro' was published in 1970, it envisaged that the maximum number of visitors the islands could handle without seriously impacting on the environment was 12,000. Today there are in excess of 200,000 visitors a year and the immediate impact is modest. The problems that the success of the industry has brought with it are twofold. Firstly the influx of people looking for jobs, as Galápagos has the highest level of income per capita of any province in Ecuador. Secondly, it is the importation of consumables, especially food and building supplies, both of which are prime sources of alien and invasive species.

Aliens

The single biggest threat to the stability of the Galápagos ecosystem and to its biodiversity comes from alien species. These have, without exception, been introduced by man, either deliberately or accidentally. The most obviously destruc-

234   *Volcanic Cinder Quarry, Santa Cruz.*

Rubbish dump, Santa Cruz.

tive aliens in Galápagos are goats, which were introduced in the nineteenth century by whalers, looking for an alternative source of meat. Goats are, after man, the most destructive animals on the planet. In 1965, Miguel Castro, conservation officer of the CDRS started the first systematic goat eradication programme starting with the island of Santa Fé. Ten years later, the last goat was culled and the vegetation is now so dense that it is difficult to walk anywhere off the trail. The native rice rat is thriving, as are the Land Iguanas. The recovery of the island is impressive.

Isabela and Santiago are two more success stories. In 1969, goats were either introduced to northern Isabela, or managed to cross the Perry Isthmus. Prior to operation Isabela, there were estimated to be in excess of 100,000 goats on Northern Isabela, In 1975 the rim of the caldera was densely covered in thorny scrub, largely Cats Claw *Zanthoxylum fagara.* By 1990 it was a large open plain with hardly a bush in site except where the endemic tree ferns *Cyathea wetherbyana,* had been fenced off to protect them.

Starting in 1997, Operation Isabela first eradicated pigs and goats from Santiago, and then eradicated the goats and donkeys from Isabel, with the last goat being shot in 2006.

The problems caused by goats, pigs, rats, cats and other mammalian pests are obvious, and these species are relatively easy to control or eradicate; far harder are the numerous plant and invertebrate species. One success against the invertebrate invaders is the case of the Cottony Cushion Scale *Icerya purchasi.* This inadvertent Australian introduction rapidly started to damage the coastal vegetation, especially the Jeli or Black Mangrove in Puerto Ayora. With no natural control agents, the National Park introduced, after much research and testing, another insect the Vedalia Ladybird beetle *Rodolia cardinalis* to combat the pest. The introduction was very successful, and the coastal vegetation has fully recovered.

Harder still are the invisible aliens like pathogens, but if we are to conserve Galápagos we need to tackle all of them. Some of the most damaging and dangerous are:

Feral goats.

235

Invasion of Quinine Tree, El Puntudo, Santa Cruz (top) and Cottony Cushion Scale.

Quinine Tree and native Miconia (red).

Invertebrates

Little Red Fire Ant	*Wasmannia auropunctata*
Tropical Fire Ant	*Solenopsis geminata*
Destructive Ant	*Monomorium destructor*
Parasitic Flies	*Philornis downsi*
Blackfly	*Simulium bipunctatum*
Cottony Cushion Scale	*Icerya purchasi*
Yellow Paper Wasp	*Polistes versicolor*
Dark Paper Wasp	*Brachygastra lecheguana*
Cockroaches	At least 11 introduced species

Plants

Quinine Tree	*Cinchona succirubra*
Guava	*Psidium guajava*
Elephant Grass	*Pennisetum purpureum*

The Galápagos National Park is becoming a world leader in the development of processes to control invasive species. The ongoing control and eradication of these species will require enormous financial and human resources, but if Galápagos is to remain the amazing place that it is, then funds will have to be found and the work done.

Marine Conservation

Just as important as the conservation of the terrestrial ecosystem is the protection of the marine environment. Many of the most iconic and visible species such as marine iguana, sea lion, penguin and the boobies are marine species. In 1986 the Galápagos Marine Reserve was established, but little was done until 1998 when the 'Ley de Galápagos' was passed by the Ecuadorian Congress after much pressure and politicking. There are however forces at work seeking to undo some of its key features: an indication that the battle to preserve the islands is far from won. Only by having a strong law and a strong National Park can we hope to preserve the Galápagos as we know them, and would want future generations to know them too.

NOTES FOR THE VISITOR

This is not a general guide for the visitor, but these notes may be helpful when planning your trip to Galápagos.

Galápagos is a province of Ecuador. Most visitors must travel via mainland Ecuador. Some nationalities are required to obtain visas before arriving in Ecuador. Check with your travel agent or the local Ecuadorian Consul. There are daily flights to the island of Baltra, San Cristóbal. If you arrive in Baltra and do not board your boat there, then you must travel by bus and ferry to Puerto Ayora on the island of Santa Cruz. Puerto Baquerizo on San Cristóbal, and Puerto Ayora and Villamil on Isabela have hotels and guesthouses. Reservations are recommended especially during peak seasons, December through March and June through August.

You have three basic options, 1). Take a scheduled 3–15 night cruise on one of the many boats available. 2). Stay in a hotel and take day trips by boat as well as some by land. 3). Take a combination trip that may involve camping, kayaking and backpacker accommodation. There are many organised groups which charter boats and you can organise your own charter. Virtually all boats now have a two week itinerary, so to see the whole archipelago you need to take two consecutive one week cruises. Some tour

Tourists enjoying the Galápagos wildlife.

operators offer specialised trips for divers, ornithologists or photographers. In general the live aboard boat trips are best as they enable you to see the islands early and late, when most wildlife activity occurs. Boats visit at least 2 sites a day and frequently offer snorkelling opportunities in between. Remember that you are close to the equator and the sun rises around 0600 and sets at about 1800 every day, all year round, so an early start is always recommended. Some of the larger boats remain on continental time to ensure an early start.

There is no 'best time to visit', but it is warmer and may be wet from December through April and cooler with some garua, from June through November. The one endemic species that is absent for a period of the year is the Waved Albatross *Phoebastria irrorata*, which arrives in April and leaves by mid-December. If you are worried about seasickness, consider a larger boat and remember that the sea is generally calmer in the warm season than in the garua season.

Darwin's first thoughts on the islands were not complimentary: 'The country was compared to what we might imagine the cultivated parts of the Infernal regions to be.' He was, I think you will agree, being singularly ungenerous. The Galápagos Islands are a very special place and will have a very special impact on you.

VISITOR SITES

There are a large number of visitor sites in Galápagos. We have included the 51 most popular ones with useful information on the nature of the sites and what you may see and do there. The key for the symbols used on the maps can be found on page 243.

Site no.	Site name	Island	Guide needed	Snorkelling	Page no.
1	La Lobería	San Cristóbal	✗	✗	240
2	Jardines de Las Opuntias	San Cristóbal	✗	✗	241
3	Cerro San Joaquin	San Cristóbal	✗	✗	241
4	Laguna El Junco	San Cristóbal	✗	✗	241
5	La Galapaguera de Cerro Colorado	San Cristóbal	✗	✗	241
6	Puerto Chino	San Cristóbal	✗	✓	241
7	León Dormida	San Cristóbal	✓	✓	242
8	Puerto Grande and Cerro Brujo	San Cristóbal	✓	✓	242
9	La Galapaguera Natural	San Cristóbal	✓	✗	243
10	Puerto Baquerizo Moreno	San Cristóbal	✗	✓	244
11	Isla Lobos; Playa Ochoa	San Cristóbal	✓	✓	245
12	Punta Pitt	San Cristóbal	✓	✓	246
20	Punta Suárez	Española	✓	✗	247
21	Bahía Gardner	Española	✓	✓	248
23	Barrington Bay	Santa Fé	✓	✓	249
30	Punta Cormorán	Floreana	✓	✓	250
31	Bahía Post Office	Floreana	✓	✓	251
32	Black Beach	Floreana	✗	✗	252
33	Asilo de la Paz and Highlands	Floreana	✗	✗	252
40	Puerto Villamil	Isabela	✗	✓	253
41	Volcán Sierra Negra	Isabela	✓	✗	254
42	Los Tuneles	Isabela	✓	✓	255
43	Punta Moreno	Isabela	✓	✓	256
44	Bahía Elizabeth	Isabela	✓	✗	257
45	Bahía Urvina	Isabela	✓	✓	258
46	Caleta Tagus	Isabela	✓	✓	259
47	Playa Tortuga Negra	Isabela	✓	✗	260
48	Punta Vicente Roca	Isabela	✓	✓	261
49	Punta Albermarle	Isabela	✓	✗	262
50	Volcán Alcedo	Isabela	✓	✗	263
60	Punta Espinosa	Fernandina	✓	✓	264
65	Playa Darwin	Genovesa	✓	✓	265
66	Prince Philip's Steps	Genovesa	✓	✓	266
70	James Bay, Puerto Egas	Santiago	✓	✓	267
71	Playa Espumilla	Santiago	✓	✓	268
72	Bahía Sullivan & Isla Bartolomé	Santiago	✓	✓	269
73	Sombrero Chino	Santiago	✓	✓	270
74	Playa Rojo	Rábida	✓	✓	271
80	Seymour and Isla Mosquera	Seymour	✓	✓	272
81	Daphne Major	Daphne	✓	✗	273
82	Isla Plaza Sur	Islas Plazas	✓	✗	274
83	Caleta Tortuga Negra	Santa Cruz	✓	✗	275
84	Las Bachas	Santa Cruz	✓	✓	275
85	Cerro Dragón	Santa Cruz	✓	✓	275
86	Bahía Ballena	Santa Cruz	✓	✓	275
87	Playa el Garrapatero	Santa Cruz	✗	✓	275
88	Puerto Ayora	Santa Cruz	✗	✓	276
89	Bahía Tortuga	Santa Cruz	✗	✓	279
90	La Galapaguera	Santa Cruz	✓	✗	278
91	Los Gemelos	Santa Cruz	✗	✗	278
92	Los Tuneles – lava tubes	Santa Cruz	✗	✗	278

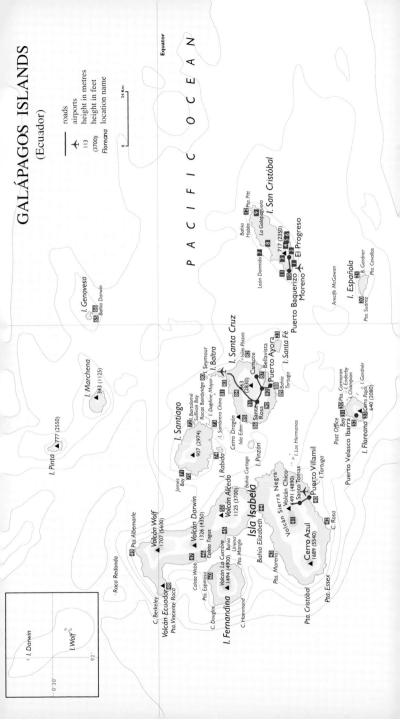

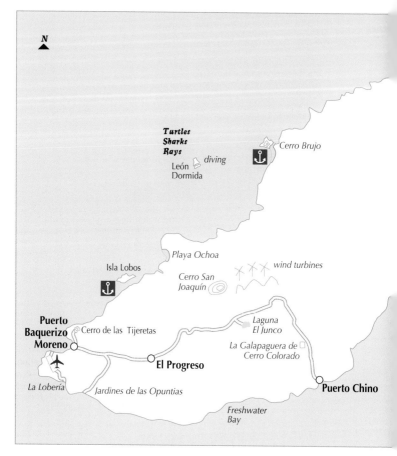

San Cristóbal – Centre and South Coast

San Cristóbal has a number of sites that are easily accessed by land. La Lobería is quite close to Puerto Baquerizo Moreno, while the other sites can be accessed from the main road that leads from Puerto Baquerizo to El Progreso, and then continues past the Laguna El Junco crater lake and on to Puerto Chino on the south coast. Some of the sites can be visited by bicycle or bus, but to reach others you will need to take a taxi.

1. La Lobería
This site, on the south coast of the island, is a 10-minute taxi drive from Puerto Baquerizo; alternatively, you can hire a bike and cycle there, or walk (about 45 minutes). At the end of the road is a short trail leading to the beach, which is mainly rocky, and from here you can walk along the top of the low cliff to a much larger sandy beach. This is a good place to see Galápagos Sea Lions and Marine Iguanas. The vegetation comprises typical Arid Zone plants; look out for the unusual Gordillo's Scalesia.

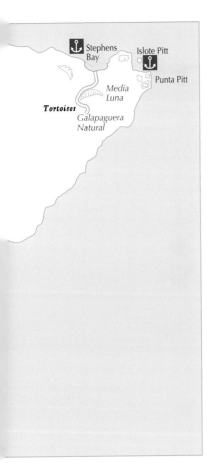

2. Jardines de las Opuntias

Take a bus to the El Cafetal ranch, just before El Progreso, then walk down the trail to the forests of cacti on the south coast (1–1.5 hours). Alternatively, take a taxi to start point of the track, which makes the walk quite a bit shorter. The prickly pear cacti here are *Opuntia echios* var. *gigantea*, the tallest of the four varieties of this amazing xerophyte. The walk is a good opportunity to observe Transitional and Arid zone vegetation and wildlife.

3. Cerro San Joaquin

Beyond El Progreso, a trail leads off to the left to Cerro San Joaquín, the site of the first windfarm in the Galápagos and part of the islanders' effort to become less dependent on fossil fuels. There is a good view from the top, which at 896 m is the highest point on the island.

4. Laguna El Junco

Just past the Cerro San Joaquín trail junction is Laguna El Junco, the only permanent freshwater lake in Galápagos. It is in the Miconia Zone, and provides the best chance to visit this unique vegetation zone anywhere in the islands. The natural vegetation is under threat from introduced Blackberry, Common Guava and other invasive alien species. The lake is a favourite haunt for frigatebirds, which come here to drink and wash. There is a short boardwalk to the top of the crater.

5. La Galapaguera de Cerro Colorado

Beyond El Junco the road heads east and south to La Galapaguera de Cerro Colorado, a large walled enclosure built by the Galápagos National Park to provide a secure location for the San Cristóbal Tortoise, and at the same time to allow visitors an opportunity to see them in their natural habitat. The trails through the area are a good opportunity to observe the wide variety of Transitional Zone vegetation. This is also the site of the park's Jacinto Gordillo tortoise breeding centre. Most organised tours to Puerto Baquerizio Moreno also take in this site.

6. Puerto Chino

Not far beyond La Galapaguera you come to the end of the road, at Puerto Chino. This small, sheltered bay on the south side of San Cristóbal is a popular swimming and snorkelling spot, and a great place to end up after visits to El Junco and La Galapaguera.

WATCH OUT FOR:

León Dormido

GREEN TURTLE
BOTTLENOSE DOLPHINS
GALÁPAGOS SHARK
HAMMERHEAD SHARK
MANTA RAY
SPOTTED EAGLE RAY
PORCUPINEFISH
BLACK-STRIPED SALEMA
REEF FISH
CORALS
OCTOPUS

■ ■ ■

Cerro Brujo

WADERS
BLACK-NECKED STILT
RUDDY TURNSTONE
WANDERING TATTLERS AND GREAT BLUE HERONS IN THE LAGOONS
BLUE-FOOTED BOOBIES DIVING ON THE SHORELINE
SMALL GROUND FINCH
MEDIUM GROUND FINCH
SAN CRISTÓBAL MOCKINGBIRD
GALÁPAGOS FLYCATCHER
YELLOW WARBLER
MARINE IGUANA
LAVA LIZARD
GALÁPAGOS SEA LION
SPOTTED EAGLE RAYS FEEDING IN THE SHALLOWS
GHOST CRABS ON THE BEACH
DRY AND COASTAL ZONE VEGETATION
POISON APPLE
GALÁPAGOS CROTON

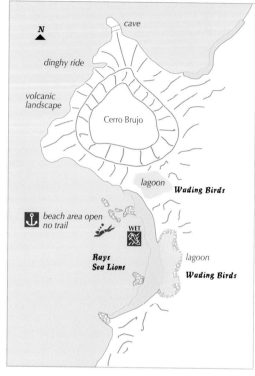

SAN CRISTÓBAL NORTH COAST

The north coast of the island has a number of very attractive visitor sites, all of which are accessible only by boat.

7. León Dormida

Lying just 3 km off the north coast of San Cristóbal, this spectacular 100 m-high volcanic plug is worth visiting just for the visual impact. Boats can sail between the two sheer cliff faces, and the site is one of the best for snorkelling in Galápagos, especially if you are keen to see sharks and rays. It is about 45 minutes by boat from Puerto Baquerizo.

8. Puerto Grande and Cerro Brujo

Immediately opposite León Dormida is the attractive sheltered beach of Puerto Grande, and just up the coast to the north is Cerro Brujo, a large tuff cone. This hill was climbed by Captain FitzRoy in 1835 while Charles Darwin took his first walk in the Galápagos bush here. There is a beautiful landing beach with a salt-water lagoon behind and cinder cones beyond, and good swimming and snorkelling. A trip here is often combined with a visit to León Dormida.

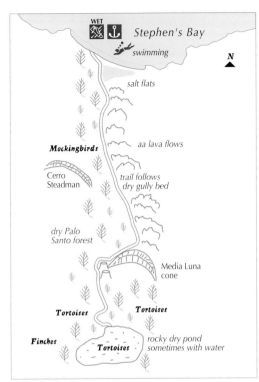

WATCH OUT FOR:

SAN CRISTÓBAL MOCKINGBIRD
GALÁPAGOS HAWK
GALÁPAGOS DOVE
GALÁPAGOS FLYCATCHER
YELLOW WARBLER
SMALL GROUND FINCH
MEDIUM GROUND FINCH
CACTUS GROUND FINCH
VEGETARIAN FINCH
SMALL TREE FINCH
SAN CRISTÓBAL GIANT
TORTOISE
EASTERN GALÁPAGOS RACER
LAVA LIZARD

DRY AND TRANSITIONAL ZONE
VEGETATION
SCALESIA INCISA
NEEDLE-LEAFED DAISY

HISTORICAL PIECES OF
GLASS LEFT OVER FROM
WHALERS AND TORTOISE OIL
COLLECTORS; MANY OF THE
PIECES OF GLASS ARE FROM
BOTTLES FROM THE 1850S

9. La Galapaguera Natural

This site, at the north of the island, is not included on most boat itineraries and is best done by launch from Puerto Baquerizo. Allow all day, including two hours each way by boat and three hours each way for the fairly easy 10 km walk to Media Luna. This is the best chance to see the San Cristóbal Tortoise in its natural habitat, along with the San Cristóbal Mockingbird and Arid Zone vegetation. Take good shoes, plenty of water and sun protection.

Key to Maps

Lava	○ Blowhole	Cinder cones
Dense vegetation	WET Wet landing site	Viewpoint
Cacti	DRY Dry landing site	Point of interest
Mangrove	Camera protection needed	Anchorage
	Snorkelling	

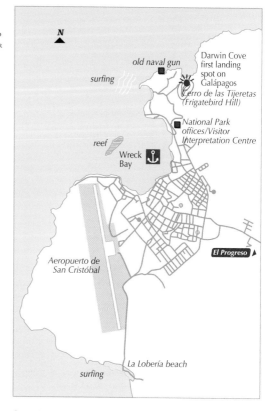

SAN CRISTÓBAL – 10. PUERTO BAQUERIZO MORENO

The second largest town and provincial capital, Puerto Baquerizo lies at the head of Wreck Bay at the northeastern end of San Cristóbal. The island's second airport is here, with regular flights from the mainland. There are also hotels, shops, bars and restaurants. The National Park has offices and a Visitor Interpretation Centre here.

There is an interesting trail from the town, to the Visitor Centre and then on to Frigatebird Hill where you can see both species of frigatebird, and also start to identify some of the Arid Zone plants. At the foot of the hill is a small beach, thought to be the site of Darwin's first landing in Galápagos.

Beyond the airport in the south coast is a beach called 'Lobería' where you can see Sea Lions, as well as Marine Iguanas, Sally Lightfoot crabs and a number of migrant shorebirds. You also get a good view of the dry and coastal zone vegetation.

From Puerto Baquerizo you can also hire a taxi or take a bus to the highlands and El Progreso and on to the only substantial permanent freshwater lake in Galápagos, El Junco.

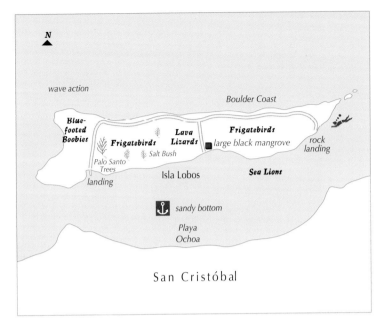

SAN CRISTÓBAL – 11. ISLA LOBOS; PLAYA OCHOA

Isla Lobos is a small rocky island under 1 km in length, lying just off the north coast of San Cristóbal, within easy reach of the town of Puerto Baquerizo Moreno, the provincial capital. It has a rather rocky trail from the landing dock at the western end of the island that runs all the way to the eastern point, where there is another rocky landing area.

The vegetation is sparse with a mixture of arid zone trees and shrubs, such as Palo Santo and Bitterbush at the western end, as well as littoral plants, such as Black Mangrove and Saltbush. The island boasts both Galápagos Sea Lions and a small number of Galápagos Fur Seals, the latter mainly on the north coast, while the Sea Lions are found mainly on the more sheltered south coast. The main ornithological attractions are a small colony of Blue-footed Boobies at the western end and two of Great Frigatebirds in the central part of the island.

At the eastern end of the island there is a good area for snorkelling where you can often sea young Sea Lions playing. It is also good for coastal rock and shore fish, and sea urchins. If you are lucky you may see a Sting Ray or Spotted Eagle Rays.

Playa Ochoa is on the coast opposite Isla Lobos and is a good swimming beach with snorkelling at either end. Behind the beach is a small lagoon and good arid zone vegetation, including Matazarna and Poison Apple, which is easily recognised by its bright green waxy leaves. Do not eat the fruit as they are poisonous, and the sap can burn.

WATCH OUT FOR:

Isla Lobos

BLUE-FOOTED BOOBY
GREAT FRIGATEBIRD
LAVA LIZARD
GALÁPAGOS SEA LION
GALÁPAGOS FUR SEAL

PALO SANTO
BLACK MANGROVE
BITTERBUSH
SALTBUSH

■ ■ ■

Playa Ochoa

GHOST CRAB
HERMIT CRAB
PENCIL-SPINED SEA URCHIN
GREEN SEA URCHIN

PALO SANTO
MATAZARNO
POISON APPLE
GALÁPAGOS LANTANA
GLORYBOWER

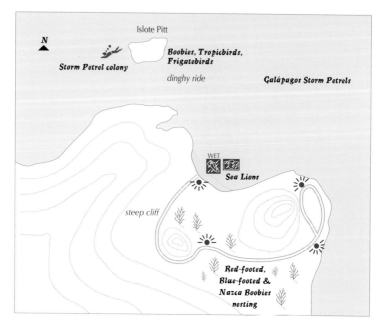

Islote Pitt

N

**Boobies, Tropicbirds,
Frigatebirds**

Storm Petrel colony

dinghy ride

Galápagos Storm Petrels

WET

Sea Lions

steep cliff

**Red-footed,
Blue-footed &
Nazca Boobies
nesting**

SAN CRISTÓBAL – 12. PUNTA PITT

A very beautiful site on the northeastern tip of San Cristóbal, this is the only place in the islands that you can see all three species of booby nesting. The landing is on a green sand beach, the colour coming from its high content of olivine crystals. The trail climbs an eroded tuff cliff around to the far side of the large eroded tuff cone that forms the point. On the way you pass the Great Frigatebird and Red-footed Boobies nesting in the trees with the Blue-footed and Nazca Boobies on the ground. The vegetation is typical of the Arid Zone and the volcanic scenery is spectacular.

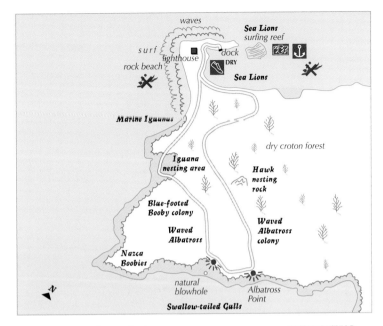

Española – 20. Punta Suárez

Española is the southernmost island in the archipelago. It is one of the oldest islands in the group and has very few obviously volcanic features. The whole of its south coast is a low cliff which makes it an ideal nesting site for the endemic Waved Albatross. The updraft along the cliff, caused by the South-East Trade Winds, enables them to take off with relative ease. This is the only location where you can see these birds that are so ungainly on land but so elegant once they take to the air. Boobies, tropic birds and Swallow-tailed Gulls also breed here. The trail takes you from a sheltered beach on the north side of the point, through low scrubby vegetation, past a pebble beach where Marine Iguanas nest, through a mixed colony of Nazca and Blue-footed Boobies and up to the cliff where the main albatross colony is located. The cliff is an excellent spot to watch albatross and other seabirds soaring. There is also a blowhole that can be spectacular with the right tide and sea conditions. The Marine Iguana, Mockingbird and Lava Lizard are specific to Española. It is also one of only two sites that you are likely to see the Large Cactus Finch.

WATCH OUT FOR:

Waved Albatross
Blue-footed Booby
Nazca Booby
Swallow-tailed Gull
Red-billed Tropic Bird
Hood Mockingbird
Galápagos Hawk
Galápagos Dove
Small Ground Finch
Large Cactus Finch
Warbler Finch
American Oystercatcher
Hood Lava Lizard
Marine Iguana
Galápagos Sea Lion
Sally Lightfoot Crab

Mesquite
Salt Sage
Desert Plum
Saltbush
Galápagos Shore Petunia
Galápagos Lantana
Desert Thorn
Common Purslane
Galápagos Carpetweed
Trianthema
Puncture Weed
False Mallow

247

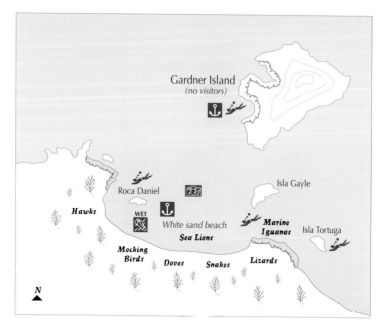

Gardner Island
(no visitors)

Isla Gayle

Roca Daniel

Hawks

WET

White sand beach
Sea Lions

Marine
Iguanas

Isla Tortuga

Mocking
Birds

Doves

Snakes

Lizards

N

WATCH OUT FOR:

WATCH OUT FOR:

GALÁPAGOS HAWK
AMERICAN OYSTERCATCHER
WANDERING TATTLER
ESPAÑOLA MOCKINGBIRD
LARGE CACTUS FINCH
SMALL GROUND FINCH
WARBLER FINCH
GREEN TURTLE
MARINE IGUANA
HOOD RACER
GALÁPAGOS SEA LION
SALLY LIGHTFOOT CRAB
GHOST CRAB

SALTBUSH
PARKINSONIA
MESQUITE
BEACH DROPSEED
PUNCTURE WEED
BEACH MORNING GLORY

ESPAÑOLA – 21. BAHÍA GARDNER

Gardner Bay has two brilliant white sand beaches separated by a rocky outcrop. The beaches are backed by a dense thicket of Parkinsonia and Mesquite. There is no trail. The beach is an open area where you will see an interesting variety of wildlife and some typical Coastal Zone plants. Watch out for the Puncture Weed whose seeds can penetrate even quite stout soles. This is a turtle-nesting beach and their tank-like tracks can often be seen during the nesting season, January to April. If you are ashore early, then you may find a female, exhausted from her exertions. Take your time here and you will see and experience more of the wonders of the Galápagos. The wildlife will approach you, especially the inquisitive Hood Mockingbird and the Galápagos Hawk. There is also a good chance of seeing a snake, the Hood Racer, here. There is good snorkelling around the small islets close to the beach.

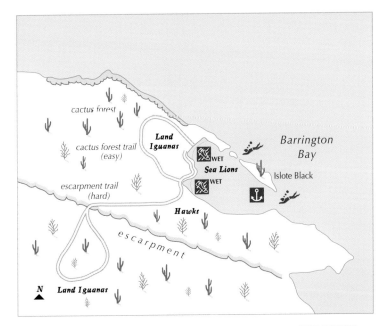

Santa Fé – 23. Barrington Bay

Barrington Bay, the visiting site on Santa Fé, is on the northeastern corner of the island. The anchorage is very sheltered, being protected by a small cactus-covered islet, 'Islote Black', named after the late Juan Black, one of the first Directors of the Galápagos National Park. The bay is quite shallow and you can often see sting rays and green turtles in the clear water. There is good snorkelling around Islote Black.

Santa Fé is noted for its large colony of Sea Lions that live on the two white sand beaches at the head of the bay. Visitors often have to find their way around groups of sleeping cows and pups. Be careful of the bull Sea Lion or beachmaster. He is normally not very aggressive, but can be during the breeding season.

On shore there are two trails. Both should give you the opportunity to view the Santa Fé Land Iguana, found only on this island, and the delightful endemic rice rat, which is particularly in evidence towards sunset. The vegetation on Santa Fé is notable for the very large Prickly Pear Cacti found here. Not quite as tall as some on Santa Cruz, it is larger and more heavily trunked than any other in the islands.

The longer trail to the top of the cliff gives an excellent view over the bay. You should also see the Galápagos Hawk and the rare Heller's Scalesia. Watch out for the dark stains on your clothes caused by the sap of the Croton bushes. This is indelible.

WATCH OUT FOR:
Galápagos Hawk
Ground finches
Cactus Finch
Central Galápagos Racer
Santa Fé Land Iguana
Galápagos Sea Lion
Galápagos Rice Rat
Sand Dollar
Ghost Crab

Palo Santo
Muyuyu
Galápagos Lantana
Leatherleaf
Prickly Pear Cactus
Heller's Scalesia
Saltbush
Spiny Bush
Galápagos Croton
Velvet Shrub
Feather Fingergrass

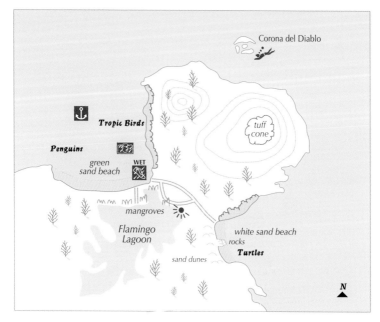

FLOREANA – 30. PUNTA CORMORÁN

Located between two tuff cones, this is an excellent site for waders and Arid Zone plants. The green sand of the landing beach is due to the presence of olivine crystals. Behind the beach are mangroves and a large salt lagoon. Flamingos nest here – their mud pie-shaped nests are often visible on the far side. Watch out for other waders and also the White-cheeked Pintail. The trail leads to a white sand beach known as 'Flour Sand Beach', due to the fineness of the sand. Turtles nest here and stingrays can be seen in the shallows. The plant life is of particular interest as several species are found only on Floreana. You should also see the semi-terrestrial hermit crab *Coenobita compressus* here. There is excellent snorkelling at Corona del Diablo (Devil's Crown), an eroded volcanic crater, just off the point.

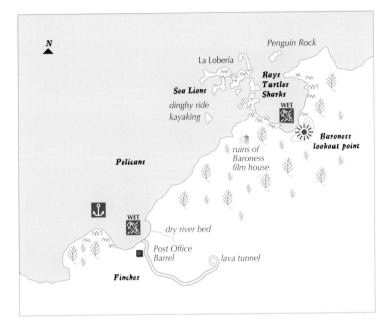

FLOREANA – 31. BAHÍA POST OFFICE, LOBERÍA AND BARONESA LOOKOUT

One of the earliest sites frequented by visitors to Galápagos, Post Office Bay is named after a barrel erected in 1792 by whalers, which served as a primitive post office for passing ships whose voyages often lasted up to five years. The barrel has now become a historical curiosity. This was also the site of an ill-fated Norwegian fish-canning factory in 1926. The trail leads through Palo Santo and Parkinsonia trees to a cave (actually a lava tube) that runs down into the sea. The lagoon at the back of the beach sometimes has migrant waders and an occasional American Flamingo. A short distance to the east is La Lobería, a Galápagos Sea Lion colony where you can also see rays and turtles, along with a small colony of Galápagos Penguins. Land on the sandy beach for the short hike up to the Baronesa Lookout.

WATCH OUT FOR:

GALÁPAGOS PENGUIN
BLUE-FOOTED BOOBY
BROWN PELICAN
AMERICAN FLAMINGO
WHIMBREL
COMMON NODDY
YELLOW WARBLER
GROUND FINCHES
GREEN TURTLE
GALÁPAGOS SEA LION
GOLDEN COWNOSE RAY

PALO SANTO
PARKINSONIA
MESQUITE
GALÁPAGOS LANTANA
GALÁPAGOS COTTON
SPINYBUSH
SALTBUSH
PUNCTURE VINE

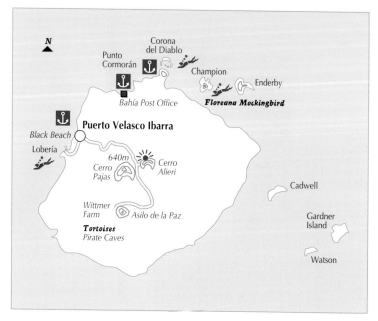

LAVA GULL
MEDIUM-BILLED TREE FINCH
LARGE-BILLED TREE FINCH
VERMILLION FLYCATCHER
GALÁPAGOS FLYCATCHER
GALÁPAGOS GIANT TORTOISE
MARINE IGUANA

SCALESIA FOREST

BLACK BEACH AND HIGHLANDS

FLOREANA – 32. BLACK BEACH AND HIGHLANDS

Floreana was the first island in Galápagos to be inhabited and has a fascinating human history. The population is around 130, who live mainly at Puerto Velasco Ibarra at Black Beach, there are two hotels here and a museum. You can walk to Post Office Bay (2–3 hours), while a 45-minute walk south takes you to La Lobería, a good place to swim and snorkel and home to a colony of Galápagos Sea Lions.

To visit the central highlands, take the bus in the morning and then walk back (2–3 hours) or hitch a ride on one of the few vehicles on the island. The highlands are the caldera of a large volcano, but the more recent cinder cones make this difficult to see. As you ascend, the 640m. Cerro Pajas, at 640m, is on your right. A short hike to El Mirador on Cerro Alieri will give you a good view of the caldera, much of it covered in *Scalesia* forest, home to the Medium Tree Finch.

Follow the road south to the Wittmer Family farm and you will come to a corral where there are tortoises (not the extinct Floreana Tortoise). Here you can visit the old pirate caves that were used by the Wittmer family when they first arrived on Floreana.

Snorkelling sites

The northwest coast has two excellent snorkelling sites: Corona del Diablo, an eroded crater that you can snorkel through; and Isla Champion, a good site for fish and White-tipped Reef Shark. You cannot go ashore on Champion, but can see the Floreana Mockingbird from a dingy.

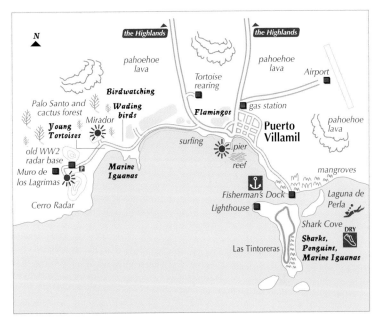

Isabela – 40. Puerto Villamil

This is the main settlement on Isabela, situated on the south side of Volcán Sierra Negra. The small settlement, which was originally a penal settlement in the nineteenth century, has grown over recent years and now boasts several hotels and restaurants, and a regular high-speed launch link to Puerto Ayora. The new airport is able to take flights directly from the mainland as well as from Baltra and San Cristóbal. To the east of the Fishermen's Dock is a small mangrove lagoon with very clear water that provides excellent snorkelling. There is also a Tortoise Breeding Centre run by the National Park.

The main wildlife interest here are the various salt and brackish lagoons close to the town which harbour a wide range of coastal and sea birds including many migrant waders. The lagoon at Quinta Playa to the west of Villamil has the largest concentration of flamingos in the islands. This is probably the best 'birding' place in the islands. It is also

the landing point for visiting Sierra Negra. The Muro de las Lagrimas (The Wall of Tears) was built by convicts from the penal colony, which was only closed in the late 1950s.

WATCH OUT FOR:

GALÁPAGOS PENGUIN
AMERICAN FLAMINGO
LAVA, FRANKLIN'S AND LAUGHING GULLS
COMMON GALLINULE
WHIMBREL
BLACK–NECKED STILT
AMERICAN OYSTERCATCHER
WANDERING TATTLER
RUDDY TURNSTONE
GREAT BLUE HERON
LAVA HERON
STRIATED HERON
PIED-BILLED GREBE
WHITE-CHEEKED PINTAIL
BLUE-WINGED TEAL
MANY MIGRANT WADERS
MARINE IGUANA
LAVA LIZARD

PRICKLY PEAR CACTUS
MESQUITE
PARKINSONIA
PALO SANTO
RED MANGROVE
BLACK MANGROVE
BUTTON MANGROVE
WHITE MANGROVE
BEACH MORNING GLORY

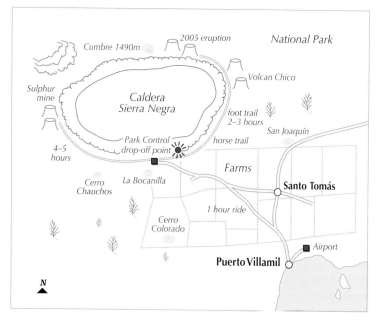

Cumbre 1490m
2005 eruption
National Park
Sulphur mine
Caldera Sierra Negra
Volcan Chico
foot trail 2–3 hours
San Joaquín
Park Control drop-off point
horse trail
4–5 hours
Farms
Cerro Chauchos
La Bocanilla
Santo Tomás
1 hour ride
Cerro Colorado
Airport
Puerto Villamil
N

WATCH OUT FOR:
GALÁPAGOS HAWK
SHORT-EARED OWL
SMALL GROUND FINCH
MEDIUM GROUND FINCH
VEGETARIAN FINCH
SMALL TREE FINCH
LARGE TREE FINCH
WOODPECKER FINCH
WARBLER FINCH
GALÁPAGOS GIANT TORTOISE
FERAL DONKEY

SOAPBERRY
HEART-LEAFED SCALESIA
RADIATE-HEADED SCALESIA
GUAYABILLO
PEGA PEGA
GALÁPAGOS ACACIA
GALÁPAGOS CROTON
LANCE-LEAFED DARWIN'S BUSH
WHITE-HAIRED TOURNEFORTIA
RED-HAIRED TOURNEFORTIA

ISABELA – 41. VOLCÁN SIERRA NEGRA

This volcano at the southeastern end of Isabela has the largest caldera in diameter of any in Galápagos, measuring 10 km by 9 km. It is well worth a visit for the scenery, the volcanic activity and the vegetation. You may also be fortunate to come across a Giant Tortoise. Volcán Chico on the northeast side of the caldera is an area of fumarolic activity and to the west there is the 'Mina de Azufre' or sulphur mine, where there is more fumarolic activity and sulphur deposits. Lava from an eruption in November 2005, on the north side of the caldera rim, flowed all around the eastern and southern edge of the caldera. There are excellent opportunities to view the Humid Zone vegetation and up to seven species of Darwin's finch. The view from the caldera rim is one of the best in the islands, in all directions!

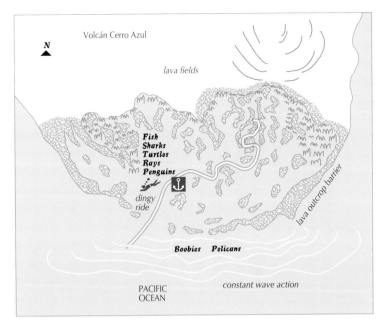

Volcán Cerro Azul

N

lava fields

Fish
Sharks
Turtles
Rays
Penguins

dingy ride

lava outcrop barrier

Boobies   Pelicans

PACIFIC OCEAN

constant wave action

Isabela – 42. Los Tuneles

Located 24 km west of Puerto Villamil is a remarkable semi-submerged lava formation known as Los Tuneles – or the Tunnels. Here the pahoehoe lava has flowed into the sea and subsequently been eroded leaving a labyrinth of passages and archways. It is a really good site for the geology, but also for the early colonizer vegetation and the wildlife, not just Marine Iguanas and Blue-footed Boobies, but myriads of reef fish as well as sharks, rays and turtles. The boat trip takes 1–2 hours each way depending on sea conditions, best visited in the calm season, December through May.

WATCH OUT FOR:

GALÁPAGOS PENGUIN
BLUE-FOOTED BOOBY
FRIGATEBIRDS
GALÁPAGOS GREEN TURTLE
WHALE SHARK (ON ROUTE TO SITE)
WHITE-TIPPED REEF SHARK
DIAMOND STINGRAY
GIANT MANTA RAY
MOBULA SPINETAIL
SPINY LOBSTER

OPUNTIA CACTUS
CANDELABRA CACTUS

LAVA FORMATIONS

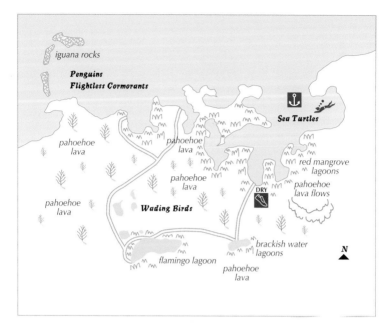

ISABELA – 43. PUNTA MORENO

One of Galápagos' many surprises, what looks at first sight to be a barren lava field, turns out to be dotted with oases – brackish water ponds where the pahoehoe lava surface has collapsed into the lava tubes beneath. There is a wealth of animal and plant life, including flamingos, ducks and waders. Invertebrates are here in strength also, with dragonflies and damselflies being the most obvious. Watch out also for a large eel-like fish. It is rarely seen and has not yet been identified. On the coast there are mangroves where Brown Pelicans nest and you may also see the Flightless Cormorant, penguins, herons and Mustard Rays.

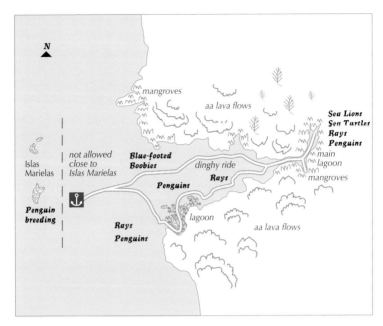

Islas
Marielas

Penguin
breeding

mangroves

aa lava flows

Sea Lions
Sea Turtles
Rays
Penguins

not allowed
close to
Islas Marielas

Blue-footed
Boobies

dinghy ride

Penguins

Rays

main
lagoon

mangroves

Rays
Penguins

lagoon

aa lava flows

ISABELA – 44. BAHÍA ELIZABETH

This large west-facing bay nestles between southern
Volcán Sierra Negra and Volcán Alcedo at the western
end of the Perry Isthmus. The Islas Mariela, three small
islands in the bay, are an important breeding ground for
the endangered Galápagos Penguin and landing is not
allowed. The shore of the bay is largely hidden by a forest
of large Red Mangroves, and you enter through a narrow
tidal channel into a peaceful lagoon surrounded by the
trees. Here you can see Golden Cownose Rays, Green
Turtles and Galápagos Penguins; Galápagos Sea Lions have
also adapted to living on the mangrove roots. The aa lava
outcrops on either side of the mangroves are good places to
see Flightless Cormorants and Blue-footed Boobies.

WATCH OUT FOR:

FRIGATEBIRDS
YELLOW-CROWNED NIGHT
HERON
GREAT BLUE HERON
GALÁPAGOS PENGUIN
LAVA HERON
BLUE-FOOTED BOOBY
FLIGHTLESS CORMORANT
GALÁPAGOS SHEARWATER
GREEN TURTLE
GALÁPAGOS SEA LION
GOLDEN COWNOSE RAY
SPOTTED EAGLE RAY
YELLOW-TAILED MULLET

RED, BLACK AND WHITE
MANGROVE FORESTS

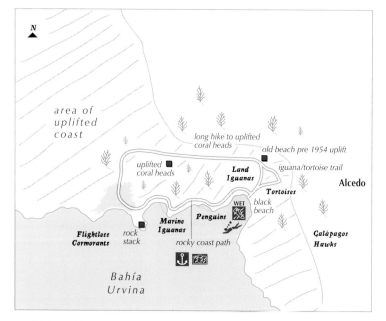

GALÁPAGOS PENGUIN
FLIGHTLESS CORMORANT
BROWN PELICAN
YELLOW WARBLER
GROUND FINCHES
GALÁPAGOS GIANT TORTOISE
LAND IGUANA
MARINE IGUANA
SEMI-TERRESTRIAL HERMIT CRAB

POISON APPLE
PALO SANTO
PRICKLY PEAR CACTUS
SALTBUSH
LANCE-LEAFED DARWIN'S BUSH
GALÁPAGOS SHORE PETUNIA
SPINY BUSH
GALÁPAGOS ACACIA
GALÁPAGOS COTTON
RED-HAIRED TOURNEFORTIA

ISABELA – 45. BAHÍA URVINA

Urvina is another rather special site. Situated at the foot of Volcán Alcedo you can see tortoises (if you are lucky), Land and Marine Iguanas, hermit crabs and a variety of Coastal and Arid Zone vegetation. You can also find coral heads several hundred metres inland.

In 1954 the whole area was raised, by up to 10 m in places. A further uplift of some 90 cm took place in 1994, which has resulted in the landing dock being unusable except at high tide. All the vegetation has grown up since then. You can still find many signs of the underwater origin of the land – shells, pebbles and sea urchin segments – and the trail leads to a raised beach where you can also find small pieces of pumice; the slopes of Alcedo are largely covered in this light and buoyant volcanic material. The Marine Iguanas found here are some of the largest in the islands.

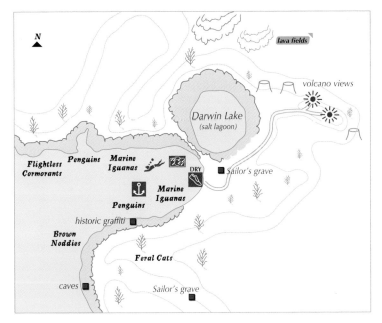

Isabela – 46. Caleta Tagus

An anchorage long used by pirates, whalers and other early visitors, Tagus Cove is a flooded valley between two large tuff cones, with the flooded crater of a third at the head of the anchorage. An historic location which still bears the inscriptions from visitors in the nineteenth century, the area has a good selection of Arid Zone plants as well as some interesting volcanic features. This is an excellent site for a dinghy ride along the coast as it is deep close to land, so that a lot of marine life is easily observed.

WATCH OUT FOR:

GALÁPAGOS PENGUIN
FLIGHTLESS CORMORANT
BROWN PELICAN
GALÁPAGOS HAWK
MARINE IGUANA
FERAL CAT
GALÁPAGOS SEA LION
SALLY LIGHTFOOT CRAB
WHITE SEA URCHIN

PALO SANTO
MUYUYU
PRICKLY PEAR CACTUS
BITTERBUSH
GALÁPAGOS CROTON
GALÁPAGOS COTTON
GALÁPAGOS LANTANA
NEEDLE-LEAFED DAISY
DARWIN'S DAISY
HAIRY GALÁPAGOS TOMATO
RADIATE-HEADED SCALESIA
GALÁPAGOS ACACIA
PUNCTURE WEED
VELVET SHRUB

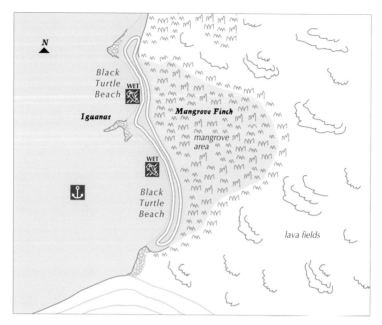

WATCH OUT FOR:

MANGROVE FINCH
FINCHES
MOCKINGBIRDS
LAVA LIZARD
MARINE IGUANA
GALÁPAGOS SEA LION

RED MANGROVE

On the northern and western sides of Isabela are three sites that are well worth a visit (pp.260–62).

NORTHERN ISABELA – 47. PLAYA TORTUGA NEGRA (BLACK TURTLE BEACH)

Just north of Tagus Cove is Black Turtle Beach, a series of black-sand beaches backed by mangrove lagoons. This is the last known habitat of the critically endangered Mangrove Finch, of which fewer than 100 individuals are thought to survive. A special permit is required to visit the site. The landing is wet and can be impossible if a north swell is running.

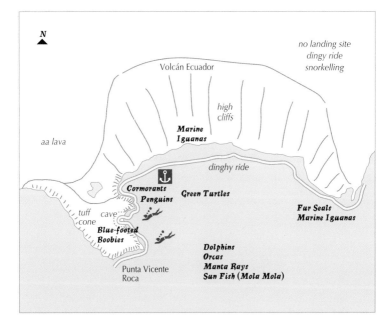

N

Volcán Ecuador

no landing site
dingy ride
snorkelling

high
cliffs

*Marine
Iguanas*

aa lava

dinghy ride

*Cormorants
Penguins*

Green Turtles

*Fur Seals
Marine Iguanas*

tuff
cone   cave

*Blue-footed
Boobies*

*Dolphins
Orcas
Manta Rays
Sun Fish (Mola Mola)*

Punta Vicente
Roca

Northern Isabela – 48. Punta Vicente Roca

Further north, at the northern tip of Bahía Banks, is Punta Vicente Roca, a very dramatic cliffscape with a tuff cone perched on the edge of Volcán Ecuador. You can't go ashore but a dinghy ride here is fascinating, with Galápagos Penguins, Flightless Cormorants, Galápagos Sea Lions and Galápagos Fur Seals being found here. If you are lucky, you may see also Orca, Giant Manta or even the giant Mola Mola – this is also a snorkelling and dive site.

WATCH OUT FOR:

Blue-footed Booby
Wandering Tattler
Galápagos Petrel
White-vented Storm Petrel
Brown Noddy
Flightless Cormorant
Galápagos Penguin
Green Turtle
Marine Iguana
Common Dolphin
Bottlenose Dolphin
Orca
Galápagos Fur Seal
Mola Mola

Spectacular lava cliffs
and ash formations

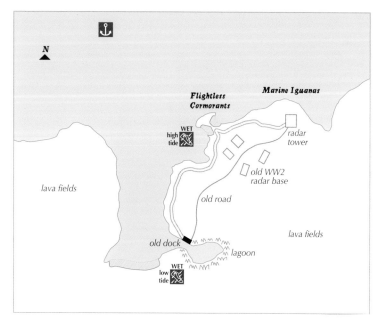

WATCH OUT FOR:

FLIGHTLESS CORMORANT
GALÁPAGOS PETREL
GALÁPAGOS HAWK
FINCHES
DOVES
MOCKINGBIRDS
GULLS
LAVA LIZARD
MARINE IGUANA
WHALES GOING BY OFF
THE COAST

OLD WW2 RADAR
INSTALLATIONS

NORTHERN ISABELA – 49. PUNTA ALBEMARLE

On the northern tip of Isabela is a site with a historical as well as natural history interest. Punta Albemarle was the site of one of three radar stations established by the US military during the Second World War. The landing can be tricky but the huge expanse of lava is impressive, as are the Marine Iguanas, which are the largest found anywhere. It is also a good spot to see Flightless Cormorants and offers spectacular views of the northern slopes of Volcán Wolf.

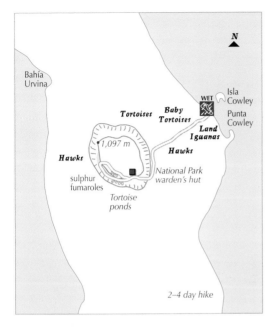

The map shows:
- N (north arrow)
- Bahía Urvina
- Tortoises
- Baby Tortoises
- WET / Isla Cowley
- Punta Cowley
- Land Iguanas
- Hawks
- 1,097 m
- Hawks
- National Park warden's hut
- sulphur fumaroles
- Tortoise ponds
- *2–4 day hike*

ISABELA – 50. VOLCÁN ALCEDO

WATCH OUT FOR:
GALÁPAGOS HAWK
VERMILION FLYCATCHER
GALÁPAGOS FLYCATCHER
GROUND FINCHES
VEGETARIAN FINCH
LARGE TREE FINCH
SMALL TREE FINCH
WOODPECKER FINCH
WARBLER FINCH
ALCEDO TORTOISE

Without doubt the most spectacular setting for viewing Alcedo Tortoises, Volcán Alcedo is the central shield volcano on Isabela and home to 5,000 of the giant reptiles. It is not on any standard itinerary and the special permit required to visit the site needs to be arranged directly with the Galápagos National Park authorities. You also have to undergo a 48-hour quarantine period, arrange your own boat transport to get you there and back, and take all of your own food and some water. You can take tents or stay in the national park cabin on the crater rim; the minimum trip time is three days.

The hike up the volcano is fairly easy apart from the last 200 m or so, which is steep. The view from the rim is exceptional, and the sight of the huge caldera with fumaroles, Alcedo Tortoises and Galápagos Hawks, along with the ubiquitous finches and flycatchers, makes this one of the most impressive visitor sites in the archipelago, on top of which it is peaceful and quiet, and there are no tourists – apart from you!

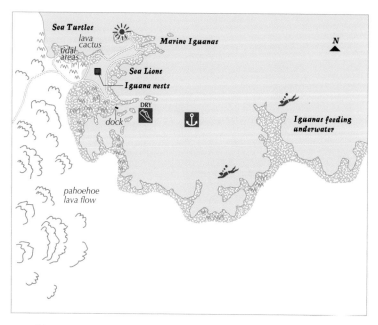

FERNANDINA – 60. PUNTA ESPINOSA

One of the most impressive and varied visiting sites in the islands, surrounded on all sides by the huge shield volcanoes of Fernandina and Isabela. It is a low point jutting out into the Canal de Bolivar. In 1994 the whole point was raised by movements of the Earth between 50 and 90 cm, leaving the landing dock inaccessible except at high tide. You can often see whales and dolphins offshore as well as large flocks of Blue-footed Boobies fishing.

For observing the marine environment of Galápagos, Punta Espinosa is unrivalled, with large colonies of Marine Iguanas, often basking impassively in the sun. Once the iguanas have warmed up after they have been feeding, they will face into the sun to avoid overheating. There are penguins here, and the ubiquitous Galápagos Sea Lion; this is also the best place to observe the most iconic of Galápagos birds, the Flightless Cormorant, hanging its ragged stubby wings out to dry. Here also you will have an excellent opportunity to observe the intertidal life with lots of tidepools and gently shelving foreshore. There is a good area of mangroves, which provides a habitat for herons, yellow warblers and just possibly the Mangrove Finch. Watch out for the Marine Iguana nesting area, snakes, lava cacti and both pahoehoe and the very rough aa lava.

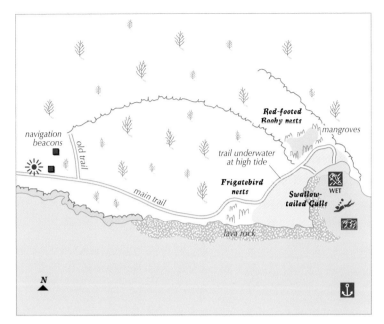

Genovesa – 65. Playa Darwin

Genovesa is a low flat island, the most isolated of the main islands. It has a limited flora and fauna but makes up for this with quantity. In particular it has large numbers of seabirds. The landing is on the white sand and coral beach where you are likely to be greeted by Lava and Swallow-tailed Gulls and Yellow-crowned Night Herons. Be careful if the gulls are nesting, not to disturb them. Behind the beach there is a small lagoon with White-cheeked Pintails and occasional waders. The trail takes you through mixed vegetation of Palo Santo, Prickly Pear Cactus and Saltbush where you will see nesting frigatebirds and Red-footed Boobies. The Marine Iguana here are very small and black. There are no Lava Lizards and only four species of finch.

WATCH OUT FOR:

Great Frigatebird
Red-footed Booby
Nazca Booby
Yellow-crowned Night Heron
Lava Gull
Swallow-tailed Gull
White-cheeked Pintail
Galápagos Dove
Large Ground Finch
Sharp-beaked Ground Finch
Warbler Finch
Marine Iguana
Galápagos Sea Lion

Red Mangrove
Palo Santo
Prickly Pear Cactus
Muyuyu
Galápagos Croton
Saltbush
Galápagos Shore Petunia
Galápagos Spurge
Heliotrope
Scorpion Weed

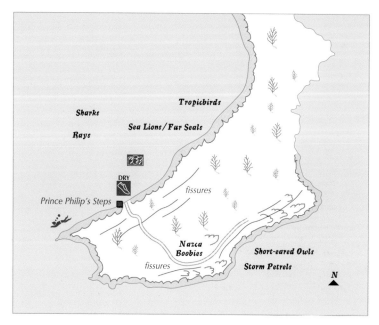

The following labels appear on the map:

Tropicbirds

Sharks

Sea Lions / Fur Seals

Rays

DRY

Prince Philip's Steps

fissures

Nazca Boobies

Short-eared Owls

fissures

Storm Petrels

N

Genovesa – 66. Prince Philip's Steps

The naming of this site stems from a visit by Prince Philip on the RY *Britannia* in 1965. The dinghy ride to the landing on the rocks at the foot of the cliff gives you an excellent chance to view the Galápagos Fur Seal. After climbing the cliff, the trail takes you past nesting Nazca Boobies, through a forest of low Palo Santo with nesting Red-footed Boobies, to the cliff top. This is bare rather hollow sounding lava, and you will find yourself surrounded by a cloud of Galápagos Storm Petrels which nest here in large numbers in the crevices and lava tubes. The same colony is occupied at night by the Madeiran Storm Petrel. Keep an eye open for the Galápagos Short-eared Owls which live here and prey on the petrels. They are not uncommon but are quite well camouflaged.

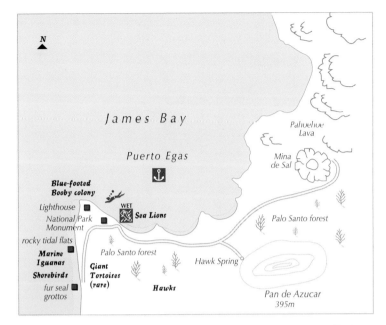

Santiago – 70. James Bay, Puerto Egas

The most prominent physical feature here is the large tuff cone to the south, Pan de Azucar (Sugarloaf), climbed by Darwin in 1835. At the base of this, there is a trail leading up to Hawk Spring. A longer trail leads to the Mina de Sal or Salt Mine Crater. The bottom of this crater is below sea level and has a salt-water lake. The salt deposits here were mined commercially until 1970.

If you are interested in the dry zone vegetation, then the area around Puerto Egas is a good place to start. The walking is easy and the vegetation quite sparse, so that identifying individual species is relatively easy.

A third trail takes you to the Fur Seal Grotto where there is a colony of fur seals which live in a series of caves and grotto-like formations formed when the lava flowed into the sea. This is the best place in the islands to watch and photograph Fur Seals. Walk back from the Fur Seal Grotto along the shore. This is an excellent area to observe shore life; there are numerous tide pools with crabs, molluscs and small fish. At low tide you can see Marine Iguanas feeding as well as shorebirds, such as American Oystercatcher and Whimbrel.

WATCH OUT FOR:

BROWN PELICAN
YELLOW-CROWNED NIGHT HERON
LAVA HERON
STRIATED HERON
AMERICAN OYSTERCATCHER
WHIMBREL
GALÁPAGOS HAWK
GALÁPAGOS DOVE
SMALL, MEDIUM AND LARGE GROUND FINCHES
CACTUS GROUND FINCH
WARBLER FINCH
MARINE IGUANA
GALÁPAGOS SNAKE
GALÁPAGOS FUR SEAL
PAINTED LOCUST
SALLY LIGHTFOOT CRAB

PALO SANTO
GALÁPAGOS CROTON
BITTERBUSH
MUYUYU
PRICKLY PEAR CACTUS
PUNCTURE WEED
SPINY BUSH
SCORPION WEED
GALÁPAGOS ACACIA
GLORYBOWER
PEARL BERRY

267

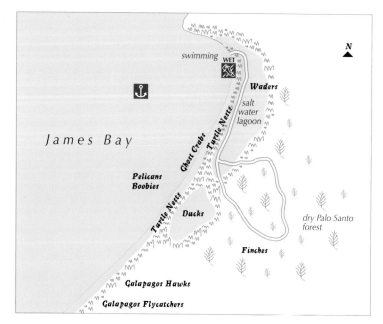

N

swimming

WET

Waders

salt water lagoon

James Bay

Pelicans
Boobies

Ghost Crabs

Turtle Nests

Turtle Nests

Ducks

dry Palo Santo forest

Finches

Galapagos Hawks

Galapagos Flycatchers

WATCH OUT FOR:

BLUE-FOOTED BOOBY
BROWN PELICAN
BROWN NODDY
GALÁPAGOS HAWK
WHITE-CHEEKED PINTAIL
BLUE-WINGED TEAL
FINCHES
YELLOW WARBLER
GALÁPAGOS FLYCATCHERS
LAVA LIZARD
GALÁPAGOS SEA LION
GALÁPAGOS FUR SEAL
GHOST CRAB

PALO SANTO FOREST
OPUNTIA CACTUS
GALÁPAGOS SNAPDRAGON
BUSHES
GALÁPAGOS TOMATO
BLACK MANGROVE
WHITE MANGROVE
BUTTON MANGROVE

SPECTACULAR LAVA
FORMATIONS

SANTIAGO – 71. PLAYA ESPUMILLA AND BUCCANEER COVE

Located on the northern end of Santiago, these two sites are among the oldest visitor sites in Galápagos, having been used by the buccaneers in the 16th and 17th centuries. Buccaneer Cove was used as a site to careen and clean their ships. Today you can take a dinghy ride along the coast. Of special interest are bands of red ash and lava, sketched by Charles Darwin who camped here during his stay on Santiago in 1835. Espumilla is a long red sand beach, an important nesting site for Green Turtles, with a lagoon behind which used to have flamingoes. However, changes caused by El Niño caused them to leave. The trail runs along the back of the beach and does a loop through the dry *Bursera* forest. The whole area is recovering from the eradication of pigs and goats, allowing the native vegetation to flourish.

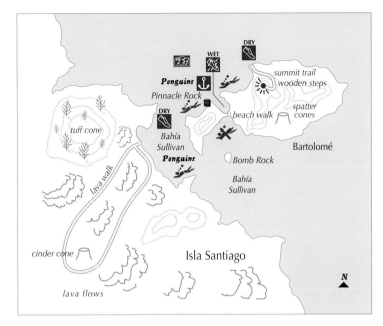

N

SANTIAGO – 72. BAHÍA SULLIVAN AND ISLA BARTOLOMÉ

Bahía Sullivan

The chief attraction at this site is the large black lava flow created by an eruption in 1889. The trail takes you from the small sandy beach, across the lava, with dramatic examples of pahoehoe or ropy lava, to a series of small cinder cones. The shapes and formations of the lava are remarkable and it looks so fresh that it might have been formed last week. Moulds formed by Leatherleaf trees are visible in the lava. This is an excellent site to see the very first plant colonisers of bare lava, particularly *Mollugo crockeri* and Lava Cactus *Brachycereus nesioticus*.

Isla Bartolomé

This is the classic beauty spot of the Galápagos. The view from the top of the island of the volcanic landscape is spectacular. It is reached by flights of wooden steps, and is the most photographed view in Galápagos. Pinnacle Rock is the eroded remains of a tuff cone. A small submerged crater can be seen just offshore. To the east are a series of small spatter cones. You may swim from the beach on the north side of the island and the snorkelling is excellent close to Pinnacle Rock. A trail leads across a sandy isthmus to a sand beach on the south side. Swimming is not allowed here but you may see a small school of White-tipped Sharks close to the beach. Turtles nest here from January to March. There are many interesting Coastal and Arid Zone plants.

WATCH OUT FOR:

Bahía Sullivan

LAVA LIZARD
SALLY LIGHTFOOT CRAB
CANDELABRA AND LAVA CACTI
WHITE MANGROVE
STEWART'S SCALESIA
SPINY BUSH
MOLLUGO
LEATHERLEAF
GREY MATPLANT

■ ■ ■

Bartolomé Island

GALÁPAGOS PENGUIN
GALÁPAGOS HAWK
GREEN TURTLE
WHITE-TIPPED SHARK
GHOST CRAB
GREY MATPLANT
RED AND WHITE MANGROVES
SALTBUSH
LAVA CACTUS
PRICKLY PEAR AND LAVA CACTI
GALÁPAGOS SPURGE
BEACH MORNING GLORY
MOLLUGO
OILY PECTIS
STEWART'S SCALESIA
SPINY BUSH

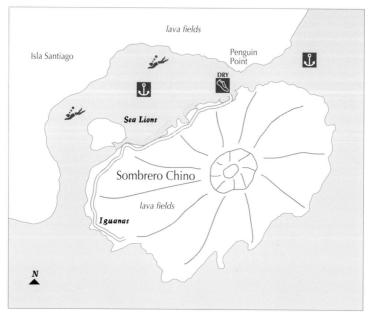

WATCH OUT FOR:

Lava Heron
Striated Heron
Great Blue Heron
Galápagos Hawk
Lava Gull
Galápagos Penguin
Marine Iguana
Lava Lizard
Sally Lightfoot Crab

Lava Cactus
Portulaca

73. Sombrero Chino

Tucked in close to the south coast of Santiago is the appropriately named Sombrero Chino, a small almost circular volcanic island with a single prominent volcanic cone and crater. This is a small protected anchorage and a good site for snorkelling. On shore the trail runs along close to the beach and gives you an excellent opportunity to see the amazing lava formations. There are small lava tubes, shiny metallic areas, lava toes and 'hornitos' or little ovens. As always there are sea lions and Marine Iguanas and with luck you will see Lava Gulls here. On the Santiago shore there are often small numbers of Galápagos penguin.

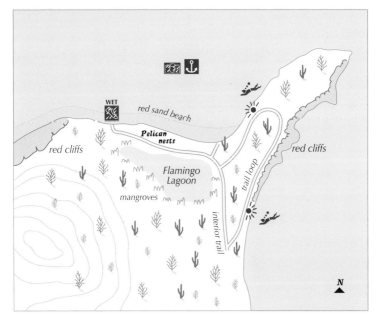

Rábida – 74. Playa Rojo

A small island just south of Santiago. The source of the red sand beach is easily explained. The cinder cone to the west is the same colour, showing that it contains a high proportion of iron. It is a good site to become acquainted with the spines of the Prickly Pear Cactus as they are soft here. Behind the beach is a lagoon with flamingos and other wading birds as well as duck. The trail from the beach up onto the red cinder cone gives an excellent selection of Arid and Coastal Zone plants. There are nine species of Darwin's finch on Rábida. There is good snorkelling at the foot of the red cliff.

WATCH OUT FOR:

Galápagos Penguin
Blue-footed Booby
Brown Noddy
American Flamingo
White-cheeked Pintail
Galápagos Hawk
Darwin's finches
Galápagos Sea Lion

Black Mangrove
Saltbush
Leatherleaf
Prickly Pear Cactus
Palo Santo
Muyuyu
Galápagos Croton
Hairy Galápagos Tomato
Galápagos Milkwort

Sombrero Chino.

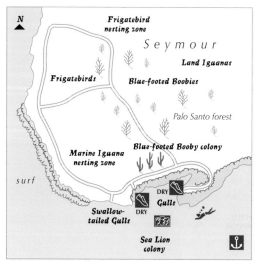

WATCH OUT FOR:

Seymour

GREAT FRIGATEBIRD
MAGNIFICENT FRIGATEBIRD
BLUE-FOOTED BOOBY
NAZCA BOOBY
RED-FOOTED BOOBY
BROWN PELICAN
SWALLOW-TAILED GULL
LAVA GULL
COMMON NODDY
WADERS
GROUND FINCHES
LAND IGUANA
LAVA LIZARD
STRIPED GALÁPAGOS SNAKE
MARINE IGUANA
GALÁPAGOS SEA LION

DWARF PALO SANTO
PARKINSONIA
PRICKLY PEAR CACTUS
MUYUYU
LEATHERLEAF
SALTBUSH
SPINY BUSH
GALÁPAGOS CARPETWEED
SEA PURSLANE
GALÁPAGOS CROTON
HAIRY MORNING GLORY
HAIRY GROUND CHERRY
PUNCTURE WEED

80. SEYMOUR

Lying just to the north of Baltra, Seymour is a low island consisting of uplifted submarine lava. It is covered with a forest of Dwarf Palo Santo trees and is the breeding site of both frigatebirds and two of the boobies. The trail leads from the small dock, along the coast, past an area where Marine Iguanas nest and then loops into the Palo Santo forest past nesting frigatebirds and both Nazca and Blue-footed Boobies. You may also see a Red-footed Booby here though this species does not nest on Seymour.

The Land Iguanas here are actually from Baltra from where they were brought in the 1930s. Some have recently been returned to Baltra as the original population was wiped out during the period that Baltra was a US military base. You can often see young Sea Lions surfing in the large waves off the rocky beach.

80. ISLA MOSQUERA

This small sandy island sits in the middle of the Canal del Norte that separates Baltra from Seymour. Named after Aurelio Mosquera President of Ecuador from 1938 to 1939, it is an open area and is best known for its large colony of Galápagos sea lions as well as Marine Iguanas, occasional shore birds and some excellent tidal pools on the eastern side.

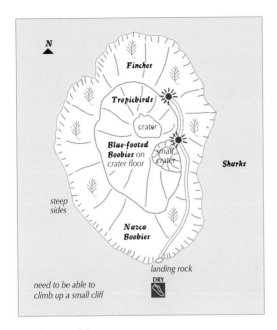

81. DAPHNE MAJOR

Located just 8 km off the north coast of Santa Cruz and west of Baltra are two tuff volcanoes. The smaller of these, Daphne Minor, is inaccessible thanks to its sheer cliff, but is an excellent snorkelling and dive site. The large island, Daphne Major, is a near-perfect cone with a deep crater that is the favoured nesting site of a colony of Blue-footed Boobies. The landing site is at the southern end of the island and the trail snakes up the side of the cone to reach the rim on the eastern side. On the flanks of the volcano you may find Nazca Boobies, and on the cliff inside, nesting Red-tailed Tropicbirds. The sparse vegetation comprises mainly *Opuntia* cacti and Dwarf Palo Santo, which is found only here and on Baltra and Seymour islands. The ground finches on Daphne Major here have been studied for the last 40 years by a team led by Peter and Rosemary Grant, whose research has shed significant light on the processes of evolution.

WATCH OUT FOR:

Isla Mosquera

WANDERING TATTLER
OYSTERCATCHER
GREAT BLUE HERON
FRIGATEBIRD
SWALLOW-TAILED GULL
MARINE IGUANA
GALÁPAGOS SEA LION
(YOUNG SURFING)
SALLY LIGHTFOOT CRAB

■ ■ ■

Daphne

BLUE-FOOTED BOOBY
NAZCA BOOBY
FRIGATEBIRDS
SWALLOW-TAILED GULL
RED-BILLED TROPICBIRD
BROWN NODDY
SMALL GROUND FINCH
MEDIUM GROUND FINCH
LARGE GROUND FINCH
LAVA LIZARD

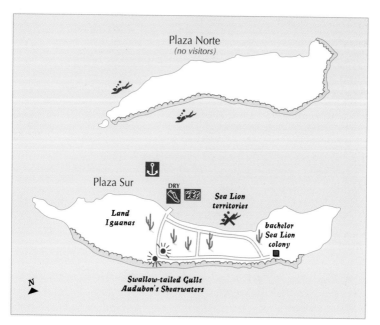

Plaza Norte
(no visitors)

Plaza Sur

DRY

Sea Lion
territories

Land
Iguanas

bachelor
Sea Lion
colony

Swallow-tailed Gulls
Audubon's Shearwaters

N

82. ISLA PLAZA SUR

The two Plaza islands lie just off the eastern tip of Santa Cruz. They are formed from uplifted marine lava. Only the southern of the two islands is open to visitors, but this is one of the most concentrated wildlife sites in the islands.

The trail takes you up from the small dock, frequently occupied by Sea Lions, past the rather droopy Prickly Pear Cacti with their yellow flowers, and up to the cliff from where you can often see a shoal of the endemic Yellow-tailed Mullet *Mugil cephalus rammelsbergii*. The cliff is an excellent place to view the Swallow-tailed Gull and the Red-billed Tropic Bird, both of which breed here, and which along with boobies and frigates, use the updraft for soaring. At the eastern end of the islands is an area where the bachelor bull Sea Lions congregate. There is a colony of Land Iguanas here as well as Marine Iguanas, and you may also see a hybrid of the two species.

At certain times of the year, the Galápagos Carpetweed which covers much of the eastern end of the islands turns a brilliant red-orange, adding a welcome touch of colour.

83–87. Santa Cruz

Santa Cruz has a number of smaller sites; some of these can be accessed by land, while others can be reached only by boat, but all can be done as a day trip from Puerto Ayora.

The low-lying coast of Santa Cruz is interrupted by a number of eroded volcanic ash or tuff volcanoes, a feature associated with water. On the western tip of the island is Bahía Ballena (Whale Bay – 86) and a volcano that has a rather whale-like appearance. The Bay was much frequented by pirates and other passing sailors as it offers a good anchorage and a useful lookout point. Land here on the green olivine-sand beach and take the trail around the base of the hill, excellent for Arid Zone vegetation, ground finches and mockingbirds, and also for swimming and snorkelling. The walk takes 1–1.5 hours.

Just up the coast is another eroded tuff volcano, Cerro Dragón (85), home to the only colony of Land Iguanas on Santa Cruz. Again you land on the beach, behind which are small lagoons that occasionally attract American Flamingos. The walk to the iguana colony is about 1 km through the dry Palo Santo and *Opuntia* cactus forest. This is also a good place to see ground finches, mockingbirds and Lava Lizards.

Continuing around the north coast, you come to Las Bachas (84), a pair of sandy beaches so named because the remains of two large steel pontoons or barges can be found there, left over from when Isla Baltra was a US military base (*bachas* is a corruption of 'barges'). This is a well-known turtle nesting site, and American Flamingos and other waders may be found in the lagoons at the back of the beaches.

Right next to Las Bachas is Caleta Tortuga Negra (83), a peaceful mangrove lagoon that has to be visited by dinghy. Here, you can have close encounters with Green Turtles, clouds of Golden Cownose Rays, fish and herons. It is best visited in the early morning, when it can be magical.

Playa el Garrapatero (87), on the southeast coast, can be visited by land or sea. Land access is via Bellavista and El Cascajo. It is a beautiful beach with an attractive grove of Poison Apple trees. There is a National Park warden here during the day and camping is permitted.

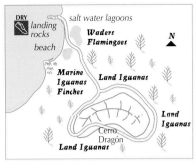

Cerro Dragón.

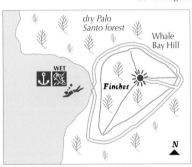

Las Bachas.

WATCH OUT FOR:

BLUE-FOOTED BOOBY

GREAT BLUE HERON

LAVA HERON

GALÁPAGOS MOCKINGBIRD

WADERS IN THE LAGOONS AND ON THE BEACH

WHIMBREL

WANDERING TATTLER

BLACK-NECKED STILT

WHITE-CHEEKED PINTAIL

GROUND FINCHES

LAND IGUANA

MARINE IGUANA

GALÁPAGOS SEA LION

SALLY LIGHTFOOT CRAB

CACTUS FOREST

PALO SANTO FOREST

CERAMIC FRAGMENTS FROM PIRATES AND WHALERS

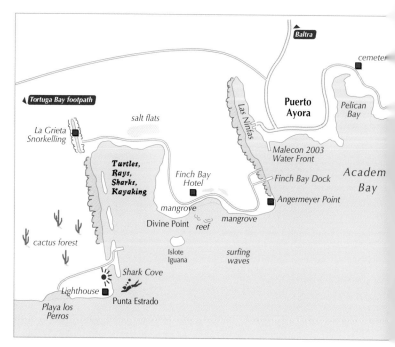

WATCH OUT FOR:

BROWN PELICAN
BLUE-FOOTED BOOBY
MAGNIFICENT FRIGATEBIRD
LAVA GULL
GREAT BLUE HERON
LAVA HERON
STRIATED HERON
GROUND FINCHES
CACTUS FINCH
MARINE IGUANA
SALLY LIGHTFOOT CRAB

CANDELABRA CACTUS
PRICKLY PEAR CACTUS
RED MANGROVE
BUTTON MANGROVE
BLACK MANGROVE
GALÁPAGOS ACACIA
MUYUYU
SPINY BUSH
PALO SANTO
LEATHERLEAF
VELVET SHRUB
SEA GRASS
GLORYBOWER

SANTA CRUZ – ACADEMY BAY AND PUERTO AYORA (88)

Situated at the head of Academy Bay, Puerto Ayora is the largest town in Galápagos and is the centre of the tourism industry. The main airport in the islands is on Baltra, just to the north. This was linked to Puerto Ayora by a road in 1975. It is also the home of the Charles Darwin Research Station and the Galápagos National Park. As a result, it is on the itinerary of virtually all visitors. The town has a number of hotels, bars and restaurants as well as numerous small shops. There is a bank, hospital, several dentists, a 'supermarket' and other delights of civilisation that are entirely absent elsewhere in the islands.

The public dock is a good place to observe pelicans, frigatebirds and Blue-footed Boobies fishing in 'Las Ninfas' the inner anchorage and in Pelican Bay especially when the fishermen are cleaning their catches. To the west of the town towards Punta Estrada is Bud's Bay and Las Grietas (The Cracks). A dinghy trip to this area is well worthwhile. Here you may see Common Noddies, Blue-footed Boobies, herons, and migrant waders. Marine Iguanas and Sally Lightfoot Crabs are also easily seen on the rocks on Angermeyer Point. They often bask on the roofs on the houses here.

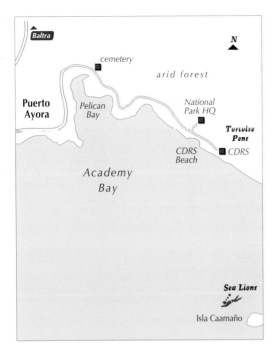

SANTA CRUZ – NATIONAL PARK AND CHARLES DARWIN RESEARCH STATION

The Charles Darwin Research Station (CDRS) is situated at the eastern end of Academy Bay. The Galápagos National Park (GNP) offices are next to the CDRS. You can get there by sea or by road from the town of Puerto Ayora. The sea approach can be difficult at low tide. To walk there takes some 15 to 20 minutes from the public dock. The road is paved all the way.

The walk to or from the CDRS is strongly recommended with a good selection of coastal and arid zone plants as well as the possibility to view the elusive Dark-billed Cuckoo. The main interest is the Tortoise Breeding Centre. This is the only place where you have the opportunity to compare the different shapes of carapace of the various Galápagos Tortoise. CDRS also has a breeding programme for Land Iguanas.

The Van Straelen exhibition hall is named after Victor Van Straelen, the first President of the Charles Darwin Foundation, the parent body of the CDRS.

Here you can see displays illustrating different aspects of the Galápagos ecosystem, the conservation problems and the programmes that the CDRS and the National Park have in place to combat them.

WATCH OUT FOR:

DARWIN'S FINCHES
YELLOW WARBLER
DARK-BILLED CUCKOO
GALÁPAGOS MOCKINGBIRD
GALÁPAGOS GIANT TORTOISE
LAND IGUANA
MARINE IGUANA

SALTBUSH
PRICKLY PEAR CACTUS
CANDELABRA CACTUS
PARKINSONIA
RED MANGROVE
BUTTON MANGROVE
BLACK MANGROVE
WHITE MANGROVE
LEATHERLEAF
POISON APPLE
MUYUYU
RED-HAIRED TOURNEFORTIA
SPINY BUSH
PALO SANTO
THREAD-LEAFED CHAFF FLOWER

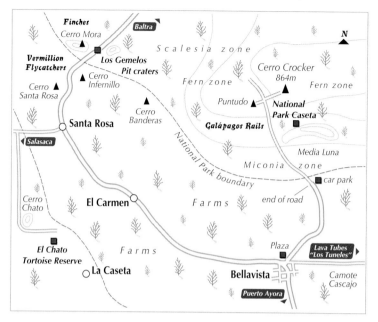

WATCH OUT FOR:

GALÁPAGOS RAIL
SHORT-EARED OWL
VERMILION FLYCATCHER
LARGE-BILLED FLYCATCHER
YELLOW WARBLER
SMALL TREE FINCH
LARGE TREE FINCH
WOODPECKER FINCH
VEGETARIAN FINCH
CATTLE EGRET
SMOOTH-BILLED ANI
SANTA CRUZ GIANT TORTOISE

MICONIA
TREE SCALESIA
QUININE TREE
BALSA
SILKY INGA
SPANISH CEDAR
COMMON CORAL BEAN
SOAPBERRY
CAT'S CLAW
GALÁPAGOS MISTLETOE
PRICKLY POINCIANA
ANGEL'S TRUMPET
COMMON GUAVA
GALÁPAGOS PEPEROMIA
GALÁPAGOS ORCHID
WHITE LEADWORTT

SANTA CRUZ – 90–92. HIGHLANDS

Los Gemelos are a pair of collapsed or pit craters, one on either side of the road in the Scalesia Zone. Here you get an excellent opportunity to see *Scalesia pedunculata*. There are also many mosses, ferns and other epiphytes on the trees. Watch out for the Woodpecker Finch and the Small and Large Tree Finches. From Los Gemelos the road descends in a straight line to South Channel, which separates Santa Cruz from Baltra. Almost immediately it turns into the Transitional Zone and then, in marked contrast to the south side, there is a very long Dry Zone.

From the village of Santa Rosa you can hike down through the Guayabillo forest *Psideum galapageum* to the Tortoise Reserve, though it is easier to view them on one of the farms where they share the fields with cattle. Watch out for the only 'Tortoise Crossing' signs in the world!

From Bellavista there is a trail up to Media Luna, an eroded and overgrown crater, and eventually on to Cerro Crocker, the highest point on the island. This takes you through the last remnants of the Brown Zone, into the Miconia Zone, and finally to the Pampa or Fern Sedge Zone. In the Miconia Zone you can see clearly the threat posed by the introduced Quinine tree. The Miconia, which is key to the breeding of the Galápagos Petrel, will only survive if the National Park continues its programme to eradicate the Quinine tree. Watch out for El Puntudo, a very pointed volcanic cone. On a clear day, the views alone are worth the effort.

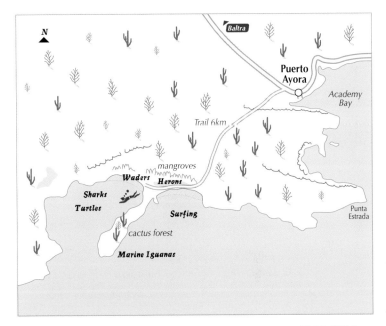

Santa Cruz – 89. Tortuga Bay

Tortuga Bay is a beautiful white sand beach with a mangrove lagoon behind situated some 5 km west of Academy Bay. There is an excellent trail which starts from the main street of Puerto Ayora. You take the second street on your left after the hospital. Once you have climbed the steps up the cliff the trail is on the level and trainers are suitable. From the top of the cliff you will get a superb view over Academy Bay. The walk will give you an excellent opportunity to view the Coastal and Arid Zones vegetation. You should also see Darwin's finches, mockingbirds and yellow warblers and if you are very lucky, a Santa Cruz Giant Tortoise.

The beach is backed by sand dunes which offer further examples of coastal vegetation and beyond the beach is a lagoon backed by mangroves. There is a very good stand of Prickly Pear cactus here, a good place to see the Cactus Ground Finch *Geospiza scandens*. This is a good swimming area. Do not swim off the beach as the undertow can be very strong. You may swim in the lagoon where you can often see the White-tipped Reef Shark *Triaenodon obesus* which is clearly identifiable by the white tip on the dorsal fin. These shark are not aggressive. There is a salt lagoon behind the mangroves, this is an excellent bird-watching site where you should see flamingos and other waders.

It is best to leave early in the morning to visit this site.

WATCH OUT FOR:

Lava Heron
Brown Pelican
Whimbrel
Black-necked Stilt
Various migrant waders
Cactus Ground Finch
Galápagos Green Turtle
White-tipped Reef Shark
Mustard Ray
(Pacific Cownose Ray)
Galápagos Horsefly

Black Mangrove
White Mangrove
Red Mangrove
Poison Apple
Prickly Pear Cactus
Heller's Scalesia
Mesquite
Spiny Bush
Saltwort
Saltbush
Heliotrope
Scorpion Weed
Beach Morning Glory
Inkberry
Common Carpetweed

BIBLIOGRAPHY

This is not intended to be a comprehensive list and includes no travel guides.

Anderson DJ *et al.* Population size and trends of the Waved Albatross *Phoebastria irrorata*. *Marine Ornithology*, 2002.

Angermeyer, J. *My Father's Island*. Pelican Press, 2003.

Anhalzer, JJ. *National Parks of Ecuador*. Imprenta Mariscal, Quito, 1987.

Awkerman, JA *et al.* Foraging activity and submesoscale habitat use of the Waved Albatross (*Phoebastria irrorata*) during the chick brooding period. *Marine Ecology Progress Series* 291, 289–300, 2005.

Beebe, W. *Galápagos – World's End*. Dover, 1988.

Berry, RJ. *Evolution in the Galápagos Islands*. Linnean Society & Academic Press, 1984.

Black, J. *Galápagos, Archipiélago del Ecuador*. Imprenta Europa, Quito, 1973.

Bowman, RI (ed.). *The Galápagos. Proceedings of the Symposia of the Galápagos International Scientific Project*. University of California Press, Berkeley, 1966.

Carlquist, SJ. *Island Biology*. Columbia University Press, New York, 1974.

Castro, I, and Phillips, A. *A Guide to the Birds of the Galápagos*. Christopher Helm/A&C Black, 1996.

Constant, P. *Marine Life of the Galápagos: A Guide to the Fishes, Whales, Dolphins and other Marine Mammals*. Constant, 1992.

Constant, PC. *The Galápagos Islands*. Odyssey Publications, 1995.

Conway, A, and Conway, F. *The Enchanted Islands*. Geoffrey Bles, 1948.

Darwin, C. *On the Origin of Species*. John Murray, London, 1859.

Darwin, C. *The Voyage of the Beagle. Journal of Researches into the Natural History and Geology of the Countries visited during the Voyage round the World of HMS 'Beagle' under Command of Captain Fitzroy, RN*. John Murray, London, 1845.

De Roy, T. *Galápagos Islands Born of Fire*. Airlife, 1998.

De Roy, T, and Jones, M. *Galápagos, Wild Portraits*. Imprenta Mariscal, Quito, 2006.

De Roy Moore, T. *Galápagos Islands, Lost in Time*. Viking Press, New York, 1980.

D'Orso, M. *Plundering Paradise*. Harper Perennial, 2003.

Epler, D, White, A, and Gilbert, C. *Galápagos Guide*. Imprenta Europa, Quito, 1972.

Fritts, TH, and Fritts, PR. *Race with Extinction, Herpetological Field Notes of J.R. Slevin's Journey to Galápagos 1905–06*. Herpetologists' League, 1982.

Grant, PR. *Ecology and Evolution of Darwin's Finches*. Princeton University Press, 2000.

Boletin Cientifico y Technico, Instituto Nacional de Pesca, Guayaquil, Ecuador, 1984.

Grove, JS, and Lavenberg, RJ. *The Fishes of the Galápagos Islands*. Stanford University Press, Stanford, California, 1997.

Harris, MP. *A Field Guide to the Birds of the Galápagos*. Collins, London, 1974.

Harrison, P. *Seabirds, an Identification Guide*. Christopher Helm, London, 1993.

Heinzel, H, and Hall, B. *Galápagos Diary*. A & C Black, 2000.

Hickin, N. *Animal Life of the Galápagos, an Illustrated Guide*. Ferrendune Books, 1979.

Hickman, CP Jr, and Finet, AY. *Field Guide to the Marine Molluscs of Galápagos*. Sugar Spring Press, 1999.

Hickman, J. *The Enchanted Islands: The Galápagos Discovered*.

Anthony Nelson Ltd, 1985.

Horwell, D, and Oxford, P. *Galápagos Wildlife, A Visitors Guide*. Bradt, 2005.

Humann, P. *Reef Fish Identification Galápagos*. Libri Mundi, Ecuador, 1993.

Huyvaert, K, Anderson, DJ, and Parker, PG. Mate opportunity hypothesis and extra-pair paternity in Waved Albatrosses (*Phoebastria irrorata*). *The Auk*, April 2006.

Jackson, MH. *Galápagos, a Natural History*. University of Calgary Press, Calgary, 1993.

Kricher, J. *Galápagos*. Smithsonian Natural History Series, 2002.

Lack, D. *Darwin's Finches*. Cambridge University Press, London, 1947.

McBirney, AR, and Williams, H. *Geology and Petrology of the Galápagos Islands*. Geological Society of America Memoirs, 118, 1969.

McMullen, CK. *Flowering Plants of the Galápagos Islands*. Cornell University Press, 1999.

Merlen, G. *A Field Guide to the Fishes of Galápagos*. Wilmot Books, London, 1998.

Moore, A, Moore, T, and Cifuentes, M. *Guide to the Visitor Sites of Parque Nacional Galápagos*. Servicio Parque Nacional, Galápagos, Ecuador, 1996.

Moorhead, A. *Darwin and the Beagle*. Penguin, Harmondsworth, England, 1971.

Nelson, B. *Galápagos: Islands of Birds*. Longmans Green and Co Ltd, 1968.

Nelson, JB. *The Sulidae*. Oxford University Press, London, 1978.

Nicholls, H. *Life and Loves of a Conservation Icon*. Palgrove MacMillan, 2006.

Patzelt, E. *Fauna del Ecuador*. Ediciones del Banco Central del Ecuador, Quito, 1989.

Perry, R (ed.). *Galápagos (Key Environments)*. Pergamon Press Ltd, Oxford, 1984.

Pritchard, PCH. *The Galápagos Tortoises Nomenclature & Survival Status*. Chelonian Research Foundation, 1996.

Robinson, G, and del Pinto, EM (eds). *El Niño in the Galápagos Islands – The 1982–1983 Event*. Charles Darwin Foundation, Quito, Ecuador, 1985.

Ryan, PR. *Oceanus, The International Magazine of Marine Science and Policy* **30**(2). Woods Hole Oceanographic Institute, 1987.

Schofield, EK. *Field Guide to Some Common Galápagos Plants*. Ohio State University Research Foundation, Columbus, 1970.

Schofield, EK. *Plants of the Galápagos Islands*. Universe Books, 1984.

Swash, A, and Stills, R. *Birds, Mammals and Reptiles of the Galápagos Islands*. Christopher Helm, Wild Guides, 2005.

Swingland, IR, and Klemens, MW. *The Conservation Biology of Tortoises*. IUCN Species Survival Commission, 1989.

Thornton, I. *Darwin's Islands: A Natural History of the Galápagos Islands*. Natural History Press, Garden City, New York, 1971.

Treherne, JE. *The Galápagos Affair*. Jonathan Cape, London, 1983.

Vonnegut, K. *Galápagos, A Novel*. Dell, New York, 1994.

Weiner, J. *The Beak of the Finch: A Story of Evolution in Our Time*. Jonathan Cape, London, 1996.

Wellington, GM. *The Galápagos Coastal Marine Environment*. Unpublished report to Department of National Parks & Wildlife, Quito, 1975.

Wiggins, IL, and Porter, DM. *Flora of the Galápagos Islands*. Stanford University Press, Stanford, California, 1971.

Wittmer, M. *Floreana*. Anthony Nelson Ltd, 1989.

GLOSSARY

annual	a plant that lives only one growing season
axillary	growing out of the upper angle between leaf or branch, and the stem or trunk
bipinnate	doubly compound leaves with leaflets; results in a feather-like leaf
calyx	all the sepals – the outside of a flower bud
coccid	aphids and other scale insects
endemic	particular to a geographic region, and found nowhere else
epiphyte	a plant that grows on another plant, but takes no nutrients from it
feral	domestic animal that has 'gone wild'
garua	light drizzle; Scotch mist
genus	group of closely related species
gravid	pregnant; with eggs
introduced	brought from another region by people, intentionally or accidentally
lanceolate	lance-shaped, much longer than wide, and tapering
lepidoptera	order of insects, comprising butterflies and moths
lore	area of bird between eyes and base of bill – also same area on fish or snake
native	occurring naturally in a region
olivine	olive-green, translucent volcanic mineral, magnesium iron silicate
parasite	plant or animal living on or in, and taking nutrients from, another plant or animal without causing the host's death
perennial	lasting year after year
pinnate	compound leaf, with leaflets growing opposite each other
plastron	bony undershell of tortoise or turtle
primaries	main outer flight feathers of a bird's wing
raceme	spike of flowers
radial symmetry	symmetrical about a central point, like a sea urchin or an apple pie
rhizome	horizontal underground stem, with buds and aerial shoots
rhomboid, rhombic	more or less diamond shaped
scapular	small shoulder feathers
scientific name	means of identifying all recognized life forms using two Latin words
scientific order	framework for categorising and describing all living life forms
scorpoid	curved backwards like a scorpion's tail
scute	individual plates on tortoise or turtle shell
speculum	an iridescent patch of colour on the wings of ducks and some other birds
sporangia	spore case
spyhop	a whale or dolphin putting its head vertically out of the water
sp., spp.	abbreviation for species – one or many
tramp	homeless or nomadic ant
whorl	leaves arranged in a circular pattern

INDEX

HOW *YOU* CAN HELP THE GALÁPAGOS

Visiting the Galápagos is a very special experience, but the reason that you are able to visit and view the amazing biodiversity is because of the time, effort and money that has been put into protecting and preserving the islands. First and foremost is of course the Galápagos National Park Service which has done a truly remarkable job, ably supported by the Charles Darwin Foundation, an international charity set up in 1959, which shouldered the initial burden until the Government of Ecuador established the Galápagos National Park. Join us in shouldering the international responsibility for preserving Galápagos for the future.

Charles Darwin Foundation/Fundacion Charles Darwin
Charles Darwin Foundation
Juan Gonzalez N35-26 y Juan Pablo Sanz
Edificio Vizcaya II, Torre Norte, Piso 5, Oficina 5C
Quito-Ecuador
Telephone: +593 2 244 0918
Email: cdrs@fcdarwin.org.ec
Websites:
www.darwinfoundation.org.ec
www.facebook.com/darwinfoundation
www.twitter.com/darwinfound

In Canada
Galapagos Conservancy CANADA
PO Box 55056
Victoria, BC, V8N 4G0
Phone: +1 250-385-5727
Email: member@galapagoscanada.org
Website: www.galapagoscanada.org

In Germany
FOG Germany is in a development stage; contact either the UK, Swiss or Netherlands organisations.

In Japan
The Japanese Association for Galápagos
5-10-7 Setagaya-ku, Tokyo 155-0032
Tel/Fax.+81 70 6429 4770
Email: info@j-galapagos.org
Website: www.j-galapagos.org

In the Netherlands
Stichting Vrienden van de Galápagos
De Toltoren 39
3912 AG Rhenen
Tel. +31 6 224 62591
Email: info@galapagos.nl
Website: www.galapagos.nl

In New Zealand, Australia and Oceania
Friends of Galápagos New Zealand
PO Box 11-639
Wellington
Tel +64 7533 2040
Email: info@galapagos.org.nz
Website: www.galapagos.org.nz

In Switzerland
Freunde der Galapagos Inseln
c/o Zoo Zurich, #202 Daizawa, Zurichbergstr. 221
CH-8044 Zurich
Tel: +41 (0)1 254 26 70
Email: galapagos@zoo.ch
Website: www.galapagos-ch.org

In UK and the rest of Europe
Galapagos Conservation Trust
Charles Darwin Suite
28 Portland Place
London W1B 1LY
Phone: +44 207 399 7440
Email: gct@gct.org.uk
Websites:
www.galapagosconservation.org.uk
www.discoveringgalapagos.org.uk

In USA and the rest of the world
Galapagos Conservancy
1150 Fairfax Boulevard, Suite 408, Fairfax
VA 22030
Tel: +1 703 383 0077
Email: darwin@galapagos.org
Website: www.galapagos.org